THE POWER OF V

AND THE ROLE OF THIRD
WORLD DEVELOPMENT AND AID

Dedicated to Guillermina.

Thanks to Danilo and Chapita, and friends in Nicaragua – for all you have shared with me over many years. Thanks to Sally (the editor), Pat, Jo and Richard – amongst others – for sustaining humour and ideas. Thanks to all those development workers who talked to me.

THE POWER OF WHITENESS

RACISM IN THIRD WORLD DEVELOPMENT AND AID

Paulette Goudge

Lawrence & Wishart
LONDON 2003

Lawrence and Wishart Limited
99a Wallis Road
London
E9 5LN

First published 2003

British Library Cataloguing in Publication Data.
A catalogue record for this book is available from the British Library

ISBN 0 85315 957 2

Text setting E-Type, Liverpool
Printed and bound by Bookcraft, Trowbridge

CONTENTS

PREFACE

'Third World' development and aid are, when given any attention at all, perceived as peripheral to serious issues of real global concern and import (i.e. 'First World' elections and economies). Representations of development and aid usually feature Western nations magnanimously doing a favour for the poorer nations of the world; this is often accompanied by arguments that more (or less) should be done – but invariably along the same lines. The overall message runs something like this: 'If only those countries could get their act together, stop fighting vicious civil wars amongst themselves, throw out their corrupt governments, organise themselves more efficiently and, what's more, be on time for once – *then* they could start to make progress and modernise themselves.'

What this version of world history and geopolitics omits, of course, is the role of the West itself, which is – and has been since at least 1492 – absolutely central to ensuring (intentionally or otherwise) the underdevelopment of the 'Third World'. And, looked at the other way round, the conception that the 'Third World' is inferior in every way – economically, socially, culturally, morally – is critical in establishing and consolidating the West's own view of itself as correspondingly superior. The role performed by the 'Third World' as undeveloped junior is not marginal to those of us who inhabit the so-called 'First World'; it is central to our existence, in terms both of self perception and – of course – the level of extracted material benefit.

What this book attempts to do is to show how these relationships of superiority and inferiority, constructed globally, are imbued with and buttressed by processes which are thoroughly racialised. Global relations generally, and relations within the ambit of development and aid in particular, can be situated within the context of a white/black binary (though this is often unexpressed, and its potency thereby enhanced); this black/white binary is easier to acknowledge in relation to the long-passed era of overt, colonial racism, but it has definitely not miraculously disappeared at some stage in the meantime. Racialised processes may have been transmogrified over time, but that does not render them less powerful in determining the nature of global relations – who benefits and who loses. This book offers evidence for this assertion, and in so doing attempts to contribute to the spaces currently being opened up by the proliferation of protest movements against the current world order and its impact on 'Third World' countries.

It is perhaps not an easy contribution to make, and Clare Short was to some extent right when she pointed out that most of the Seattle and Genoa protesters were 'young and white and middle class'. But so am I and so is she – at least white and middle class. And it certainly is a contradiction that they/we wear Nike trainers, and not only on demonstrations. Such contradictions should not be ignored, as there is no doubt that Western consumerism contributes cumulatively to deepening poverty in much of the 'Third World' (rapidly bolstered by ever increasing levels of consumption amongst the Westernised elites of the 'Third World'). The purpose of this book is to ask *all* white Westerners (young and older!) to consider the part *our* whiteness plays in establishing and maintaining unequal power relations; and to begin to take serious and concrete steps to challenge the greed and acquisitiveness of the West, which is one of the main causes of poverty elsewhere. This applies at both individual and corporate levels – it does matter how we live as well as what we say. Above all there is a need to challenge the West's assumption of its right to consume a disproportionate percentage of the world's resources, an attitude which is based on – conscious or unconscious – feelings of the superiority of whiteness.

INTRODUCTION

Our defeat was always implicit in the victory of others; our wealth has always generated our poverty by nourishing the prosperity of others ...

Galeano, 1973, p12

Our lives were worth less than those of machines or animals
We were like stones, like weeds in the road

Marcos, 2001, p109

The aim of this book is to examine the way in which much 'Third World' aid, far from contributing to the prosperity of the recipient countries, in fact serves to shore up relations of domination and subordination. My argument is that the whole panoply of development and aid contributes to the creation and perpetuation of global inequalities.

Having worked as a volunteer in a 'Third World' country – in my case Nicaragua – I have spent many subsequent years ruminating on my experiences, and questioning both my motivation and the effects of my intervention. I have come to the conclusion that my contribution – as is the case with so many other aid and development workers – did nothing to improve the lives of Nicaraguans. The work I undertook was situated within a much bigger pattern of power, which meant that my good will – though this in itself could be called into question – was irrelevant, since the overall effect of my work was the reinforcement of western superiority.

In particular I have come to see the whiteness of power – I was able to go off to a country about which I knew very little, and there to fairly quickly assume a position where I was giving out advice and assistance, because my whiteness was a badge of superiority. The more I have reflected on my experiences, the more I have realised the crucial role of notions of white superiority in the maintaining of the whole structure of global inequality. The aid industry is deeply implicated in these structures.

This book is an attempt to share my reflections and theorisations with others. My aim is to use my own experiences, and those of many of my colleagues, together with my subsequent reflection, and reading of many texts on race, power and international relations, as a small contribution to contemporary debates on aid and its effects.

THE MOTIVE

Before 1985 or so I knew nothing about Nicaragua. By the late 1980s I was living in Managua, the capital city, doing voluntary work in what would be called, in England, a residential children's home. At that time the Rolando Carazo Children's Centre was home to about 70 children, mostly under 12 years old, many of whose lives had been shattered by the ongoing war being waged against Nicaragua by the United States (see Appendix for a summary of the history of Nicaragua). Once back home, my story often provoked reactions of how brave I had been to travel alone to such a dangerous continent, but how selfless, how good-hearted were my actions. I have spent much of the intervening ten years reflecting on that journey, and specifically what it means for me – a white, middle-class, well educated, Western woman – to travel to the 'Third World' and offer my assistance in this way. A decade later and I want to ask a question – did this journey represent nothing more than an individual English woman's wish to help children in an under-developed country or does it, as I would now argue, constitute a part of the unequal power relations which exist between the 'Third' and 'First World', contributing significantly towards the maintenance of those power relationships?

In questioning my own motivation, I hope to show its ambiguous nature, something which I believe is shared with many colleagues in this field. It is important to do this, since it points to the fact that, from the very start of the process, a decision to become an aid worker is often taken – albeit unconsciously – because of one's own interests rather than those of others. The story of how I came to volunteer in the children's centre is as good a starting point as any. I was then living in a relatively affluent part of the city, where I shared a house with a number of other Europeans and North Americans. We were engaged in a range of different activities – some of us were involved in researching different aspects of society under the Sandinista government whilst others sought more practical ways of helping Nicaraguan people – working at a women's centre or with UNAG (the rural workers' union), for example. To begin with, I did not do much at all except try and learn some words of Spanish but that changed when I went to a party, with mostly non-Nicaraguans, where I met an English physiotherapist who was working in the children's centre and who, after a short conversation during which I acknowledged my social work profession, asked me to go and work alongside him. I explained that my Spanish was still very poor and, furthermore, social workers do not know very much about physiotherapy. Mike's Spanish was, if anything, worse than mine, so he said that did not matter and he would certainly find something for me to do. I started work the next day.

Looking back, I think I can begin to make some sense of the, at the time, inexplicable unfriendliness and resentment that seemed to emanate towards me from the Nicaraguan workers at the centre. From my first moment, it felt as if all of my attempts to smile and be as helpful as possible were constantly greeted with looks of disdain and I was conscious of what felt like a wall of hostility. For a while, I assumed it would get better as my Spanish, and therefore my ability to communicate, improved; but it didn't. It seemed incredibly unfair, because here I was offering my services, trying to help in whatever way I could, and willing to learn as much as possible, not least a whole new language. No-one seemed to appreciate my efforts and nothing had prepared me for such a response. I felt very miserable for a while and was unable to discuss it with any of my house-mates because they all seemed to be getting on just fine with their Nicaraguan counter-parts. I kept a diary and this entry is typical:

> I was really not sure I felt like going in to Rolando Carazo this morning. I woke up with something of a hangover – Brian and I were up late arguing and I must have drunk more Victoria [the beer] than I intended. It was even hotter and stickier than usual and the 108 bus was really crowded – I got on but was pushed and shoved until I was standing in the middle of the bus which always panics me because it's not clear that I'm ever going to be able to squeeze past so many tightly packed bodies to get out when it arrives at my bus stop in the Siete Sur. But mostly I don't want to go because I don't really know what I'm supposed to be doing and the women who work there really don't like me very much. I spend a lot of time, especially in the mornings in the building where the youngest children live – babies and toddlers – and I feel nervous anyway because I'm not used to handling babies. They seem so little and fragile. Rosa, who I think is the manager of this part of the centre, completely ignores me and when I do try and talk some Spanish she pretends not to understand me or she thinks it's funny. It doesn't do much for my confidence in learning another language. On the other hand, I cannot stay in the house all day or I will die of boredom. I am here now and I must do something with my time. Hopefully it will get better. I must talk to Mike about being given something specific to do so I can feel I'm using my time constructively.

I also had a niggling feeling that, especially because I wasn't being paid, the staff should recognise that I was voluntarily giving up my time and, indeed, money and so it had to be a 'good thing' that I was offering my services to their children's centre. The way I saw it was that I was doing them a favour and couldn't they at least be nice to me? It simply did not occur to me to try and perceive an alternative perspective on the situation. Now, more than ten years on, I wonder whether my extremely privileged position was not bound to have had an impact on the regular workers at the centre. I was privileged because of my ability to stroll in and out of the centre at will – as a volunteer, I was not given specific hours to work and could arrive on whichever days and at the hour which suited me – and indeed I could stroll in and out of the country, I could leave whenever I chose. Furthermore, I had sufficient resources to live well without having to actually earn any money. And I was working without understanding either the language or even the rudiments of what I was supposed to be doing professionally. I turned up with the expectation that I would be given a niche where I could fulfil my desire to help and be useful, without so much as a thought as to how appropriate that help would be, nor whether I would be treading on someone else's toes (did I ever do a paid worker out of a job? – I have no idea and I did not ask). It did not occur to me that simply turning up at the bequest of the English physiotherapist, with no-one knowing what I would be doing nor how long I would be doing it for, would be problematic. The Nicaraguan workers were polite enough not to point it out. Such privileges are, I shall suggest, entirely due to my Western origins and were easily obtained because my whiteness acted as a badge of convenience, allowing my 'right' to be accorded such privileges to be instantly recognised.

Imagine, for a moment, the situation the other way around – a recent arrival from a 'Third World' country arrives at your workplace, having successfully negotiated the immigration authorities. This person turns up out of the blue, having been invited by a fellow ex-patriot whom he/she met at a party the night before. The person is not paid, but has sufficient private resources to live in the best part of town and it is clear that he/she will not be expected to conform to the hours of the working day or the days of the working week. This person apparently wants to help in some unspecified way but does not speak the language, knows next to nothing of the history or culture of Britain or of your organisation, and has no idea of existing professional levels of expertise nor of expectations. And yet this person expects to be given useful, meaningful work immediately and, what's more, to be instantly socially accepted. How would you respond? In retrospect I feel somewhat embarrassed by the whole situation on a personal level, but I shall argue that this is far from being a one-off event. On the contrary, it is so widespread in terms of both individual people and organisations from the 'First World' engaging in 'Third World' development as to be accepted as the norm. Furthermore, it is indicative of the power imbalances that exist on a global basis between those countries which are largely perceived as developed (in the West or the North) and those represented as under or undeveloped (usually Southern nations). To illustrate the imbalance further – the very idea that a Nicaraguan man or woman could make an invited and respected arrival at the airport of a Western capital with a mission to advise, to offer help and criticism or to set up and run a project of her/his own choosing, in a location decided by her/him, is somewhat laughable, certainly to Western minds. It just does not happen this way around; yet this scenario occurs as routine in 'Third World' development. Even in an aspect of life in which Nicaraguans (together with many others in the 'Third World') have centuries of experience and understanding, such as surviving hurricanes and dealing with their aftermath, even when a hurricane devastated Southern England in October 1987, it occurred to no-one in authority to invite a Nicaraguan delegation to fly in and offer their services as consultants or emergency aid workers.

I will argue in this book that the apparently beneficial discourses and practices of 'Third World' development do not exist in a vacuum and are, as I have begun to demonstrate, deeply imbued with and structured by issues of power. I will also argue, and this is probably the most controversial aspect of my thesis, that the particular contribution of whiteness to global structures of power is decisive – in the sense that the whiter the person, or the nation, or the global region, the less there is to prove in relation to expertness, competency or even the assumed right to arrive in a 'Third World' country proffering advice and wisdom. I now think I was able to walk into the children's centre in Managua because I had landed from a Western nation, assumed by all to have superior knowledge and practice on tap, and such a position was never challenged. Such a position of superiority was and is undoubtedly enhanced and publicly demonstrated by my badge of whiteness. Such a badge acts as a visible marker of assumed superiority, one which can be immediately and generally recognised and acted upon.

In my case, the first of my visits to Nicaragua was in 1988 when I decided to join a Study Tour – which I had seen advertised as a combination of getting to know and understand something of the Nicaraguan political situation and travelling around the country, with the promise of a few days relaxing in the sun on a Pacific beach as the icing on the cake. A trip which is nicely summed up as 'political tourism'. Beforehand, I had read a few *Guardian* articles on Nicaragua and the Sandinista government and, together with many other Europeans and North Americans, I was intrigued enough to want to go and see for myself whether socialism was really happening there and what it involved 'on the ground'. It did not occur to me to consider whether being better informed might be a good idea. Solidarity for the Sandinista Revolution of 1979 (see Appendix), which had succeeded in overthrowing the brutal and US backed dictator, Somoza, was usually the expressed motivation for going. This was often strengthened by opposition to the US supported Contra war (fought throughout the 1980s), which was aimed at undermining the Sandinistas since their policies were essentially unacceptable to North American hegemony in the region. Sandanista policies were perceived as especially dangerous by the US because they feared they might prove generally popular throughout Central America and spread to neighbouring countries such as Guatemala or El Salvador, which would pose a potential threat to American commercial interests. I was also affected by the contrast with the atmosphere of gloom and doom in the late 1980s amongst the British left after ten years of Thatcher government: whilst Sandinista Nicaragua seemed to be offering us a message of hope and positiveness. My feelings, shared by the others who were also on the Study Tour, was that if such a tiny country could achieve so much in the face of such overwhelmingly hostile odds, then surely there was still a chance for things to improve back at home. This was undoubtedly my conscious motive for undertaking the journey and, even with the bene-fit of hindsight, I have no wish to completely deny its validity for myself nor for others. I do, however, wish to unpack it.

My current version of the motivation for my trip to Nicaragua would be considerably more complex. I would now recognise that my original decision to go to Nicaragua was very bound up with the parlous state of my life, at that time, in Britain. I was in the privileged position of having a considerable sum of money, from the sale of a flat in London at the height of the property boom, and so was able to travel without worrying about an income. The details of my personal life at the end of the 1980s are not essential – suffice it to say that I had recently left a job where I was not only unhappy but almost universally unpopular. Also, I was bitterly disappointed by the failure of yet another relationship and felt fairly hopeless about the possibility of anything really interesting or exciting ever happening to me. What I suppose might be termed a mid-life crisis hitting me in my late 30s! I needed to do something different, to give myself a challenge and, above all, to seek out some new possibilities, the more dramatic the better. The decision to go on the Study Tour, actually taken whilst relaxing in the bath one day, was based primarily on my own existential misery, with some very vague notions about life and politics in Nicaragua thrown in. I knew it was 'politically interesting' from a left-wingish point of view and, furthermore, I carried in my head a romantic, heroic image of a successful revolution which undoubtedly had strong under-tones of sexual adventure and emotional fulfilment. The figure I focused on was the sexy, charismatic Sandinista guerrilla (bearing a remarkable resemblance to the well known Che Guevara poster of my student days) who had emerged from a life of hardship in the moun-tains to take on and defeat a ruthless dictator and his army, long bankrolled and trained by the US government. The fact that they had the courage and tenacity to challenge the world's most powerful authority was very appealing to me. I do not want, in any way, to diminish the extraordinary achievements of the Sandinistas both as guerrilla fighters and subsequently when in government – rather to demonstrate how I, in a very vague and inexplicit way, constructed my own, private version of their heroism. And I had a deep hankering, which I could not have then acknowledged, for that hero to include in his list of priorities the task of rescuing me from my middle-aged doldrums. I longed to find a reason for living which would be an improvement on what I had and, given my inability to do this for myself, I was full of dreams – nebulous and unfocused but nonetheless powerful for all that – that something (or, preferably, *someone*) would happen in Nicaragua which would sort it for me! Looking back from the vantage point of the present, I can analyse, at least to some extent, what was going on for myself. I would now argue that I was feeling very restricted and my life seemed to be lacking in opportunity, excitement and danger and a trip to Nicaragua offered a potential way out. My personal desires, though, were largely sublimated and replaced by more acceptable justifications of solidarity and doing what I could to help a poor and beleaguered 'Third World' country.

The question then arises whether our motivations for helping really matter, as long as we help. Is it not more important that we give whatever help we can to individual people whenever and where ever we can, and, indeed, to those countries that are less privileged than those of us in the West who have relatively affluent lifestyles? Are our actions not the most important thing? I have had a number of informal discussions where this argument has been advanced, usually in the context of suggesting that any more major or structural changes are simply not possible. The propositions I intend to make in this book argue against this position and I present an analysis which suggests that, overall, the development and aid actions of the West are not helpful to their recipients. At best some particular interventions may achieve better conditions for a select number of individuals in a given 'Third World' country, often those who come to work in some way in the development and aid industry, and I do think that some individual development workers and agencies do achieve positive results in specific circumstances. Overall, however, there is no evidence that 'Third World' development and aid achieves its own goals and certainly poverty as a whole is not decreasing (see the debate in *Prospect*, March 2002 for an outline of the arguments for and against the notion that global poverty is decreasing). At worst, incalculable damage can be caused to many people – for example those just outside the spatial or temporal limits of a development project, who witness resources being allocated to their neighbours whilst being totally excluded themselves. In general, Western notions and practices of development and aid are not only largely failing those in less developed countries who are supposed to gain from its ministrations; they are also, in this way, actually contributing to unequal power relations. And motivations matter to the extent that the altruistic variety can act as a smokescreen, covering up unpalatable outcomes and preventing recognition of our contribution to increasing global inequalities. They also allow us to kid ourselves that we (the goodies, the development workers) are not exploiting anybody as we are there, by definition, to 'do good'.

To return to my personal story, I cannot seriously argue that my sojourn in Nicaragua actually benefited anyone to any extent – except myself. I did not find my Holy Grail in the form of a sexy Sandinista guerrilla, nor anywhere else for that matter, but I learnt more about myself and how to sort out my own happiness than many years of Western therapy could have taught me. Perhaps this concentration on our own needs is reasonable – it could be argued that at least this is more honest than the version of 'us' helping 'them', which continues to reinforce the image that we in the West are superior to people in the South.

At first sight, an example of the more 'honest' approach to motivation is the booklet published by VSO (Voluntary Service Overseas) in conjunction with the *Guardian* in March 2001, entitled '6 ways to change your life'. In order to recruit potential volunteers, it clearly aims to appeal to those with a relatively comfortable lifestyle in Britain; it bypasses extraneous entreaties to our better selves or to a need to do good for others, focusing instead almost exclusively on the anticipation of personal achievement spiced up with the opportunity for adventure and a chance to experience the exotic. The emphasis in these adverts aimed at attracting prospective candidates to serve overseas becomes increasingly focused on these latter aspects, which are more usually associated with tourism. There appears to have been an explicit decision taken, at least in the responsible ad agency, that appealing to altruism does not work any more, whereas directly hooking into a range of personal interests and desires will be more successful. This particular booklet makes no attempt to elicit any interest in the people who live in the six countries which are represented. Their needs are relegated to a single comment at the end of the several page leaflet: 'the range of placements reflects the needs in developing countries around the world'. And that is that. No where does the leaflet demonstrate how this might be the case and yet, presumably, this is the rationale behind the very existence of VSO and similar agencies. The needs and desires of the volunteers, on the other hand, are continually highlighted and are visually illustrated on every page through photos and drawings. Their greater importance is continually stressed: from enhancement of future career paths, to the 'promise of year-round sun'. The advert is divided into six sections, each one devoted to a different 'developing' country, each of which is described in terms of its 'something special' on offer to the volunteers. Kenya, unsurprisingly, is the country of big game animals, and is apparently devoid of human life, except for Carol, the volunteer already in situ, who describes her typical day as follows: 'As usual, I was woken up at around 6am by lions roaring close by. When I got up, I found the water buffaloes had burst the water pipe again. So I had to drive off to find where they had dug into it, remove the animals and fix the pipe. When I returned I found that while the compound was empty, the baboons had ransacked the place and pulled a toilet cistern off the wall.' And so on. Leaving aside the intriguing question as to how she 'removed' the water buffalo apparently single-handedly, the portrayal could be in any tourist brochure advertising exciting adventure holidays in Africa. The fascination of Zanzibar is summarised in the heading 'Get Spiritualized', whilst China holds out the more mundane pledge of offering opportunities to 'Climb the Career Ladder'. Then there is the story of Karen and Duncan who fell in love whilst on a VSO placement in Malawi. Karen comments that, 'It seems easier to meet your partner in the middle of nowhere sitting around on a crate drinking beer than down the local pub'. And she goes on: 'It was also a bit of a standing joke among volunteers in Malawi that VSO should advertise as a dating agency as they'd get a bigger response!' Precisely. Karen's use of the phrase 'middle of nowhere' is from a particularly Western perspective, implying both vastness but also unimportance in contrast to the unspecified but nonetheless very important 'somewhere'. We shall see that this kind of allusion is very frequent in development discourse. Finally, we have Alison and Paeder who met whilst teaching English in the Maldives, and for whom the major question is 'will two years in the sunny Maldives really quench their thirst for adventure?', or will they 'settle down and have a family' after their adventurous interlude? I repeat, the question of the suitability of any of this for the recipient community is entirely absent.

If, having read the alluring brochure, you decide to send off for further information, you will receive another leaflet, this time entitled 'Working Overseas with VSO – The Facts', which, on its second page, declares the 'VSO vision' of tackling poverty' to be 'a long term goal'; 'we know we cannot work miracles overnight'. But we know about the power of individuals to make a difference. The question is, will you commit two years of your life to helping others realise their potential?' The remainder of the booklet (a further 14 pages of A4 size), however, returns to the theme of the welfare and contentment of the volunteers themselves. The levels of remuneration are made clear; there is advice on how to adjust to life in a 'Third World' country, and on what to do to ensure both physical and psychological health whilst living in a developing country – 'since conditions may be fairly basic' – and reassurance that VSO will pay medical costs if necessary. The issue of taking partners and dependants overseas is discussed and VSO undertakes to support its volunteers once they have returned to the UK. All of which is very useful and valid information for potential candidates but there is no explanation at all as to what VSO means by its 'vision'. It is as if the suggestion that anyone, whether architect, bricklayer, social worker or business adviser (apparently the latter are particularly welcome these days) from the 'First World' who wants to 'help' people in developing countries must, by definition, be doing good. What kind of 'help', whether or not it has actually been requested, whether its impact on 'Third World' people is being evaluated in any way – these kinds of questions are simply not posed, let alone answered. 'Making a difference' is blithely assumed to be beneficial for those on the receiving end. Having so summarily dealt with 'the vision', more evidence is presented along the lines of the advertisement, using direct quotations from volunteers in a range of 'Third World' countries about the impact the experience has had upon *their* lives. The possible benefit to the volunteer's own life and career is again emphasised – one volunteer is quoted as saying 'there have been so many positives: not least the way my hair-cutting and culinary skills have come on in leaps and bounds': any concept of this volunteer's potential impact upon the people of Eritrea goes entirely unremarked. So, while the spotlight remains firmly on the human interest stories of how the lives of Westerners are enriched by such experiences, the question as to whether the lives of those at the receiving end of such attention were enhanced goes entirely unasked. This, I shall argue, is because the lives of the latter are invariably deemed less significant and I shall suggest that this is effectively underwritten by the assumption of the superiority of the former, embodied in our overwhelming whiteness.

It is also worth considering whether there are unintended effects on 'Third World' peoples of the constant flow of development visitors from the materially better off countries. It is possible that one of the impacts of cutting hair in Eritrea, for example, is to unwittingly transmit a message that the tools used for haircutting in the West are superior to those in Eritrea, together with all the other attributes of Western haircutting (the salons, the hair styles, the magazines devoted to the newest cut and colour). This message of superiority and corresponding inferiority, repeated endlessly in relation to all aspects of life, contributes to people believing in the idea that everything in the West is superior, and it is then a short step to wanting to go there oneself to 'better one's life'. A further example of the communication of this sense of superiority occurred when a Nicaraguan friend visited me in England. She is a scientist, has recently obtained her PhD, and hoped to improve her spoken English. Whilst watching a British TV programme about child abuse, I was surprised by her comment: 'surely that doesn't happen here'. The conversation progressed and she remarked that 'you don't have violence towards women here like we do in Nicaragua'. I asked why she thought this and found her answer to be highly illuminating in relation to North/South power relations. She said:

... because there are all these European and North American women in Nicaragua who seem so strong and sorted out. They come to tell us that it's not right to get beaten up all the time by your man. They tell us to get out of bad relationships, to leave them behind and move on into something better. They say we shouldn't put up with it because, as women, we're worth more than that. So we assume that European and North American women must have got it all sorted and they come to Nicaragua once there is no violence in your own countries. No-one says any different.

A reasonable assumption – that we would only tell others what to do once we have our own house in order. My friend's shock at discovering the downside of life in the West – the inequalities, the violence, the hypocrisy – was quite palpable.

Given the problematic nature of the outcome, it is important to pause for a moment and consider whether motivation for journeys from the 'First' to the 'Third World' matter. Certainly, the vast majority of North Americans and Europeans whom I met in Nicaragua felt similarly to myself inasmuch as they had undertaken their own journeys with the primary, and unquestioned, goal of giving and helping. In contrast to the VSO booklet, the conversations I had with my Western colleagues contained very little – if any – discussion of personal motives. I would suggest that being unaware of one's personal motivation may encourage an over-emphasis on the tendency of us (the visitors) to perceive and present our very presence as being solely concerned with 'helping or giving to them'. This dynamic underpins and supports ideas and feelings that 'we' must be superior to 'them', because 'we' are always in the position of being the helpers and givers. Certainly, ten years on, the VSO approach seems to be more aware that the actual motivations of overseas workers and volunteers are much more complicated and link into their/our personal lifestyles and ambitions to a far greater extent. VSO now apparently recognises that it has to be upfront about this in its assessment of motivations, at least when advertising for recruits. However, the recognition of the role of personal motivation apparently does not lessen the assumption of rightness and superiority of Western development and aid; nor apparently does it detract from the conviction that Westerners, whatever their personal needs and desires, must nonetheless be doing good when they/we become 'Third World' development workers or volunteers. We seem to take it completely for granted that we have every right to go to a 'Third World' country, regardless of our motivation and that, once there, almost whatever we do or say will be assumed to be for the benefit of 'Third World' citizens. Even though, in my case, the choice of Nicaragua was effectively determined by where I chose to go on holiday ten years ago, and by my urge to escape the monotony of life in Britain I nonetheless took it upon myself to engage in what we call 'Third World' development work as a volunteer – thus I could feel good about myself at the same time as hopefully embarking on a life-changing adventure. I did not, until several years later, even question my vision of myself as indubitably having something worthwhile to offer Nicaragua as, in common with all of the other Western travellers whom I have met, both in the early 1990s and subsequently, we see ourselves as being in the position of expert, of helper, of decision-maker – whatever our personal motivation for making the journey may have been.

I shall argue in this book that 'we' from the West can operate in such a way and undertake such adventures – whatever our explicit motives – because our whiteness allows us to hold onto a view of ourselves as unquestionably right and superior. It is possible to take the view that not only does development and aid not help the 'Third World' much; it also acts as a smokescreen, allowing the West to look like it cares and is help-ing by 'doing the South a favour'; this is especially important in the self-representation of the West, whilst it carries on doing what it has long done best – extracting from the Southern countries precisely what it needs to sustain its own way of life. This process may have shifted in emphasis since colonial times of dependence upon raw materials (though that is still important), with cheap, submissive labour and the provision of exotic holidays becoming more sought after. (It is perhaps not a total coincidence that advertising for development workers is taking on more of the sun, sex and excitement quality of tourist brochures.)

To conclude this section by returning to my own story – in spite of fantasies about meeting my ideal rescuer in the shape of a rugged Sandinista guerrilla figure, the reality of my existence could not have been more different. Where I actually chose to live was the most Westernised of the options available at that point, and I spent many months in a part of the capital city, Managua, called Bolonia which, before the time of the Revolution, had been inhabited by the wealthy elite of Nicaragua, the friends and business cronies of the ruling dicta-tor and his family. Such people had mostly fled to Miami in order to avoid the financial effects of the Sandinista government and their large and comfortable houses were taken over by a variety of Nicaraguan organisations, such as Trades Unions. The only private individuals who could afford to live in surroundings of such faded glamour and luxury were those of us in from the West. I lived in a spacious, light but cool, villa with a garden – heavily fenced to keep out 'undesirables', and reeking of the vividly scarlet and pink bougainvillaea. Christina was included in the rent – she did all our washing and ironing and kept the communal areas clean. Not only did I think nothing of this at the time, I, together with my housemates, saw nothing contradictory in main-taining our collective view of ourselves as only being there to help and do good. I would have been embarrassed at keeping a servant in England, and would never have thought of myself as being the type to keep servants in the English context, but somehow the issue of exploitation did not arise in Nicaragua. I cannot argue that I justified the situation – I just never thought about it from the perspective of how I was fulfilling my own needs, because the dominant discourses were concerned exclusively with our role as do-gooders.

THE CONTEXT

Having begun with a discussion of the role and importance of motivation in 'First/Third' World relations, I wish to move on to explore further issues, and especially connections across time and space, two crucially important themes for this book. Issues of 'Third World' development and aid are often approached as if they somehow exist independently of the bequests of history and the world's geopolitical powerplays, which reach backwards and forwards across the centuries. We in the West often operate as if 'Third World' development and aid exist in a secluded and reserved space, where all the nasty, exploitative features of the neoliberal world have been banned. In this space, we developers seem to believe we can think our own thoughts and do our own thing, entirely untouched by the grim realities of the political and economic forces (often summarised as globalisation) which affect all else on the planet.

The first important connection to try and unravel is the link between Western lifestyles and the conditions of life for the vast majority of 'Third World' people, which, for the most part, are getting worse on an almost daily basis. Thinking about the racialisation of North/South relations in general, and the contribution of development and aid in particular, requires the linking of the personal experience (at the level of the individual worker and agency) to what is happening on a global basis. Relationships and events which may appear to be purely personal, even idiosyncratic, such as my journey to Nicaragua, can be shown to actually form one part of a pattern. A pattern which is conditioned by historical factors of domination and by current day geopolitics. I will begin to establish the existence of such patterns with a personal story from my development diary. This entry was written as reflection, trying to make sense of experiences which I found difficult and unsettling. I had signed on at a Spanish school where part of the learning was to go and live with a 'local' family.

> Living in Paula's house was such a contradiction. I need to think through what I mean by that. She and her family are very poor. I was poor as a kid too, but there's a difference between being allowed only one piece of fruit a day (either an apple or an orange – I can hear my mother say it now) and having jam or butter, but never both. There's a

difference between that and what's going on here. The house has a dirt floor – kept incredibly clean by Paula and Myra (the oldest girl) who must sweep it at least six times a day, even in the dry season when the dust is unbearable. The roof is corrugated iron which I thought quite romantic the first time I heard the rain pounding down and making so much noise we couldn't talk to each other. I was less impressed when I discovered water had leaked through onto my suitcase.

Breakfast, lunch and dinner were always rice and beans, or beans and rice or even 'gallo pinto' (rice and beans mixed up) and an occasional egg. I am not sure the family ate three meals a day when we weren't there. A runaway pig was knocked over in the street more or less opposite Paula's house – so everyone in the barrio had pork for a few days. I learnt to ignore the ants which walked across the small rickety table while we were eating. I mostly didn't go to the toilet, I would wait until I got to the school and I avoided going into the kitchen. It's not that I thought it would be unhygienic, it's just that I didn't want to know.

The bed. Paula and Juan gave up their double bed, I have no idea where they slept. To make a few extra dollars they took on three of us students and thought that all three of us could share the double bed. They reckoned without knowing the size of us well-fed Westerners! We could barely sit on the bed at one time, let alone sleep in it. The first night was fun. We stayed awake, chatting and giggling, constantly rolling on top of each other and probably keeping everyone else awake. We enjoyed the parrot living under the bed. We thought it charming that the chickens and cockerel strolled in and out of the bedroom and the cock chose the bottom of the bed from where to make his early morning wake-up call.

After the second night we realised that one of us would have to leave if we were to have any sleep at all. In spite of my view of Paula and her family as amazingly kind, generous and hospitable way beyond the call of duty, I instantly volunteered to be the one to move out. I moved to another family close by and noticed right away the clean and in working order state of the shower and toilet. There were also stone floors. Definitely one step up from Paula's house. Not to mention a comfortable (single) bed all to myself.

Two myths were dealt severe blows by this experience. Firstly, my tendency to romanticise poverty – it is actually unrelentingly grim and hard work just holding things together (and I felt that in a couple of days!) and affects every aspect of people's lives. Health, education, social life were all visibly adversely affected. People are ill more and die younger. Secondly, my view of myself as being able to help. Actually, I couldn't stand it. Beyond giving a few extra dollars to help repair the roof, it became clear to me that their life situation was so exploited, particularly their labour, that material progress was totally blocked. It is truly amazing that they survive at all.

Reflecting further, from my current standpoint, it now occurs to me that I did not consider at all the impact on Paula and her family of my moving out. There was, of course, the financial implication but also the social effects of being deemed 'too poor to stay with'. It seems clear to me now that what Juan needed was simply a decent wage for his labour, which was hard and unhealthy work in a cement factory, not one-off handouts to mend the roof.

I want to take a further look at the meaning of poverty from a perspective totally different to my own, but one which expresses values with which I would concur. 'Let us introduce ourselves', says Subcommandante Marcos of the Zapatista Liberation Army, addressing the First Intercontinental Meeting for Humanity and against Neoliberalism in July 1996. He begins by extending an inclusive welcome to 'Brothers and Sisters of Asia, Africa, Oceania, Europe and America' to their meeting place in the mountains of Southeast Mexico, the Chiapas region, and he continues:

> For ten years, we lived in these mountains, preparing to fight a war.
> In these mountains, we built an army.
> Below, in the cities and plantations, we did not exist.
> Our lives were worth less than those of machines or animals
> We were like stones, like weeds in the road
>
> For the powers that be, known internationally by the term 'neoliberalism',
> we did not count,
> we did not produce,
> we did not buy,
> we did not sell.
>
> We were a cipher in the accounts of big capital.

The impressive book (2001) of Marcos's collected poems, speeches and other communiqués, including a number of e-mails, forms a moving testimony of views and feelings from the perspective of the world's excluded and othered peoples, those whose lives are rendered effectively worthless, 'worth less than those of machines or animals' by the forces which he summarises as neoliberalism. Paula and Juan clearly don't count in global terms and I think that, like me, much of the development and aid apparatus treats the 'Third World' poor as a separate species whose role is to be looked at, or ignored, judged to be lacking, and sometimes given what is considered 'good for them'. On some indices of quality of life, the indigenous people of the Chiapas could be ranked amongst the poorest on the planet, and in that sense Marcos could be forgiven if he insisted on focusing solely on the plight of his own people. But he doesn't. On the contrary, his writings demonstrate a profound concern and ability to encompass the condition of all humiliated and offended peoples, whatever the basis of their oppression and wherever they live. He goes on:

> Behind us, you are us.
> Behind our masks is the face of all excluded women,
> Of all the forgotten indigenous,
> Of all the persecuted homosexuals,
> Of all the despised youth,
> Of all the beaten migrants,
> Of all those imprisoned for their words and thoughts,
> Of all the humiliated workers,
> Of all those dead from neglect,
> Of all the simple and ordinary men and women,
> Who don't count,
> Who aren't seen,
> Who are nameless,
> Who have no tomorrow.

This author shares this value base, insofar as it is possible for a white, Western woman with a relatively comfortable middle-class life style to do so, and I am grateful to the Subcommandante for his eloquence and succinctness of expression. This book is not an investigation of 'Third World' poverty as such, nor about the lives of those who inhabit the 'Third World' – what it aims to do is to highlight the connections between the depth and persistence of 'Third World' poverty and Western lifestyles.[1] The overlap between the terms poverty and 'Third World' and blackness, and the affluence of the 'First World' with whiteness, is crucial to this exploration of power imbalances. Clearly, the surrounding context of 'Third World' development and aid is what Marcos terms neoliberalism, and development discourses and operations are always conditioned by that context. Discourses and practices of development and aid, simultaneously, impact on the power of neoliberalism, and not always to the benefit of people in the 'Third World'. This book is about 'Third World' poverty in the sense of trying to understand whether it might be the case that institutions and individuals who perceive ourselves, and are represented, as helping the 'Third World' poor are actually exacerbating the situation by replicating white-on-black power relations.[2]

It is not simply an unfortunate accident that, looking at the world as a whole, some people, some groups of people, some countries, some regions, some parts of the world, are disproportionately affected by what Marcos terms humiliation and offence, and which more statistically minded writers would want to illustrate utilising quantitative rather than qualitative data. It is no coincidence that these are also the regions inhabited by the black peoples of the world. It is similarly not fortuitous that the richer regions of the world in the North also happen to be the whitest. Although serious inequalities with profound implications exist within the 'First World' or the West, and there are white people who are both poor and oppressed, the overriding aim here is to highlight particular features of the big picture, of global patterns of poverty.[3] Just as the fact that the North of Britain has a number of indices of inequality and poverty which are consistently higher than those in the South does not mean that there are no rich people or places in the North, nor any poverty in the South: similarly, the identification of a pattern which suggests that there is an increasing wealth gap between North and South on a global basis does not negate the existence of destitution and distress in Northern countries, nor of affluent countries and individuals in the Southern regions of the globe. It is a question of trying to maintain the bigger picture (the global) in focus, whilst simultaneously acknowledging the dynamics of individual situations and power balances.

Issues of poverty, of inequality and injustice are routinely linked to the notion of development or, conversely, under-development. It is explicitly considered axiomatic by the majority of commentators in the West that to be poor equals being under-developed, and that what is required is help to progress along the route, previously mapped out by the developed nations (mostly synonymous with the North or the West), towards the attainment of those goals defined as essential and usually associated with modernity and progress. There is also an implicit association, as we shall see, that continuously, though often subliminally, links poverty and underdevelopment with blackness – and correspondingly links the achievement of progress and development with whiteness. This association is a highly significant one and I shall explore the implications of the links between development and those bedrock notions of white Western thought, of which progress is a central tenet, in some detail in Chapter 2. For now, suffice it to say that the desirable overall goals of 'Third World' development and aid, as defined in the West, are usually expressed in relation to the economic aspects of achieving modernity or progress. Many of the key government pronouncements of the subject in the early 2000s, for example, stress the need to eradicate poverty, or at least ensure a significant reduction. One major obstacle, however, to achieving this goal is that it would require addressing the power imbalances between North and South, entailing difficult and demanding changes in lifestyle in the West. The avoidance of such issues in the West leads to a tendency to move away from the grander, more sweeping general announcements and their unwelcome implications to, instead, focusing on more precise objectives. As expressed by specific government departments or NGOs, a different emphasis becomes apparent, and no longer is the stated goal to abolish poverty, but indices emerge which are more prescriptive towards 'Third World' countries and less potentially critical of the West. Thus abolishing poverty becomes transmuted into measures such as improved life expectancy, greater literacy, education initiatives for girls, better health, lower infant mortality rates and so on. The advantage of these somewhat narrower aims is that it allows the spotlight to be focused exclusively on the developing country and on what its people have, to date, done wrong or not done well enough, and what they might do better in the future. Often the issue of not doing things well enough or achieving certain prescribed standards is then linked, both in public and private discourse, with subliminal messages which have a racialised connection. For example, one such message is that blackness supposedly equals inefficiency and corruption, whereas whiteness invariably implies efficiency and adherence to moral standards. Thus the question of any Western responsibility for the existence of such levels of poverty is neatly and entirely avoided.

What I wish to try and do in this book is to look at the issue from a different standpoint than that of people whose lives are directly affected by poverty. This is not because I wish to minimise the centrality of that perspective, but I wish to explore the possibility that taking a different angle could illuminate aspects which thus far have tended to remain obscured. I am interested in exploring the attitudes and practice of those of us who start from the premise of wanting to see a fairer and more just world, those of us who try in a variety of different ways to help ameliorate poverty – specifically those of us located in the Western world who are engaged in some way in 'Third World' development and aid work. My hunch, which emerged from the sort of experiences I recorded in my diary, was that development and aid is not quite what it seems. It rarely benefits those it is directed towards and is never neutral in its praxis. I began to consider the possibility that it is actually one more expression of global power imbalances, similarly infused with racialised judgements, and perhaps even more dangerous because of the appearance of benignity. It also occurred to me that an exploration of these supposedly positive aspects of North/South relations will tell us a great deal about the general power imbalances between so-called developed nations and the 'Third World', and suggest reasons why change in the latter has not been as forthcoming as many would like. I stress that I include myself in this broad and, as yet, ill-defined group of 'Third World' sympathisers and helpers and I am inherently sympathetic to the intentions of the majority of those whom I quote in this book. I thus include myself as being a part of what I am concerned to critique – I have been there, done that, got that T-shirt and therefore cannot pretend that I am some kind of impartial observer who is not personally implicated.

A word about how power relations, particularly those with

racialised referents, are frequently viewed. Over the past ten years I have had numerous conversations about my research and everyone has a view, often strongly held. In my experience, most discussions with white Westerners who have encountered the 'Third World', whether travelling because of paid employment, volunteering, backpacking or just going on holiday – or even those who have no direct experience, but have read about it – will very quickly shift into a discourse which concentrates on the position of whites, almost invariably positioned as unfairly beleaguered and dominated by their 'Third World' hosts. So we have the stories of the lazy 'Third World' bureaucrat whose goal is to ruin the long planned holiday, the inefficiency or outrageous speed of the local public transport system, the inadequacy of health care services and so on. Whites are regularly portrayed as the victim, sometimes of overt hostility. In a number of recent discussions about my research, I have been categorical that my interest is in white-on-black racism. Nonetheless, the response invariably ignores this – I think mostly unintentionally – and focuses instead on situations where my discussant has felt uncomfortable in relation to her/his whiteness. The conversation goes something like:

Me   I'm doing some research into racialisation and the power of whiteness in 'Third World' development and aid.
My respondent   Oh, I know just what you mean. I was on holiday in Jamaica last year. The racism towards me was terrible. I actually got spat at in the street.

The point here is not to deny nor to minimise such experiences and the feelings they engender for the individual concerned, but to indicate how much easier it is to identify an abuse of power when it happens against oneself and one's own feelings of being oppressed by others. It is so much harder to recognise when one is doing it to others. So much harder that, in my experience, people would rather edit the point out of the conversation than address it in any way. The hardest thing of all is to detect ways in which one is oneself the oppressor. Variations on the theme of being spat at whilst on holiday in Jamaica form the almost ubiquitous response to my interest in racialised power relations. I quote Patricia Hill Collins who makes the point extremely well:

> Although most individuals have little difficulty identifying their own victimisation within some major system of oppression – whether it be by race, social class, religion, physical ability, sexual orientation, ethnicity, age or gender ... they typically fail to see how their thoughts and actions uphold someone else's subordination. Thus white feminists routinely point with confidence to their oppression as women but resist seeing how much their white skin privileges them (Collins, 1990, p229).

And furthermore, it is much easier to see and react to oppression in individualistic terms (one person abuses another) and to fail, deliberately or otherwise, to perceive systemic or institutional oppression, based on membership of societal groupings which have differential access to various forms of power. To visualise what I mean – imagine two rooms. In one room is a group of people from 'Third World' countries (essentially, Africa, Latin America and South Asia) and in the other a collection from the West. Where would the higher incomes be and where, conversely, would the greatest levels of poverty be? Who takes most of the decisions of global import, particularly in relation to trade and investment? Who constitutes the effective membership of the world's most powerful forums – the G7, the World Trade Organisation, the IMF, the World Bank? Who owns and runs the banks and the multinational companies? In which room are the people who can back up their decisions with the use of armed forces which can be deployed anywhere in the globe when required? Who makes and sells armaments to whom? Who decides who is to be considered developed and who correspondingly un-developed? Who defines who constitutes the extremists or fanatics of the world? These are all aspects of power – military power, economic power, political power, social power and even moral and spiritual power. In which room will most of the people be white? On the whole it is not black people who have these resources or take decisions which have global import – and neither is it women nor disabled people. Take any attribute of global power, and you will find it is disproportionately located in the West and largely associated with whiteness (as well as maleness and so on). But as Collins argues, we all prefer to identify or imagine our own oppression whilst ignoring or downplaying ways in which we are responsible.

In my study of development work and development workers (who are, I repeat, concerned above all to help and to improve the lives of the 'Third World' poor), I am going to approach us as members of the relatively more powerful group – as members of the self-designated 'First World'. As I have suggested above, development workers and agencies often do not feel particularly powerful – especially when the mechanisms of oppression are not the obvious ones of previous eras but the immeasurably more subtle processes of neoliberalism and globalisation, and the perhaps even more pervasive, though often indirect, power plays of development and aid. However, the power imbalances are built into the development and aid process from the point of conception, for it is within the 'First World' that definitions of who is developed and who is under- or un-developed are formulated. It is here that decisions are made about which country, which region, or which group of people, should receive what kinds of aid input and how much help towards the goals of more and better development – goals which are also largely defined by Western organisations. The majority of

personnel directly or indirectly involved in development work originate in the 'First World', and those that do not will almost inevitably
have received a Western based education in 'Third World'
Development Studies (and these can increasingly be studied on a
distance learning basis so that the necessity for actual attendance at a
Western academic institution is minimised). Ironically, it is even the
Western workers and agencies who decide whether or not there should
be 'local participation' in the setting up of a development project and,
if so, what form it should take. In fact, the very concept of development can be argued to have emanated from the time of the European
Enlightenment and to be inextricably linked to ideas of rational
thought, science and the onward march of progress (see chapter 4).
There are of course challenges to this distribution of power, and most
organisations concerned with aid and development now issue statements about their intentions to be more inclusive of a Southern point
of view. My argument is that, although important, such changes are not
altering the fundamental distribution of power in its manifest forms,
and are unlikely to so in the foreseeable future. And, crucially, I have
come across few challenges to the racialisation of power relations.

To summarise the argument so far. This book takes for granted that
many of the institutions associated with the West have generally
exploitative impacts upon the 'Third World' and that sufficient information and analysis has been presented about the activities of the IMF,
the World Bank and the multi- or trans-nationals and all the rest of the
powerful institutions of the 'First World', rendering it unnecessary for
these arguments to be repeated here (see, for example, George, Hayter,
and Korten, 2001). Suffice it to say that such institutions are not necessarily intentionally exploitative, but their impact is demonstrably
oppressive, disproportionately affecting the people of the 'Third
World'. I am less concerned with those institutions regarded by many
as almost by-words for exploitation and oppression; my focus is on
aspects of the relationship between the North and the South which are
generally assumed to be beneficent (or at worst, neutral) in their
impact. Development and aid are generally considered to be unquestionably 'a good thing', with any criticism usually focusing on
insufficient amounts being donated, or the suspicion that such funds as
are available are not being used properly; most argue that the processes
of development and aid are designed to redress global power imbalances, at least to some extent. My proposition, however, is that the very
concept of development buttresses and underpins global inequalities,
including racial inequality. It is not just a matter of faulty practice,
though there is plenty of that; it is a question of interrogating the very
concept of development. The notion of development contributes to
global power imbalances because it contains within it the necessity for
its own opposite: by definition, describing oneself, or one's country, as

developed necessarily entails characterising others as less developed – otherwise there is nothing and no one to measure 'developed' against. It is not possible to conceive of development without the existence of its converse. The existence of the one side of the coin requires that the other side exist, and establishing a superior point of view presupposes that there is an inferior one. And white is persistently associated with superiority and black with inferiority.

I shall illustrate my argument thus far with an example taken from my daughter's geography text book, which visually depicts the connections between discourses of progress and modernisation and white on black racialisation (Waugh and Bushell, p92). The illustration is full page (A4 size), in colour, and is headed 'The road to development'. The summary tells the reader: 'There are great differences in levels of development around the world. It has become increasingly difficult to improve living standards for people in the poorer countries'. The implicit suggestion is that it is those of us (who are the consumers of the book) in the 'First World' who are finding it 'increasingly difficult' to help those in 'the poorer countries'. The argument I present in this book suggests that the relationship is much more complex than this summary would have us believe, and involves difficult power relationships.

These power relationships are not explicitly drawn in this illustration. But they are there nonetheless. Imagine the following picture. The page is divided into three sections, each containing a scene purporting to represent a stage on the road to development. In the bottom section, in the right hand corner there is a chunk of rain forest, and in the left a village of round huts with straw roofs. Surrounding the village are a number of fields. The scene is peopled by black people, some of whom are working in the fields, using only hand-held tools. Two people, closest to the viewer, are seated in a wooden cart being pulled by oxen. These two have their backs to us, and one of them, it is clear, is semi-naked, without a shirt.

Half-way up the page is a picture of an industrial landscape – row upon row of factories and chimneys, producing a great deal of smoke and grime. The colours are exclusively muddy browns and greys and the overall impression is not designed to attract the reader.

At the top of the page we find a portrayal of nirvana. It consists of a cityscape – lots of bright shiny multi-storey buildings surrounded by a well designed road system. There is a limited amount of greenery; the roundabaouts are planted with a few trees and some grass; no people are visible, but there are a dozen or so cars on the roads. We know this is paradise because the sun is shining down and there are no clouds in the sky. The countryside just outside the cityscape consists of a single block of green – presumably grass.

Through these three sections there runs a 'road'. The picture as a whole is set out like a board game, with the road divided into squares, presumably so that children at school can become interactive with the illustration. Should they throw a dice and land on square No 4, they will be told: 'United Nations aid programme helps with new health scheme. Move on 1'. Should they be unlucky enough to land on square No 6 they will find 'Cost of imported manufactures goes up. Go back 3'. It will be evident from this that the START for our players is the black people's village and the finish line is the desired city-state populated only by cars. The instructions for playing the game are very clear (p92) and 'the winner is the first to reach the end of the road'. The illustration graphically shows how being developed and therefore superior is equated with being white, whereas black figures are utilised to convey under-development, in all respects implied as a less desirable state. It illustrates a view of development whereby there is one road, and one road only, leading to the nirvana of development. It also gives a clear idea of the acceptable parameters of development in that the preferred state is urban as opposed to rural and so on. The motif of the 'road' becomes particularly poignant when juxtaposed with Marcos' metaphor quoted above, where the poor and oppressed are likened to unwanted stones and weeds in the road – people who are quite literally in the way. A closer study of this representation of development illustrates some interesting and pertinent issues. Firstly, the fact that this road has one end, where people should preferably wind up, necessitates having an starting point, the implication being that from here people can only travel (and travel they must) forwards and upwards towards the ultimate goal. Furthermore, the implication is that everyone, and all nations, must be situated at some staging post on this road – for there is no other route available to take. And staying at home doesn't appear to be an option either. It is crucial, for the argument of this book, to acknowledge who is visually located at the outset of the road, the setting out point, who is seated in the ox cart, and their surrounding context. The travellers' destination, where, having surmounted the obstacles en route, the lucky ones will arrive is, as described above, a place where the sun is shining in a cloudless sky. The urban-scape as represented here has left behind the grime and pollution of heavy industry and moved onto a higher plane of clean technology and science. The pollution present in the heavy industry stage has miraculously vanished. The implication is clear – life is better at the top than at the bottom of the page. This book takes as a central proposition another feature of this picture – that it is not by chance that the people at the bottom of the picture are black (the most likely location to come to mind for a British child looking at this would, I suggest, would be Africa). The city is visually people-free, though this visual absence does not mean that the city will not be peopled by the Western imagination. And I suggest that the people associated in the Occidental mind with this kind of superior achievement would be largely white. The overwhelming presence of the white, often there but not acknowledged, and its links with the power plays of development and aid, are one of the central concerns of this book.

I consider the design of this geographical aid as neither coincidence nor deliberate conspiracy. It is, though, part of an overall pattern, which is deeply ingrained by history and geopolitics. I argue that such a pattern of the superiority of that which is to be desired, with its corresponding pole of inferiority, is regularly, though frequently subliminally, linked to images and discourses of white and black. This geography textbook offers the first piece of evidence for asserting that there is such a pattern.

Other motifs are used to reinforce the pattern. In this case, the motif of transport, of moving from one place to another (or even, as indicated by the image, from one time to another), is a resonant one which also re-emerges in many guises in later chapters. The people at the start of the development game, who are in the wooden cart or toiling in their fields, are black, whilst those moving around the cityscape in cars remain hidden and must be imagined. Cars, together with the rest of the accoutrements of urban, modern-day travel, are presented as inevitably and unquestionably superior to the humble ox-cart – regardless of environmental costs or suitability to local context. But the point here is not specific arguments relating to better or worse forms of transport, but the manifest and apparently incontrovertible racialised assumptions behind such a portrayal. Which is also, by the way, being routinely taught to all our school children. To summarise: apparently, better = faster = white, whereas black (read 'Third World') people and their ox-carts are locked forever in a seemingly timeless portrayal of inferiority.

Interestingly, even closer analysis of the picture divulges some telling and somewhat wry contradictions. The countryside attached to the desired state of urbanisation is completely devoid of life, so much so that it has a distinctly post foot-and-mouth feel to it. It is not at all clear what the viewer is supposed to admire in this totally empty portion of the representation, in contrast to the more obviously lush and vibrant vegetation (which is at least alive) of the landscape portrayed in the bottom right hand corner of the picture. I would argue that this slip in the intentionality of this image is crucial – it gives the game away and opens up a crucial space to begin to question some of the underlying assumptions and values which determine the overall power balances.

Permission to reproduce the illustration in this book was denied by the publishers on the grounds that my interpretation is not 'fair and representative'. The publisher argued that I had taken the illustration out of the context of the rest of their work on development. However, I will amply demonstrate in this book that this illustration is not a unique or unusual portrayal of the power relationships involved in development. Throughout this book I use many similar examples to depict a wider context which does indeed demand recognition – that of white on black racialisation.

The publishers of the illustration also pointed out, in their letter of refusal, that I 'fail to show that, on the opposite page (p92), Figure A uses black people as representative of a developed country'. The illustration they refer to consists of a number of faces (both black and white), each with a speech bubble commenting about development and aid. The letter makes the point, more succinctly than I could, that black people are simply being 'used' here, I would imagine to give an impression of fairness. A further comment suggests that I do not take into account that, in other places, their Key Geography textbook series treats 'the subject of development and aid ... without any reference to race or colour'. Much of this book is devoted to arguing that 'race' (or rather racism and racialisation) is present and affective in such discourses whether or not this is explicitly recognised.

THE ARGUMENT

To begin this section I intend to discuss some of the potential challenges to my argument. Firstly, I am aware of the view that I am arguing that the lives of black, 'Third World' people should be relegated to the ox-cart whilst those of us in the more privileged West continue to enjoy the benefits of consumerism. I do not take the view that all progress or development is, by definition, a bad thing, and it seems perfectly reasonable to hold a position whereby people choose for themselves which bits of the 'modern' world they want to buy into. It is clear, however, that we cannot continue to assume the unquestioned benefits of all aspects of progress – and one of the main representations of modernity in my daughter's geography book illustrates the point. The car is a potent symbol of power but its benefit as a tool of mobility must be judged alongside its costliness to the world as a whole. Its costs and benefits need to be thought through much more carefully than is currently the case, and related to global power differentials – this would include assessing the number of car-related deaths and injuries and to whom, their contribution to pollution, their impact on city life, the absorption of raw materials and the conditions of labour employed in their manufacture, particularly in 'Third World' factories. Having thought these issues through, my judgement is that I, as a 'First World' consumer, must downsize somewhat and, at the minimum, use cars as a means of transport as little as possible. The argument is, crucially, about what we in the West choose to do, rather than offering prescriptions to the poorest and most beleaguered nations of the world.

Secondly, a possible interpretation of my thesis might be that I am opposed to helping those in distress and that I would be prepared to leave people in conditions of misery. There is indeed a difficulty with the very concept of helping, but only, I maintain, when it is help which is imposed on someone else. It seems almost impossible, within current structures of aid and development to envisage a world where we all help others at their request and when it is required, instead of continually imposing Western-determined targets and methodologies. My proposition is that, from a value base of a belief in the injustice of poverty – shared by most development workers and agencies – those of us who are relatively comfortable need to develop theories of development which highlight the role of the Western world in the creation and maintenance of poverty, and which do not conceptualise development as a linear activity, equally applicable to all countries regardless of history or geopolitics. Perhaps we could even begin to think in terms of what constitutes enough, instead of assuming that progress must always equal more growth, and everything improving by becoming bigger and faster; we should concentrate on applying the concept of enough initially to ourselves in the West. We must couple this with a recognition that a significant part, at least, of Western comfort and privilege derives from what we have taken in the past, and continue to take in different ways in the current day, from the 'Third World'

I suggest in this book that the personnel and apparatus of 'Third World' development does not, indeed cannot, achieve what it purports to, and that, far from ameliorating the negative impacts of capitalism or globalisation on the poorer nations, it actually and unwittingly compounds them. The theory and practice of development are partly structured by processes of racialisation which permit the justification of the attribution of inferior and superior, in all aspects of life, to different regions of the globe – roughly speaking, the undeveloped countries of the Southern hemisphere are consistently represented as inferior whilst the developed areas of the West are routinely assumed to be superior. Apparently paradoxically, I argue that the theories and practices of development and aid work, far from contradicting this, instead feed into and buttress these fundamental power imbalances, and contribute significantly to the racialisation of the superior/inferior binary.

The bulk of this book provides the evidence for proposing such a link between racialisation and the discourses and practices associated with aid and development. As I have already indicated, I do not consider that development and aid (either theoretically nor in practice) exist in a vacuum, and I shall make some connections with discourses from other arenas, particularly in relation to tourism in the 'Third World'. If I can persuasively demonstrate that those of us from the North who set out with the best of intentions are implicated in racialised relations of inferiority/superiority, then it seems to me that the entire structure of North/South relations would need to be re-conceptualised. The connections need to be made across what are at present seen as different 'disciplines', and I shall take a moment here to look at the overlaps and recurring patterns in another major, and increasing, aspect of North/South relations – that of tourism. I shall use an example which relates to Kenya in order to begin to reveal how the similarities of the Western gaze are replicated not only across the 'Third World' but also across different types of relationships between the 'First World' and the 'Third World'. The racialisation of this relationship, inscribed in development discourse, is also present in discourses associated with tourism.

I referred to myself earlier as a political tourist, by which I meant that I had come to look at the interesting and unusual political situation which then pertained in Nicaragua. I also, of course, took advantage of the opportunity to do some of the more 'normal' things associated with tourism – it did not take me long to discover the best beaches in Nicaragua and I gloated over how totally unspoilt they were (notice the 'were' – some ten years on increasing levels of exposure to both international and Nicaraguan visitors are now visible). I ventured into neighbouring countries as my confidence grew and my Spanish vocabulary increased sufficiently. Certainly the opportunity to travel and to 'see something' of Central America was an important part of the motivation for being there, and future travel plans, as well as stories of journeys completed, formed a major topic of ex-pat conversation. Thus I would argue that discourses of tourism overlap significantly with those of development and aid, both in the theoretical sphere as well as in our everyday lived realities. Hence I moved from political tourism to development tourism.

Tourism, in common with development, is represented in the West as invariably positive for the host countries of the 'Third World'.[4] The visitors – hopefully – benefit from having a good time and the peoples of the 'Third World' from increased amounts of revenue. I would like to take a moment to unpack some of this, because there are significant features in common with views of development. Not only is there the problem of the potentially destructive impacts discernible in quite concrete terms (for example, the effects of numbers of people on frequently sensitive environments, in terms of the amounts of the amounts of rubbish generated, particularly the ubiquitous plastic water bottles), but we also see here, once again, the assumptions of Western superiority that feature in much that is said and written about tourism in the 'Third World'. To return to Kenya for a moment, let us take as an example an article written in *The Guardian* by Claire Armistead, where she asks the question: is it safe to take the family on safari? Her observations on Kenya as viewed from the safari lodge are particularly pertinent:

> at the safari lodge ... you don't feel sealed off from the outside world ...
> It is all an illusion, of course: the dollar-rich tourist is a million miles
> from the Masai schoolchildren, walking barefoot from their villages to

the tin-shed communal schools – but to see them in their grubby ging-
ham frocks, the lucky ones clutching footballs (though their villages
have no electricity and they can never have seen a football match) is to
witness a moment of history that is unlikely to survive into my children's adulthood.

The imagery in this short quote is so commonplace in relation to the
'Third World' that most British readers would barely notice it, let alone
actively question its validity. Some of the images are really quite bizarre
– what is a school if not 'communal' (Oxford English Dictionary definition – benefiting a community, for common use); yet the use of the
word has a very specific ring about it in the Kenyan context. It somehow reeks of being old-fashioned, of being amateur rather than
professional, of not educating children for the modern world. And this
is re-enforced by the description of the school as a tin-shed and the
children themselves are inevitably grubby and barefoot. But the real
conflict with the so-called developed world comes with the assumption
that it is 'lucky' and therefore better to be carrying a football – a fortunate or even blessed talisman of Western culture – and that the children
must be aspiring to this to such an extent that they are already 'history'.
In the absence of any further explanation for such a sweeping dismissal
of the future of an entire people, the reader is left to assume that the
conquering power of football is representative of the superiority of
Western culture and way of life generally; and that it will, within a
generation, naturally and somehow inevitably, come to replace such an
inferior existence.

This approach to development and aid issues is nothing new, though
VSO (see previous section) are perhaps a little more honest than most
of us about what it is that lures Britons to seek out development work,
whether as a permanent way of life or as a temporary volunteer. This
kind of relationship between Britain and the rest of the First World
with developing countries, where the latter are perceived and portrayed
primarily in terms of what they can provide for the benefit of
Westerners – whether it be the sun, wild animals, romance, exotic
things and people to look at or a chance to improve one's career
prospects by cutting one's teeth on 'unusual' challenges – this is not a
new relationship. It is actually a continuation in a different guise of the
old colonial relationship whereby the colonies were regarded as essentially providers of what the 'mother-country' needed and desired. Only
in those days it was slaves, sugar and cotton rather than exclusive beach
holidays and character-building safari adventures. The exploitation of
raw materials from the Third World has not gone away, it is simply less
visible and supplemented by other forms of domination, discernible
primarily in the contexts of tourism and development and aid work.

This book argues, then, that development and aid contributes to a fundamentally unequal power relationship between the First World and the Third World and helps to maintain those global power structures more commonly associated with colonial times. Furthermore, I shall present a case for suggesting that the First World/Third World development relationship also embodies a particular aspect of power relations – that of racialisation and white racism. I want to look at this feature because it has been ignored as an aspect of international relations more generally, and specifically within the arena of development and aid.

Thus this book will approach the issue of 'Third World' development, not in terms of its impact or lack of impact on levels of poverty in the so-called 'Third World', but from the perspective of that part of the globe generally portrayed as the beneficent donor, that part of the world which is largely represented as the source of solutions to the problems of the South. I want to think about what the provision of aid and development means to those of us located in the North who are in some way associated with both the theory of development and its practice, and who see ourselves (see pvi) as at the top of the road, where the sun is apparently shining, and thus in a position to send enlightenment back down the path to those at the bottom (of the page in this instance).

There are, of course, commentators who are simply dismissive of the whole panoply of Third World development, whose opposition is based – overtly at least – on grounds of cost, and who argue a position that peoples in faraway countries should cease to be 'provided for' in any way but should learn to stand or fall according to their own ability to compete successfully in the global economy. This is not the argument of this book and I would characterise this viewpoint as reasonably typical of those whose expressed fundamental beliefs are that the creation and operation of unrestrained free markets and free trade leading to unhindered economic growth for those who take advantage. From such a standpoint, it follows that any aid designed to assist development in Third World countries constitutes an inadmissible distortion (thought it should be noted that neoliberals frequently argue for state intervention to secure 'favourable' market conditions). Though I will refer to such views, I place them at the extreme end of a continuum of Northern attitudes towards the Third World. Their contribution to the exploitation of the 'Third World' has been well documented and does not need to be repeated again here.

I wish rather to consider and investigate those of us who would describe ourselves as, at least on the whole, positioned at the sympathetic end of the continuum, trying in some way to be responsive to the needs and concerns of the majority of the world's population who live, broadly speaking, in the Southern part of the globe. Development and aid are usually firmly linked in the public perception (at least in Northern discourses of development) with charity, with beneficial actions and good intentions, and if it doesn't work, this is assumed to be because either the sums of money are insufficient or there is a fault in the system. The association is almost invariably with doing good, or at least attempting to do so, and any apparent failure to ameliorate the levels of poverty, or to lower infant mortality rates (one of the commonest of the various indices used to measure 'quality of life') is generally explicable either in terms of deficiencies in the aid budget or recipient countries' inability to respond positively enough to the offers of help. The proffered reasons for such inability vary; it could be lack of democracy or 'good governance' in 'Third World' countries; or the endemic bribery and corruption also to be found in 'Third World' governments and bureaucracies, and occasionally in aid agencies themselves; it could be their lack of institutional capacity (to use one of the current buzz words in development) and infrastructure; all of these are perceived to hinder growth and development. We shall see how, when identified in the South, such matters tend to be attributed to a nationality or a region ('African leaders are ...'), with a distinctly racialised basis. In contrast, the responsibility for similar misdemeanours when uncovered in Northern states is laid at the door of the individual, with others around exonerated. An example would be media coverage of the relationship of the Conservative Party to Jeffery Archer. The suggestion is that such levels of corruption in Britain are entirely due to the actions of an individual, and that even those in his immediate surroundings could not have been expected to be aware of what was going on. Similarly, newspaper headlines of the corruption in the Enron corporation do not refer to such corruption as being a North American trait, or as being endemic in Western society. However, when it comes to understanding such processes in the South, the argument is that generalised 'Third World' corruption, coupled with other identified features such as the lack of viable democracies, renders it impossible for Northern donations and assistance, no matter how generous, to be effective in achieving the aims of poverty reduction. Occasionally explicit but more often underlying the apparently technical arguments as to why development has failed to achieve its goals is an implication that those at the lowest section of the route to development are, for some reason, resistant to a full appreciation of its benefits or are just incapable of taking full advantage of what is on offer. It seems that it is the fault of 'Third World' countries in some way if they become stuck at the beginning of the race and do not complete the circuit around the monopoly gameboard. And, as with the example from the geography textbook, blackness is always associated with factors such as corruption and lack of democracy, and hence with being situated at the beginning of the road to development rather than having arrived at the peak. Very rarely is the concept of Third World development itself critically examined in media coverage or, perhaps unsurprisingly, within aid and development agencies.

Some writers (the ideas of several of them, such as Escobar, Esteva and Sachs, will be drawn upon later in the book) argue that development is, overall, a Northern imposition, designed and implemented with little real regard to Southern needs or values in spite of the rhetoric of participation and empowerment, and then blaming the victim when it fails to deliver the goods. Devastating though these critiques may be, in my view they omit a significant aspect of Third World development – that is, the extent to which, in both its discourses and its practices, it constitutes an active participant in the racialisation of the relationship between those regions of the world which may be broadly characterised as North and South. This relationship is clearly one of overall unequal power relations, and can be characterised as being similar to that which prevailed in the time of imperialism and colonialism (the term neo-colonialism refers to a situation where the forms of imposition may be different and more subtle but the overall results are not clearly distinguishable from what went before). But one aspect of the colonial relationship which many assume to have undergone a transformation is that of white-on-black racism. And this is precisely the aspect which I wish to highlight, as well as the extent to which the development relationship remains essentially racialised. I deliberately employ the term racialised as distinct from racist, as I want to emphasise that much of this is entirely unintentional, and even ostensibly benign in origin. Nonetheless, as I shall demonstrate, the outcomes are clearly racialised, inasmuch as one part of the world – that where the majority of the population is white – is consistently treated as superior to an 'othered' region which is consistently represented as inferior in all aspects – that part of the world where the majority of the population is black. Such differences are apparent in all aspects of life – economic, political, intellectual, moral and even emotional – it is generally regarded as impossible to live in the 'Third World' and be happy or content! And, as I shall explore, I believe that much of this binary approach is underscored and legitimised at a subterranean level by continuing and pervasive concepts of racial superiority/inferiority. These are less overtly expressed than in the more outspoken eras of imperialism and colonialism, but they nonetheless retain their authority. The potency of white and black as markers of superiority/inferiority have not disappeared with the official disbanding of empire. Much writing has hitherto focused on the use of black skin colour (and other physical traits) to delineate inferiority and/or subservience in various contexts, but in this book I attempt to focus on the significance and power of being white.

The following extract from my diary (summer 1995) in Nicaragua relates a story which could have been situated in any country in the 'Third World'. It reveals my discomfort at my position, which was part of the trigger for subsequent thinking and research.

We travelled today from Granada on the ferry to the Isle of Omatepe in search of some rest and relaxation. We are staying in a new hotel, actually called 'The Paradise Hotel'! I can't decide what I think about it. On the one hand it is really comfortable, whilst being pretty basic and of course beautifully situated right on the beach with a lovely terraced garden. Just the stuff tourist brochures are made of. It is run by a Swedish woman, her Nicaraguan partner seems very much in the background, and this worries me though I don't know why.

I was completely fascinated by this scene which took place on the on the ferry. It's quite a large boat, especially by Nicaraguan standards, and I'm glad it was because Lake Omatepe is enormous and it feels more like being out in the open sea. The ferry was mostly full of Nicaraguans, most of whom looked like they were returning to the island from working on the mainland or possibly selling agricultural produce, such as plantains and other fruits for which Omatepe is quite famous. Anyway, they were all clearly exhausted and as soon as possible they had spread rugs and other pieces of cloth wherever they could and slept for most of the 5 hour voyage.

However, there was also a handful of gringos on board. 10 or so – mostly backpackers from the States but also a few development workers (one woman from Spain whom I recognised) looking for sun, beach and who knows what else. Most of them have turned up at the Paradise! It was extraordinary how all of us ex-pats gravitated towards one another on the ferry – a completely unspoken but powerful coming together, drawn by the visual identification of shared skin colour and enhanced by our recognition that even the most cash-strapped of us was distinguishable by the expensive rucksack, money belt and the ubiquitous camera. Thus we marked each other and ourselves out from the rest. And we proceeded, almost by stealth, to stake our claim to the most comfortable part of the boat where there was a kind of large, raised platform more comfortable to sit on. Those Nicaraguans who had already taken up residence on the wooden slatted platform simply melted away and found themselves somewhere else. The result was much more comfortable for us, with considerably more space. All this happened without a word being spoken. The demarcation was complete, obvious to all, mentioned by no-one. The only one of us to break ranks and spend a good part of the journey chatting to (up?) a young Nicaraguan guy was the Spanish woman. The rest of us stayed well and truly together.

Clearly, the beginnings of an explanation of my interpretation of whiteness is required here. Skin colour is an important component in establishing power relations, as illustrated in my story above. This is particularly obvious in situations where stranger recognition is the issue. Though critically important as a visible marker in situations such as this, the skin colour binary of black/white is neither literal nor uncontested. Though I consider myself to be white in terms of what happened on the ferry, my actual skin colour is pinkish grey, turning a little red or brown upon exposure to the sun and, as my daughter says, rather splotchy. Thus I am using whiteness in an ideological or political sense, to indicate a socially constructed, racialised process whereby a particular power relation is established. Perceived physical attributes, most often skin colour, but also including for example hair texture, are employed to establish in and out groups. Cultural and moral attributes are also used in a similar way to indicate that one group is to be defined as superior to another. The Omatepe ferry scenario illustrates the immediate impact of skin colour, reinforced by economic and cultural attributes. The rucksack is the travellers' emblem, indicating the wealth of being able to travel in such a way. There was also a moral dimension in terms of who claimed the right to occupy the superior space on the ferry. A racialised power relation effortlessly came into being, acutely in evidence on board the Omatepe ferry. Such perceptions of greater and lesser worth clearly have real effects, which impact on the material lives both of those deemed superior on the basis of attributed whiteness (we got more leg room and somewhere to sit) and those deemed correspondingly inferior. There are also emotional and psychological benefits in that it feels good to be treated as superior, adding to a personal sense of self-esteem and self-worth.

Being visibly, politically white is critical, for the possession of 'white' skin is an immediately recognisable passport to power which can override a range of other attributes of power such as wealth or education, as I shall illustrate in later chapters. It is no coincidence that, in much of the 'Third World' such as Africa and Latin America, the more powerful and the more wealthy elites are also generally the lighter skinned. Power does not always operate in the same way for all individuals at all times and, for example, a white development worker can feel powerless in certain situations; but I would argue that an appreciation of her/his individualised reality has to be balanced alongside the wider, global picture of unequal power relations between the North and the South – what I shall refer to as the bigger picture. White is not coterminous with Northern (or Western), but the overlap between them is critical and, furthermore, the association of both white and Western with the concepts of modernity and development are central to this study. The overlaps with other attributes of power, such as class, gender and, I would add, consumerism, are important and they will feature in later stages of the book. The central feature, though, is whiteness, for, as Alistair Bonnett points out: 'the emergence of white racial identities is an integral component of the development of modernity across the world' (Bonnett, 2000, p2). Bonnett stresses the links between words such as 'civilisation', 'European', 'Western' with the identification of a European white 'race'. I shall argue that this remains the case in current day international relations and I shall explore its prevalence in an arena where one would least expect to find it – in aid and development.

It is not easy to demonstrate the existence of something which is, on the whole, kept well-hidden, and of which most of us who are in some way implicated are entirely unaware, though it nonetheless constantly and profoundly impacts upon both what we say and what we do. In order to establish and maintain the sense of superiority/inferiority which pervades most North/South interactions and relations, racialised discourses have to be present in some form and be recognisable as such by all parties. Everyone involved has to know their place, as on the ferry. And the more everyone just knows what their place should be, the less need there is for any explicitly racist statements. Furthermore, the absence of overt recognition of imbalanced power relations renders them less likely to be subject to any form of challenge.

The incident on the Omatepe ferry could be interpreted as a particular, unique experience, determined by a particular combination of environmental factors and the personalities who happened to be on board at that conjuncture. But this incident is just one in an already well-established pattern. Such individual snapshots of life take place as part of the texture of wider, global inequalities; and such particular instances of wider racialised power relations are legitimated by the everyday power plays which resonate across global space – what we term geopolitics – and across the centuries of historical time. There are two main tributaries feeding into and informing the creation and maintenance of racialised global power structures. The first is primarily a question of geopolitics, the second a matter of history. Neither institutions nor individuals operate in a geopolitical vacuum, separate and distinct from other global and regional power relations, whether expressed through the use of armies, the threat of force or economic exploitation. In this world where economic motivations and outcomes are the predominant determining factors in global relationships, and where there is a flow of resources and capital from South to North – including the provision of 'exotic holidays' and, increasingly, of cheaper and cheaper labour – development agencies cannot be and are not neutral bystanders. They/we are not outside of that relationship. For example, many of us benefit directly from the purchase of cheaper clothes and shoes, and do not think twice about trying to afford a holiday in the tropics, no matter how critical we may be in theory. And history is important in its sanctioning of racialised power solutions. As we have seen, colonial attitudes may be expressed a little more subtly in current times – whether on safari holidays in Kenya, or on the Omatepe ferry – but their effectiveness seems undiminished.

THE EVIDENCE

This book is about demonstrating the existence of powerful patterns – patterns of white-on-black racialisation in history and in geopolitics – and their appearance where they would be least anticipated. The aims and intentions of 'Third World' development and aid are usually regarded as positive by both practitioners and the general public. An assertion that this is a sphere where unequal power relations based on racialised differences operate would therefore come as a genuine shock to many. But the core of the evidence for this proposition comes from a number of interviews which I carried out with development and aid workers between 1996 and 2000, both in the field and at headquarters offices (mostly London-based). The workers themselves were not all white, but each was asked how s/he would define him/herself, since the object of the interviews was to explore how individuals perceived themselves as white, Western workers practising in a 'Third World' country, and whether the issue of unequal power relationships impacted on their view of themselves and their work. The interviews outside Britain were undertaken in Nicaragua, for no other reason than that I had contacts already in place there, and would not have to start from scratch. These formal interviews are supplemented by many informal discussions over the period of a decade, with workers and volunteers based in many 'Third World' countries, including World Bank officials. The informally obtained material cannot be directly quoted, as there was no awareness that I was undertaking an interview as such, but it provides invaluable background information.

It is also crucial to indicate how I locate myself within the emerging pattern. I have already indicated that my journeys to Nicaragua are thoroughly implicated in the racialised discourses and practices which I shall be highlighting, and I have attempted to incorporate myself throughout the discussion. Of course this is not easy; one is always tempted to exculpate one's own actions and one invariably understands the reasons for one's own actions better than those of others. And I have no desire whatever to indulge in a 'white guilt' syndrome just for the sake of it – throwing one's hands up in horror in a 'mea culpa' kind of a way seems to me to be of extremely limited value unless it leads to some active change on the part of the sinner. The chief reason for including myself is simply, as I have already mentioned above, that I too was brought up in a society where I received the drip-drip effect of racialised ideas of superiority and inferiority. My mother, rightly considered by all who knew her to be the gentlest of souls, nonetheless could and did invoke the image of the 'black man' as an object of fear and punishment. The advent of a black majority government in South Africa was the occasion for serious tut-tutting and premonitions of the direst forms of black-on-white violence. No reason was offered for these predictions other than the very 'nature of the black'. I offer these as examples of patterns of thought that were, and still are, routinely resorted to in discussions of superiority and inferiority. Images supporting such views bombard everyone from every angle of life – the media, advertising, the way school classes are taught, the predominance of whites in any relatively senior position and the racially unbalanced profile of management in both public and private institutions. So, as a child and now I have been as imbued as the next person with racialised ideas of inferiority and superiority.

A further important reason for including myself is to emphasise that I am not interested in establishing a blame culture. Though some of those whom I quote directly (and I do not identify them in order to avoid as much as possible any pointing of the finger at particular individuals or agencies – all names and some other details have been changed) may recognise themselves from the interviews, I want to stress that the views transcribed here are fairly characteristic of attitudes to the 'Third World', as I indicate through the use of a range of different sources of material. Development and aid workers are certainly not responsible for racialised approaches to the 'Third World'. On the contrary, they often see themselves as doing their very best to alleviate some of the worst effects of Western inspired processes (colonisation, modernisation, globalisation) on the South. They/we are, however, totally imbued with racialised attitudes and this cannot help but influence discourses and practice in the 'Third World'. All of us who benefit in whatever way from unequal global relations (tropical holidays; garments, shoes, carpets, manufactured in sweatshop conditions; use of raw materials, especially wood and minerals, exacted at a price usually unknown to Western customers; the consumption of ever cheaper coffee, tea and sugar, etc) must take responsibility for the effects of our actions and the need for effective change. Development and aid workers certainly have a responsibility to be aware of the implications of their role, and are perhaps in a unique position to point out the effects of Western processes to those who have somehow remained unaware of the effects of exploitation and poverty – but beyond this I suggest that they/we are no more and no less liable than the rest of the West.

This book, as I have said, is about patterns and connections. In relation to historical factors, I try to show that colonialism and imperialism have not reached an end point – on the contrary, many of the attitudes of white colonists towards colonised peoples (particularly in relation to concerns for the welfare of the subjugated) resonate on, and with, today's discourses of development. Thus there are connections across time as well as those across space. There has been a repetition of discourses of inferiority and superiority across the globe. Of course there are significant differences in power relationships in different parts of the globe, but there are also striking similarities. I shall refer to this pattern as the role of geopolitics.

I also want to establish links between discourses apparent in development and aid and those that emerge in other spheres of life. I have already indicated some of these in relation to tourism, and I also utilise texts and materials taken from a wide range of sources – academia, British governmental politics, popular authors, newspaper and magazine articles – to indicate how these discourses re-emerge time and time again, constantly acting to reinforce one another. What these sources all have in common is that I have selected them because they are identified as being sympathetic to Latin American or other 'Third World' peoples. And, as I have said before, if discourses of racialised inferiority/superiority are apparent in these contexts, how much more so will they define what goes on in the arenas where sympathy is not even on the agenda?

Two points to stress here. Firstly, I do not consider racialisation to be the only affective power relation either globally or in any other sphere. I am aware of the role of other relationships and discourses of dominance, for example in the spheres of gender, class, sexuality and physical ability. But these are not my main concern here, and I would argue that the impact of whiteness in development and aid has remained, certainly in the West, totally unacknowledged. There is, for example, a significant contrast between the attention paid to gender issues as a power relation within the development and aid world and the total absence of issues connected to 'race'. My aim, therefore, is to consistently and actively challenge the myriad ways in which negative images and stereotypes of blackness are identified and disseminated by the dominant (Western) culture, while whiteness is not even given a name in many contexts – at least, not in white dominated contexts. As Toni Morrison points out, whiteness is perceived – or, to be more accurate, *not* perceived – as 'mute, meaningless, unfathomable, pointless, frozen, veiled, curtained, dreaded, senseless, implacable' (1992, p59). The resounding silence which surrounds whiteness cannot be explored head-on, but rather through an approach which investigates and unpacks, at close quarters, those discourses and practices which in some way touch upon it, overlap or even elide it. This would include exploring discourses and practices of power, of development, of expertness – even discourses of solidarity, of the very concept of helping. Marianne Gronemeyer (1992, p53) goes as far as suggesting that the very idea of helping should be problematised and seen as 'a threat, as the precursor of danger'.

Secondly, I have no doubt that Nicaraguan people (or people elsewhere in the 'Third World') have a great deal to say about the impact both of Western development models and practice and would express a range of views about the role of whiteness in the racialisation dynamic. The comparative absence (though not total) of Nicaraguan or other 'voices from the South' from this particular work should not be taken to mean I consider them insignificant. Following this trajectory

would be important work, but it is not within the remit of this particular research. It seems to me that critiques from the less powerful can
run the risk of being dismissed by the relatively powerful, as resulting
from a 'chip on the shoulder' or just plain envy. I want therefore to
focus on evidence directly from, as it were, the horse's mouth. It is so
much harder to deny or minimise critique when the horses ourselves
acknowledge (albeit unwittingly) our role in creating and maintaining
unequal global power relations.

The impact of whiteness is a highly problematic area to explore. As
I have already illustrated, whiteness is rendered invisible in the
discourses and practices of development (as, indeed, in many other
spheres of life). But it is embedded in attitudes and assumptions which
are important not only for their own sake, but because they have material impact on peoples' lives. It is embedded in attitudes and
assumptions which people, particularly those of us engaged in 'doing
good', do not like to admit to, and which we would much rather allo-
cate to explicit racists or to bygone colonial and imperial eras. This is
the reason for the very close analysis of texts presented in this book –
whether of interviews explicitly carried out with the aim of exploring
attitudes to whiteness, or of the range of other texts, and my own material, primarily in the form of diaries kept during and after my trips to
Nicaragua. It is only through close and detailed analysis that various
themes emerge which can be linked to racialised discourses and, in
particular, to the superiority of whiteness.

Lastly it seems necessary to say that I do think things can change.
There has long been both debate and action in relation to racism and
racialised relations within the borders of Britain and the US (and
indeed, within European boundaries). There seems every reason to be
optimistic that, once on the agenda, racism operating between regions
of the world, on a global basis and apparent in all aspects of that relationship can be addressed and tackled just as forcefully. This is not to
say that racism has been overcome within the 'First World', but that
actions can lead to change.

NOTES

1. As well as 'voices from the South' such as that of Marcos, there is currently
   a thriving industry involved in the production of life stories of the
   poverty-stricken and the marginalised and I do not intend to present here
   yet another version of life from the perspective of the oppressed (or, more
   accurately, a chronicle of life from the perspective of the oppressed as
   interpreted by myself). There is now a massive accumulation of data –
   both in the form of 'hard' statistical evidence as well as the more literary
   first hand accounts such as that of Marcos – which, between them, offer
   ample documentation of the existence of global inequalities and injustices

and their impact on the real lives of 'simple and ordinary men and women'. It seems to me there is more than sufficient material available and readily accessible demonstrating why and where poverty exists, its destructive repercussions on all aspects of peoples' lives and, what is more, plenty of ideas as to how best and by whom it might be tackled.

2. The terminology used in this book – black/white; 'Third World'/'First World'; South/North – is not meant to imply the existence of absolute, impermeable binary divisions. It is certainly not intended to reinforce those divisions. The available language is imperfect but, as this book illustrates, it is reflective of existing power imbalances on a global scale, in both the discursive and material realms.

Furthermore, the use of such terms is not intended to encapsulate or portray any of those aspects of identity which may exercise individuals and groups. I am conscious that for many the descriptions 'black' and 'white' are unwelcome. It is important to recognise that I am not using black and white in the sense of attributing identity. The issue for this book, to reiterate, is power relations and, crucially, the racialisation of inequalities of power. In this sense, I consider the discursive and operational division of the world into black (inscribed as inferior) and white (self-portrayed as superior) to be absolutely fundamental in determining global power relations.

3. It is interesting how frequently conditions of poverty or deteriorating public services (the health service or transport services, for example) in Britain are described as 'Third World', usually without the need for any further comment as the phrase itself is apparently sufficient to indicate the direst of situations.

4. Exceptions are the literature of Tourism Concern and Returned Volunteer Action, both of which are highly critical of the 'First World' approach to the 'Third World'. See especially RVA's *For Whose Benefit – Racism and Overseas Development Work* 1991.

1

THE EVIDENCE OF WHITE POWER: INTERVIEWS AND DIARIES

It was the promise of the politicians, the justification of the technocrats, the illusion of the outcast. The Third World will become like the First World – rich, cultivated and happy if it behaves and does what it is told, without saying anything or complaining. A prosperous future will compensate for the good behaviour of those who died of hunger during the last chapter of the televised serial of history. WE CAN BE LIKE THEM, proclaimed a gigantic illuminated board along the highway to development ...

Galeano, 1997, p215

This chapter draws primarily upon on the material which I have collected from interviews carried out over several years, which were specifically designed to unpack and investigate connections between whiteness and power.[1] I also use examples taken from a trawl back through my own diary, kept for more than a decade to record events in which whiteness seemed to be implicated in some way, and, perhaps more importantly, later reflections on those events. I have kept this diary ever since my early days in Nicaragua when it began to strike me that there was something interesting and important, but unspoken and unacknowledged, going on, which had a profound effect on relations between those of us from the North and Nicaraguan people. The material is, therefore, necessarily personal, in the sense that each portion of interview or diary which I choose to present originates from a particular individual's point of view, and from a particular moment in time. Clearly I make decisions to deliberately select those sections which touch upon the argument I am proposing. However, it becomes clear, over a number of interviews and diary entries, that significant patterns emerge, or indeed remain submerged, which are testament to particular and consequential ways of approaching issues of whiteness and power. To draw out these patterns requires very close and continual analysis of the textual material. I have already stressed how this book takes as its subject those of us in the West who are expressly sympathetic to the needs of 'Third World' people, and it is therefore unlikely, though not impossible, that explicit expressions of overt racism and white superiority will be apparent. But it is only with a detailed examination of what we say, and sometimes of what we leave out, that our deeply held attitudes, often rejected and denied any existence at the conscious level, become apparent and can be accorded their due level of importance. An exploration of such perceptions, though often disconcerting, and at times even painful, is not only important for its own sake but because there are serious consequences for the lives of both black and white people as lived in the material world. Development practices in particular, and wider North/South interactions in all their manifestations, can be shown to be thoroughly and intensely infused by racialised power relations. Thus I use, as the first piece of evidence, a precise scrutiny of selected fragments of text taken from relatively informal dialogues (I include my diary recordings in this description), as I consider this the best way to search out indications of largely hidden referents.[2] This accumulation of identifiable themes, each of which contributes crucially to the significant overall pattern, can then be combined with the evidence presented in the next chapter, which is, in contrast, taken from discourses circulating widely and available to all. However different the material, the emergent patterns are disturbingly similar.

The selected quotations presented in the ten sections of this chapter are taken from interviews in which discussion of issues related to whiteness and power, and the links between them, was quite clearly stated to be the purpose of the interview. The outcome of the interviews, taken overall, indicates that whiteness as a power construct is largely absent in any explicit way from development discourse; it is also frequently and vehemently denied that whiteness has any importance at either conceptual or praxis level. This is not in some ways surprising as there is little overt recognition of racialised relations in the development world generally, or, indeed, in any discussion of current-day global relations. The only exception to this, and one of the few contexts in which whiteness is routinely and unquestioningly acknowledged and, indeed, headlined, is when the representation is one of 'whites under threat from blacks'. Thus whites were so identified (and identified themselves) during press debates on the so-called 'race riots' of 2000 in northern British towns such as Bradford and Oldham; and oppression of self-categorised whites in Zimbabwe has been similarly standard newspaper fare in recent years. (This exception is also apparent in the interview excerpts, especially those quoted in Section 6.) Nonetheless, the issue of whiteness is demonstrably present throughout the interviews in underlying and highly affective forms, emerging through the more common patterns of white-on-black formations of power relations, as I shall illustrate throughout this chapter.

In contrast to its almost total absence as a subject for discussion on the global stage, there is some limited discussion of whiteness in domestic British and North American cultural arenas. Richard Dyer, for example, seeks to deconstruct the imagery of whiteness as represented in (Western) photography and film. He does allude to 'those in power in the West' (1997, p9), but is not concerned to elaborate on this as a global relationship. Though not the object of his concern, what he says about whiteness is nonetheless relevant in the wider context:

> The equation of being white with being human secures a position of power. White people have power and believe that they think, feel and act like and for all people; white people, unable to see their particularity, cannot take account of other people's; white people create the dominant images of the world and don't quite see that they construct the world in their own image; white people set standards of humanity by which they are bound to succeed and others bound to fail. Most of this is not done deliberately or maliciously ... goodwill is not unheard of in white people's engagement with others.

Many of the extracts from interviews and other sources already quoted reflect a number of these themes: the creation and maintenance of dominant images of the world; the apparent desire to construct the world in the image of the powerful; and the formulation of standards, and the making of judgements, by which both white people and those defined as others succeed or fail – and there is also ample evidence of goodwill in development work, as I readily acknowledge.

The urge to help was also present in imperial adventures, but this does not in any way negate the existence of attitudes of white superiority. The assertion of goodwill by those involved in development and aid contexts can be problematised: it should not be automatically taken as synonymous with the belief that no deliberate malice is intended. Joel Kovel's comment on the abolitionist movement, that the 'actual aim of the reform movement, so nobly and bravely begun, was not the liberation of the black, but the fortification of the white, conscience and all' (1988a, p202), is an insight amplified by bell hooks (1990b, p125), when she critically examines the role of white women in the anti-racist movement. Such critiques do not destroy the notion of 'good will', but they point to the fact that people's motivations are complex, and often informed by unconscious feelings and desires, sometimes linked to a need to establish superiority.

This chapter sets out to explore the racialisation of development discourses as it emerges through the interviews and my diary material. It will already be clear that such issues are unlikely to be discussed in a upfront, straightforward way. Rather, my task has been to scrutinise closely my diary and the interview transcripts, and to extract relevant themes, codes, recognitions and disavowals, showing where there are links with discourses of colonialism and imperialism and the racialisation of the global North/South relationship. The effect of the evidence must be taken overall and not in isolated chunks, for its importance is accumulative rather than immediate – by which I mean that the impact of each individual statement or allusion (or book, or TV programme) may be almost imperceptible, but taken together such racialised referencing adds up to a consistent and seemingly unbridgeable division of the world into superior and inferior. The dynamic sometimes operates subliminally, but nonetheless it always conforms to the patterns of global racialisation.

In this chapter, I identify a number of ways in which white racism and the racialisation process seem to come close to being recognised but are then immediately disavowed or denied. I organise the discussion into ten sections, each of which considers a particular theme of disavowal. Firstly, I demonstrate how in many instances white racism simply is not (in contrast to gender issues) placed on the development agenda and this remains relatively unchallenged. Secondly, I consider the technique of allocating responsibility or blame for everything which goes wrong within national boundaries (in this case, Nicaraguan) – from the macro-economic to the bus being late; this allows the contribution of the West to be defined not as part of the problem, but only as the solution. Thirdly, I look at the tendency of such acknowledgement of white racism as there is to be located securely within the borders of Nicaragua (again the use of national borders), thus avoiding any potential global implications. Fourthly, I explore how concepts of hybridity and identity may be used to render situations more complex but, at the cost, I would suggest, of obscuring overall power relations. Fifthly, the technique of arguing that someone else abuses their power more than we do is also a common enough technique, and I give examples of the willingness of many people (including myself) to 'blame' the US whilst choosing to ignore the pivotal role consistently played by the British in Nicaragua. Six, I consider how issues of class and money are interwoven with those of racism and how class, like gender, can act as a distraction. In section seven, I show how personal emotions, particularly the feeling of being threatened, emerge in discussions of whiteness and I argue that this serves to allow whites to strategically position themselves as relatively powerless and in a victim role. Whilst possibly an experiential actuality for the (white) individual in a particular moment, this is a reversal of the overall power balance and an example of the narcissism which can take over even the most altruistic of development workers. Finally, I offer some examples of sexualised stereotypes of Nicaraguan men and women, demonstrating the highly ambivalent nature of some of the relationships recorded in these interviews and diary entries.

1.1 ON THE AGENDA?

This section explores the direct and indirect connections made by the interviewees when answering questions I posed expressly about what they perceived and how they felt about issues of whiteness in relation to their role as development workers in Nicaragua. Unless I indicate otherwise, all of the interviewees here self-identified as white. I asked the majority of my respondents a direct question as to whether they considered the issue of 'race' or racism to be on the agenda – either their personal agenda or that of the organisation for which they were working – and they all, without exception, said that it was not. Jan said that, even though 'most of the development workers you see are white, middle class and … within their recruitment structures [the agencies] haven't made a lot of effort to branch out',[3] she nonetheless felt that issues around 'race and racism' were 'hard to see, because it goes out of your mind being here – you're not confronted with it on a political level like you are in Britain'. Joanne made a very similar comparison with her involvement with issues around racism in Britain:

Gender is on the agenda but racism isn't. Perhaps it gets obscured behind the question of culture. For example, in the job interview you are asked about cultural sensitivity, about how you would deal with cultural situations and on the preparatory course before going overseas, you are told about not offending with dress or behaviour. One way racism manifests itself is a lack of respect for someone's culture. But it goes far deeper than that and organisations should tackle it more.

People with *extreme racist attitudes disqualify themselves*,[4] because they wouldn't want to come to a country like Nicaragua but, on a more subtle level, it hasn't been tackled by organisations.

I haven't discussed racism before in Nicaragua. I've discussed it in Britain and I've been to workshops and became quite aware of racism within myself. One particular experience I remember. I went to the golf course with my Mum and I saw a black man playing golf with a white caddie and it was such a visual shock – afterwards I realised why – it was indicative of my own internalised racism.

So it was a big issue in Britain. But out here it's not addressed at any level. The only time it's been talked about is when people talk about *encountering racism from Nicaraguans but I've never heard about Europeans being racist.* It's somehow because we want to be here, because we're working here, because we have something to offer, it's assumed that we can't be racist. I find myself thinking about Nicaraguans; 'oh, they're all so childish', and then I stop and think 'this was what was said about Africans in the last century' and I realise this is my own racism coming out – I'm perceiving them as being childish whereas in fact they have very good reasons for feeling the way they do and on an intellectual level I can appreciate all that – but when it comes to the emotional level, I think 'oh, *they're being childish*'.

Other interviewees were considerably less forthcoming than Joanne, who, in the above quotation, has been very open about the early influences in her life and willing to acknowledge the possibility of her own racism. The mechanism of comparing 'Third World' peoples to children is, as she indicates, a fairly prevalent mode of expressing racialised sentiment, though its relevance is often assumed to have been relegated to the colonial era. Another important aspect which she mentions is the interpretation of racism as something experienced only, or primarily, by whites or Europeans. This tendency to project the expression of racism onto Nicaraguans is a theme I shall return to later in this chapter. Her idea that people with 'extreme racist views' would disqualify themselves from development work is also interesting. My experience suggests that people often travel from the 'First' to the 'Third World', not with an open mind, but, on the contrary, a determination to find evidence to support their preconceived notions as to, for example, what causes 'Third World' poverty. And one does not have to be marked as an extremist for this to be the case. It is not difficult for the 'First World' traveller to utilise every late bus, every street robbery, every bank queue, as concrete proof of inferiority.

For the present, I wish to emphasise the mechanism of avoidance – the way white-on-black racism is simply not placed on the agenda. Paul offered an interesting example of this – we had just had a discussion about global inequalities between the North and the South, and I ask:

Me Do you think it is reasonable or not to argue that racism plays a part in that?

Paul Well, historically, yes. The process of colonisation was a racist process and what we call the North and the South is now defined as a result of that colonisation process by the various European powers. So I think, historically, yes. The extent to which one can say that it's fuelled by racism *now* would be more difficult to define. I think that, well, the attitude exists that anybody from Nicaragua must be of less capacity for doing the job than somebody in Britain That attitude exists, right. It's based on ignorance because, you know, *they haven't come across people like the educated sector here,* who despite disadvantages in access to education and so on, you know globally and at national level, they're just as capable if not more, with probably a far better perspective on things than the average person from Britain, so there are attitudes which persist.

Me But you wouldn't go quite as far as I would and call that racism?

Paul (long pause) Well, it is a racist attitude, because it differentiates people according to their colour, race or nationality. There are mixtures of all three, but it's a racist attitude. It's people making an assumption, illogical assumptions based on ignorance.

Me So when you said earlier that you would certainly agree that historically the relationship was based on racism, colonialism and so on, that's less true now. It may be less true now, but you would still say that are kinds of attitudes and ways of perceiving in the North that you would see as being quite racist?

Paul I think there's more awareness or more concern *about being identified as a racist amongst people from Britain*. For example, I think the issue of racism has grown in importance over the last two hundred years and hopefully over the last twenty years it's started accelerating. But I'm not sure if I'm qualified to say or not, but I mean that's an optimist's point of view.

Me In your experience, does it get talked about much in the context of white people from Britain working here in Nicaragua?

Paul I don't think that the word racism comes up with frequency, but there is another way of, I'm just trying to think of, if people avoid the term racism and I think that's true, I think that *represents a problem*.

Me In the way that people don't avoid the word gender or even the word sexism.

Paul Well, they're the trendy themes of the day, aren't they, of course. I think I'm agreeing with you. Frankly, the issue that is going to attract funding today is gender. *Racism doesn't seem to have the same priority amongst NGOs that gender has* and I wouldn't, I mean you'd have to ask an NGO what they think about it. I mean like NGOs will say 'we have an Equal Opportunities statement policy', but special attention is given to gender, and I think that's fine, absolutely correct, and *I'm not saying that the issue of racism is not of significance*, talking in circles here aren't I?

Talking in circles or not, Paul makes some important points here which illustrate some of the mechanisms of avoidance. Firstly, he implies that racism was certainly a feature of colonial and imperialist times but has (mysteriously) disappeared from the 'now' during the intervening years, though no evidence is offered to support such a major transformation. Secondly, he goes on to agree that there are 'attitudes' which he would call racist although he is clearly unhappy about using the actual word 'racism' and, if it does exist, it must be based on ignorance – 'they' (i.e. those with racist attitudes – note, exclusive of 'us') only persist in holding on to such views in the absence of meeting those individuals who would disprove it, in Paul's schema the 'educated sector'. He also mentions that people from Britain are now more concerned about being 'identified' as racist, which does not necessarily imply any real change. However, on pushing him a little, he acknowledges such avoidance 'represents a problem'. He finishes this particular quote with a classic double negative, though, which has less impact than saying racism is significant. Double negatives are useful in keeping something off the agenda.

1.2 THE PRESENCE OF GENDER AND THE ABSENCE OF WHITENESS

Interest in gender as a power relation is very evident in discourses of development. Both in the consciousness of individual workers and in official pronouncements of the agencies, it has a high profile. One of my female interviewees, Amanda, has been involved for many years in gender issues, though she says gender was not 'an in word' when she first went to Nicaragua:

> ... the Nicaragua experience of seeing how women are organised made me further consolidate that interest and I'd always had an international interest and the two things came together and I thought let's go and try this out ... try and see where *it takes me*.

Me   Can you say what is meant by the feminisation of poverty?

Amanda The fact that poverty resides, you know, that it's, I suppose that in it there is a suggestion that more and more, it is becoming increasingly women who are bearing the brunt of poverty. Just thinking about it, perhaps it's always been the case, perhaps it's always been the feminisation of poverty, you know, structural adjustment, there has been a lot written about how it has impacted even more so on women. So to some extent there is an increase in the numbers of women who are becoming impoverished as a result of the massive reductions in public spending programmes.

Me   It's not saying that men aren't poor too?

Amanda It's saying that there are a far higher proportion of women than men who are poor and a very high proportion of people who are classified as poor, in that income bracket, are women who are trying to manage to raise children on their own, you know single mothers and their wages are ... and so on and so forth ...

This quote indicates both the scope and the intensity of the concern for women. It encompasses a personal experience leading to a degree of identification which is then substantiated with a theoretical framework articulated in terms of the feminisation of poverty, though I wonder whether a degree of Western narcissism is not implicit in the trajectory of 'where it takes me'. There is also much written on the need to focus particularly on 'Third World' women. For example, Momsen puts forward a convincing picture of the persisting inequalities that 'Third World' women face relative to their men and states that this has implications for development strategies: 'The alternative vision, recently put forward, of development *with* women, demands not just a bigger piece of someone else's pie, but a whole new dish, prepared, baked and distributed equally' (1991 p3).

As part of their contribution to the 'new dish' a number of the development and aid agencies publish material which is solely concerned with gender issues. In One World Action's list of publications (September 1996), three out of ten titles are exclusively about gender and three of the remainder have chapters specifically written on gender issues. During my visit to the CIIR (Catholic Institute of International Relations) offices in London, I noticed that two complete bookshelves were devoted to books about women and the 'Third World', more than any other single topic. Oxfam also publishes a great deal specifically focusing on gender and one of their published authors, Helen O'Connell (1993, p60), argues that although there are differences between North and South, and 'the legacy of centuries of systematic exploitation and colonialism cannot be dismissed', nonetheless, she feels that 'women all over the world share some common problems; discrimination; greater poverty amongst women; the triple burden of family, paid work, and community; the sexual division of labour; male violence; and marginalisation from political decision-making. They also share a concern for the global environment'. It is noteworthy that potential divisions between 'First' and 'Third World' women are dealt with summarily whereas shared aspects are heavily emphasised. I shall return to this tendency to subsume differences or even potential conflicts in order to establish connections which I would argue are to some extent imaginary – what Gilroy calls 'pseudo-solidarity' (2000, p41).

Pertinent here is the role of the NSC (Nicaraguan Solidarity Campaign), which is somewhat different from the majority of NGOs involved in Nicaragua, in that its remit is not overtly to promote or encourage development as such but rather to build a relationship of solidarity. This relationship has undergone some major changes during the 1990s and Denise describes them thus:

> I think the NSC in the 1980s was very much working with what we saw as a political project, something that solidarity movements throughout the world saw as a symbol of hope for people who were oppressed throughout the region, so yes it was a political project, working alongside the FSLN. Things have changed since all the allegations of corruption, and especially with the sexual abuse charges against Ortega. It's not so easy to work with them now.

So, we changed our focus and now we're working in solidarity with a number of different organisations including, we still have contacts with the FSLN, but we also work with women's groups, community groups, voluntary groups and with groups working around the autonomy process on the Atlantic Coast. So that political project and people's perceptions of it in Nicaragua is very, very fragmented and Sandinismo means different things to different people.

One of the major ways of expressing such a change in direction for the NSC has been to focus increasingly on community groups, of whom women's groups are an important example. Schumann argues that the NSC is an example of people-centred and community based development, which includes the requirement for communities in the North to mobilise their own citizens for political action and change; he says: 'Southern and Northern communities can work together through people-to-people relationships that are non-bureaucratic and motivating' (1994, p3). He presents the solidarity network which Northern based organisations, such as the NSC, built up with Nicaragua as among the most successful CDIs (Community Based Initiatives) and argues that currently, 'Northerners of any political viewpoint can find plenty of opportunities for partnership' as Nicaraguan organisations 'are desperate for the most basic kinds of technical assistance' (p48). Angela Hadgipateras (1997) discusses the increasing threats to women's organisations from Nicaragua's current neo-liberal government and its newly set up Ministry of the Family. One of the growing side-effects of the international solidarity movement and its antagonism to such moves from the Nicaraguan government has been an increasing willingness to circumvent official bodies in order to reach and fund Nicaraguan NGOs directly – whether this undermines one of the stated goals of development to build up democracy is an important question, but beyond the scope of this book.

Thus attempts to create solidarity with women's groups and organisations have intensified over recent years as an apparently unproblematic replacement for the currently less acceptable links with Daniel Ortega and the official section of the FSLN. An NSC pamphlet says that the women's movement is one of the most active social movements in Nicaragua today and the Women's Network Against Violence is the most dynamic expression of that movement (NSC Special Report, 1999). NSC and CAWN (Central America Women's Network) aim to achieve their goals 'through campaigning and lobbying in Britain and the development of political, material and moral solidarity at all levels with partner organisations and communities in Nicaragua' (p4). From the perspective of this research, the important effects of such links built around gender is not only concerned with what these relationships entail but also with what is left out. Unlike O'Connell (quoted above), I would argue that if differentials in power between men and women require attention and challenge, then so do other power relationships, including those which may implicate white Western women. Their/our engagement in the politics of solidarity, admirable though this may seem, does not absolve us from the commensurate exigency to interrogate and actively try to change those power relationships in which we play a part.

Some of the interview participants did share their observations and comments on a number of pertinent power relationships in addition to that of gender, and talked about their impact upon their role as development workers. A number of complicating features emerge. For example, Peter makes the point that gender is not equivalent to women's issues when describing his workshops on 'Popular education in masculinity'. The focus is male identity and issues of discrimination: 'why *we* discriminate especially against women and the methods we use to discriminate ... *We* try and relive, simulate certain experiences for the men in the group so that *they can experience* in the workshop being discriminated against or remember when they've been discriminated against'. It is interesting that Peter moves from a 'we' identification with the Nicaraguan men into a demarcated, distanced 'they', but the major point I wish to emphasise here is the intense and all-embracing commitment to working with gender issues. Peter says the group leaders try to put the experiences of the group members:

> ... within the context of gender theory and analysis and the issue of homosexuality always comes up ... (which) most men live as a real fear ... most men in Nicaragua from the time they have been told and taught, you mustn't ever show any behaviour that people might think is homosexual. It's an absolute fear, terror that other people might think that they're homosexual. This dictates their behaviour towards women and towards other men. (In) one of the first workshops we did an exercise, we put men into small groups to discuss what had caused them most shame in their lives. In the plenary the number one fear was being raped by another man. Not what we were expecting, we expected being a thief, or beating up or raping a woman. It was quite shocking for most of them to realise that one of the biggest fears was being raped by another man, just the sense that if another man penetrates you, it's taken away totally your masculinity. The workshop tried to unravel *all these myths and prejudices* that go towards making up male identity in Nicaragua and looking at other male identities, not just the stereotypical identity that *society imposes on men in Nicaragua.*

I quote this in order to indicate how serious, almost fervently so, this gender work is intended to be. And how entirely and how precisely the 'myths and prejudices' are located within Nicaragua, whilst the potential solution is to be brought in from the outside. The nature, the qualifications, the relevant experience of the outside agent are nowhere specified by Peter but he and I (as the listener) share an assumption that any intervention must be for the best. Clearly his aim is to have a major impact on the attitudes and behaviour of the men who attend the group sessions.

Vicky is another interviewee who was involved in working with a range of power issues (my italics indicate the wide range of power issues covered in her work), and she introduces a perspective on 'race'.

> ... we are working on internal institutional development from a diversity perspective – diversity with equity really, although we began with a gender focus and then looking at inter-generational focus, but increasingly it's moving towards looking at much more complex issues of power and so that's why we're going on to diversity with equity. That's what we're saying – it's a bit of a slogan but that's the way we're kind of, you know group it all together
>
> So the first 8 or 9 workshops – the key was, the cross-cutting issue was sexuality and power and then we looked different themes – like violence, abortion, religion or theology, health, sexuality in itself and I can't remember all the others at the moment but that's the way it was, but then we repeated them, and making changes each time ... and that's (about) the transformation of power relations in daily life, mainly about men and women but also about adults and young people and about sexual options and, increasingly about looking at other issues, about *issues of disability and race* and such like ... there's long been a concern about going beyond gender and looking at the way power relations inter-link and then there's a whole kind of concern about, if you're going to build strong, active and civil society – what kind of actors are they?
>
> Me So where's the race stuff going to come in and impact?
>
> Vicky Well, the way that's come in is really through the work – there's a programme which is called – there's a lot of work with young people, there's one training programme which is 'Training for Youth' and that's where they've done most work on looking at the way young people experience the cross over in their different identities. So they've begun to look at, you know, *gender issues, obviously, class issues, issues of sexuality* and begun to work more seriously on disability this year and race. They began to work on *race issues* last year, because here, I mean particularly the issue of black/white, it's not black/white, I mean it's a question, that's the thing, you could see it as black/white, but it's Atlantic Coast and Pacific Coast. But there is a lot of *ingrained anti-Coast prejudice.* So they're just developing a methodology to work with young people to look at the way all these power relations, get them to look at them altogether. So, for example, every year, for the last two years there has been a youth camp for young people which lasts

about twelve days and each day they are looking at a different set of power relations. So it's kind of an intensive experience for these young people who come from all kinds of organisations, from church organisations, from environmental organisations, from community organisations and they come together with young trainers as well. There's very few adults, there's a real emphasis on handing over to young people so that they speak for themselves and the way it's dealt with here, they call it adultismo, because there's a preference for adult knowledge, and young people adopt that as well. So they are working on that *anti-adult focus*, like letting young people develop a sense of self and developing their own voices. So, anyway, I mean I didn't manage to get to the youth camp but I would love to have done. I was meant to go as an extra person for methodology and stuff, but in the end I didn't. But everybody who goes on this says it's really amazing because its twelve days out of normal life and working on all of these key issues at once so that not one gets precedence. And what happens is you get a transformation. It's quite incredible, I've talked to some of the young people afterwards, and it's just really interesting, the way looking at them all together is, like something happens, like a click. Very moving. A lot of young people come out.

One of the things they did say this year was, whereas last year the whole race issue hadn't been very strong, this year, when it got to the day when they were going to be dealing with race issues, the people from the course were saying 'tomorrow's our day, tomorrow's our day' because there's much more of an awareness now. *Racism was not discussed, during the Revolution it was not discussed – well, you know, 'there's no racism here'. It was denied.* And now that it's beginning to be discussed, it's like creating an environment, a fertile environment for people to begin to stand up and be counted, the same way as prejudice against women was not discussed and violence wasn't discussed in the mid-80s. And by now you've got like a critical mass where people don't accept it anymore. You know, it will take some time.*

I have indicated the wide range of power relationships considered by Vicky to be important, in addition to gender. Racism is specified but it is important to note that it is perceived in black/white terms only as applicable to relationships between Atlantic Coast people and Pacific Coast people (I look at this in more detail in Section 1.4). She is clearly not avoiding the use of an uncomfortable duality as she is happy to use this construct in relation to several different power relationships (young person/adult to name just one example from the above extracts); her avoidance stems from racism being thought of as existing only within the national boundaries, in this case Nicaragua. The possibility of white racism as a component of the development relationship, in which she and I and other development workers may be implicated, is entirely absent. I return to the significance of this in the concluding section of this chapter.

1.3 KEEPING WITHIN BOUNDARIES

One of the issues which struck me whilst living in Nicaragua was the frequency with which after dinner conversation would be spattered with references as to how Nicaraguans as a people and as a country do not succeed in establishing standards which, the comparison insists, one would expect in Northern, developed or 'civilised' countries. Comments varied from the sublime, with an entire thesis being written critiquing the propensity of the Sandinista government for constructing large projects (such as sugar refineries) which then did not have the capacity (in this case the raw sugar cane) to function properly; to the apparently ridiculous, with my housemates arriving home from work hot, tired and angry because their bus was severely overcrowded. And all this would be somehow the fault of Nicaragua. Even though we knew the political and economic constraints in theory, this failed to translate into everyday conversation, especially when one's personal comfort was affected. On a remarkably consistent basis, both macro economic issues and more minor, everyday irritations would be discussed, usually moaned about, with no reference whatever to the surrounding context. And, remember, we were a group of people basically sympathetic to the Sandinistas and, as I say, sufficiently informed in theory to offer an excellent seminar on the economic impact of the US blockade and the Contra War, both of which lasted throughout the 1980s. In my experience, such identified 'lacks' or deficiencies (economic know-how, comfortable buses) are rarely placed into any historical or geopolitical context, but instead provide the grist for a good end-of-day grumble. It is a serious matter, though, because this process allows the implication to settle that the total responsibility for whatever lack is identified belongs within Nicaragua, though the power to identify and pass comment invariably belongs with the West.

The following quotation provides an example of this tendency. This interview took place in 1998. I quoted this worker earlier and, as with my housemates, he does establish an overall political and economic context, and, in theory at least, he is well aware of the impact the unequal relationship has had over time on the lives of Nicaraguans and other peoples of the 'Third World'. And yet, when he is talking about what makes life difficult for him personally in Nicaragua he reverts seamlessly to allocating responsibility to forces within the boundaries of Nicaragua, and therefore apparently within the control of Nicaraguans:

If we take the telephones ... there are various reasons why our partner organisations are not on the phone. Firstly, it's because of a lack of funds, they get cut off when they can't pay, but secondly, it's because there's no telephone lines being installed to mention. This house has been waiting for a phone line for 3 and a half years, still with no sign of anything happening, *and that's not anything to do with Nicaragua as such,* apart from the fact that the *Nicaraguan government is going along with the privatisation* of Telcor and they're storing up the bank of demand for when the company is privatised. So this is neo-liberal policy in action and the effects of it.

The lack of telephones are, initially, 'not anything to do with Nicaragua' but the overwhelming impression by the end of the discussion is the culpability of the Nicaraguan government. The impression is given that the Nicaraguan government is a free agent in terms of whether or not it supports the privatisation of Telcor and the imposition of neo-liberal policies. The phrase 'going along with' suggests there is a real alternative path which could be followed if the present government so chose. What goes unmentioned is the impact of the IMF (see below) in ensuring such policies are implemented, and the critical role of the US, backed by the UK, in establishing and supporting the current neo-liberal Nicaraguan government in the first place. However, on a more abstract level, and when the topic of conversation is less about personal issues, then this worker offers a critique of the role played by the West in determining conditions in Nicaragua. Thus one way of keeping discussion of issues like poverty within national boundaries is to essentialise, not only the actors, but the whole process, so that allusions may be made, allocating blame and responsibility to the poverty sufferers themselves and thus encouraging a victim-blaming approach.

As the above example illustrates, many individual development workers are well aware of the general outline of the geopolitical context in which Nicaragua, together with other 'Third World' countries, has to operate. The foreign debt is one part of the equation – by 1994, Nicaragua owed some $11 billion. This meant each man, woman and child owed $3,000, the highest per capita debt in the world. Since then, some creditors have cancelled parts of the debt to about half but debt repayments remain an unmanageable drain on the economy as a whole (Plunkett, 1999). When the Sandinistas lost the election in 1990, the efforts to 'integrate' into the world market economy had begun in earnest. In that year, a stabilisation and structural adjustment programme was instituted in order to qualify for IMF loans. The result was the beginning of several years of huge cuts in public services and the selling off of state assets (as with Telcor, described by the previous interviewee). The Sandinistas had spent some 59% of Gross Domestic

Product on public expenditure (ibid, p47) and within three years this was reduced to 27%. In April 1994, the Nicaraguan government signed a letter of intent with the IMF for a 3 year Enhanced Structural Adjustment Facility. Some $500 million in aid was promised from the US and other sources – much of which never materialised. In return, the government agreed to sacking a further 13,500 workers (the government had already fired 25,000 public employees – it helps when reading these sorts of figures to bear in mind that Nicaragua's population is 4.5 million). Education and health spending levels were frozen and fees introduced, electricity and water rates rose and most state owned assets sold. In sum, a fairly recognisable IMF package (Green, 1995). The effects are familiar from other 'Third World' accounts of relations with the IMF, and some sweeping critiques of global organisations such as the World Bank and the IMF have been published. Susan George (1986) describes how both their policies and practice are heavily biased towards the interests of the developed nations and are 'irrelevant or downright harmful to genuine development' (p xiv; see also Hayter & Watson, 1985). As one example, she shows how food aid is used to promote commercial sales from the 'First' to the 'Third World' and how local food production is undermined by the dumping of surplus food-stuffs resulting from over-production in the North. Other writers have gone further, arguing that the current development model actually causes poverty to deepen because it is inextricably linked into unfair terms of trade and ever declining prices for primary exports. Free trade and liberalisation mean that the most basic foodstuffs can be freely imported into 'Third World' countries, thereby destroying the liveli-hoods of small farmers, whilst the developed countries insist on protecting their own farmers (Bendana, 1999). This pattern is clearly repeated across other countries in the 'Third World' (Ransom, 2001 & Ellwood, 2001). Thus aid and development, in Nicaragua and else-where, cannot be seen as somehow independent initiatives which can stand or fall outside of other global power relationships.

A general awareness of these issues is often apparent in the inter-views, as with Paul above, but the implications do not necessarily filter through into everyday narratives. To offer a further example from another development worker: Mary describes her experience of North/South relations when she graphically portrays a particular aspect of IMF policies impacting on her project:

> It's a big problem with the sort of thing we were doing – the Ministry of Health, in that region, we went to their meetings sometimes. There was somebody in charge for that region; now he's got things to do, hospitals to run, he's got immunisation campaigns ... and his money is being *cut and cut because of structural adjustments* and everything. His staff is being laid off and he can't pay wages – so he has got his priorities and he

would really like to get our money. And one of the big problems was, and it was a problem for me as well, was that we were getting paid much more than the woman, for instance, who ran the hospital. You could argue very well that health promotion and health preventive work never really gets the funding and that it was important to put money into it and that it *could be done* by us from outside, even outside of wherever, even outside of the system, not necessarily outside of the country. But, in fact, if you looked at *how much of the money was going on us and flying us in and out,* then it would be much more *difficult to justify.*

Mary's analysis of the situation would seem to argue against resources being put into such outside intervention, offering as she does a critique of the IMF approach and an acceptance that her project is also implicated with 'how much of the money was going on us ... difficult to justify'. It is often the case in development and aid work that Western governments and aid agencies seem to spend inordinate amounts of money on ensuring that Westerners are transported to the chosen 'Third World' location rather than handing the money over directly to, in this case, a Nicaraguan organisation or even directly to the poor. The unspoken implication is that Nicaraguans simply would not know how to use the money effectively, which is, of course, highly contradictory when we consider how much is spent on the panoply of necessary accoutrements for incoming Western development workers (transport and living costs, sometimes including dependants, higher wages, health insurance). Informally, I once asked a development worker why resources could not be directly given to the poor. 'The men would drink it' was the reply. The use of the phrase 'flying us in and out' I find particularly telling as it seems to imply a level of wastefulness and indulgence which would stand in complete contrast to the lives of the majority of the local population who would be unlikely to have such a claim on resources. Having the choice of 'in' or 'out' is a peculiarly Western luxury, but one which is rarely acknowledged. The choice of phrase 'flying us' also absolves development workers of personal responsibility for what is happening, as they/we are being flown. In spite of an analysis which would apparently argue for devolving the finance to grassroots level, Mary and the rest of us continue to fly out there, absorbing precious resources. The very fact that she, and other Western workers and researchers, are physically present and undertaking development work in one form or another suggests that there is an alternative analysis, conflicting with her explicit one and establishing instead the inevitability and naturalness of a presence which does not really need to be explained nor justified and which can withstand even an internally contrary logic.

It is also important to the coherence and strength of this argument that Mary presents the oscillating issues of the impact of the IMF and her own presence in Nicaragua as if they were individualised, discrete sets of actions and discourses. In some respects clearly they are but this transaction is also an exemplar of the West taking with one hand, with IMF cuts as only one of a sophisticated range of extractive strategies (see above example), whilst giving back – considerably less – with the development other, a pattern re-iterated all over the 'Third World'.

This quote, from a worker who has spent many years in Nicaragua, offers an example of the importance of boundaries to her and what is thereby included and excluded:

> You don't feel in Britain, that the country is about to *slip off the edge* and you feel that here in Nicaragua. You just don't see a future. You talk to people about their experiences of, you know, their kids in school or the treatment they get in health centres and you just realise that *where do you begin?* And I sometimes wonder that this work that we're doing with organisations and such like, what can you really hope to achieve when people are struggling from day to day to survive or they work night and day, when basic levels of education are minimal and the quality of education is very, very poor. So there's a whole lot of stuff that, you know, they just can't grasp because *they haven't learned certain skills*. And so it's limited what you can do in this situation, without structural change, without overall policies – *that perspective between the local and, let's say, the more general or the national.*

The empathy with poor Nicaraguans evident in the first part of this extract slips, unnoticed by me at the time of hearing, into a reflection on how hard it is for development workers to achieve, though their goals remain unspecified. Empathy with Nicaraguan people 'struggling to survive' moves onto basic standards of education being low, which then becomes their responsibility because 'they haven't learned certain skills'. The skills can remain unspecified, as this links into the discourses around Western expertness which I will explore in more detail later. The crucial phrase in terms of establishing responsibility and, in this case a degree of blame, is 'where do you begin?'. It is important in conveying a sense of geographical and temporal lost-ness and has a resonance, at least in Britain, of hopeless resignation. The use of the complicit 'you' draws me, the listener, into a state of more empathy with the problems of achievement facing the worker and away from consideration of what might be causing a country to be in such a dire state as to be close to slipping 'off the edge'. Thus, we stay focused on Nicaraguans and their problems which are defined solely in terms of their (Nicaraguan) contribution. And the positive achievements 'begin' in the West. Any suggestion that, at the micro-level, the work itself might not be appropriate or, on a more macro scale, that the West, including Britain, may be contributing to Nicaragua's proximity to 'the edge' is effectively forestalled. The 'edge' in itself is a very resonant metaphor; conjuring up ideas of marginality and 'pre-Enlightenment' notions of the earth being flat encouraging the imaginary of 'falling off'.

Furthermore, the speaker makes it clear that the required structural change, the (revised) overall policies, are nationally based, thus ensuring once again that not only are the causes of the problems kept within Nicaraguan national boundaries but so are the potential solutions, though they must be determined and initiated by those who 'begin'. The direction of this debate then moved into a lengthy discussion of how the NGOs do not pay 'dignified salaries' to those working in the South, and the power differentials between country-based staff and London staff, who are described as thinking that 'we're playing out here really and we're like volunteers'. This power differential, which clearly touched upon her own interests, made her angry and indicated a degree of narcissism, a theme which I shall return to.

This tendency of explanations being confined to what happens within national borders, and abstracted completely from any sense of historical or geopolitical context, is a mechanism which occurs persistently and I shall return to its importance. It allows for the exercise of global power relations to be significant in their effect and yet to remain hidden and thus go largely unchallenged, at least by those who benefit from the system thus sustained. The following section explores another aspect of the use of national boundaries – that of a preparedness to acknowledge racism, but only that which exists between othered peoples, in this case Nicaraguan peoples.

1.4 NICARAGUAN RACISM

There are, in Nicaragua, as in any part of the globe, differences of ethnicity and culture which sometimes become the basis for varying degrees of antagonism and hostility. Within Nicaragua, the fusion of those indigenous peoples who survived the period of European conquest with the incoming Spaniards resulted in a population of which three-quarters are mestizo. The inhabitants of the Pacific coast are almost entirely mestizo, with a few small and scattered Indian communities. In contrast, the Atlantic coast has a number of diverse ethnic groups. The Miskitos are the largest of the indigenous groups and are concentrated in the north-east of the country. They have resisted incorporation into Nicaragua since it became an independent country in 1821 and prefer to identify with other Miskito people who happen to live the other side of, for them a meaningless border, in Honduras. There are smaller groups of indigenous peoples, including the Mayangna Indians, who are sometimes pejoratively known as Sumo, the word for cowardly in their own language, and the Rama. Further south, particularly in the Bluefields region, live the Creole descendants of slaves who were taken there by the British in order to work on plantations, and abandoned when the plantations turned out to be unprofitable. The Creoles are English-speaking and often perceive themselves as having more in common with the islands of the Caribbean than with the rest of Nicaragua. The British hunted the Mayangna and Rama Indians, using them too as slave labour. They were also subject to the usual missionary interventions. This section illustrates how much easier it was, in the interviews, to identify and comment upon that racism which occurs within Nicaraguan borders than to discuss that which impacts from other countries. In the literature too, the aspect of racism which has received the most attention as it impacts on Nicaragua has been that between Pacific coastal peoples and the Atlantic seaboard (see Lancaster below and Plunkett, 1999).

Since national independence in 1821, the various Nicaraguan governments, based on the Pacific coast in Managua, have tended to neglect the Atlantic coast region, except when there were natural resources to exploit. Minerals and timber have long been targeted by both Nicaraguan and outside entrepreneurs and the coastal peoples have rarely benefited. This inevitably aggravated already existing tensions between the two parts of the country. The Sandinistas, who were themselves mostly of Pacific-coast origin, acknowledged what they initially referred to as the 'Atlantic Coast Problem' (Hooker, 1985); this presented particular difficulties when some of the Miskitos joined the Contra forces to fight against the Sandinista government. The situation was undoubtedly made more complex by the refusal of the Miskitos to recognise national boundaries, as ties with other Miskitos in Honduras were greater than those with the rest of Nicaragua, and there they received military training from the US along with other Contra forces. After the Revolution, there was a real attempt to implement autonomy on the Atlantic coast, but there was some tension between this initiative and the need to maintain and enhance national identity. William Ramirez explains the Sandinista position thus: 'There are Nicaraguan Miskitos, as there are Nicaraguan Sumos, Nicaraguan mestizos, Nicaraguan Ramas, Nicaraguan Creoles. So we have our differences, but these differences have a common denominator – Nicaraguan nationality' (1985, p393). Moves were made to encourage the re-instatement of indigenous and Creole languages, and Bluefields culture was, for a number of years, much appreciated by the younger and international set in Managua, but little was done to challenge, or even acknowledge, the racism exhibited towards peoples of the Atlantic coast (see Rooper & Smith, 1986 for an alternative view).

What is significant, from the point of view of this author, is the tendency to focus solely on the racism/s which are a feature of the situation within Nicaragua's borders, as briefly described above. Even though I explicitly stated that I was interested in white-on-black racism, the responses frequently slide very quickly into a discussion of the complexities existing between the different ethnic peoples of Nicaragua. Thus a further mechanism for avoiding discussion of the existence of white racism and its impact is to make an assumption that what we are really talking about is that racism which exists between Nicaraguans.

Vicky, for example, who organises and runs workshops with young people (as described in the previous section) discussed questions of race solely in terms of the relationship between the Atlantic and Pacific coasts, arguing that it was not so much a black/white question as an Atlantic/Pacific one. The following quote from Peter illustrates further how the words 'race' and racism are taken to mean issues within Nicaragua:

> *Me*   How much attention do you pay (in the workshops) to issues around 'race and racism?
>
> *Peter*   Very little. Absolutely none. Because there aren't any men from the Atlantic Coast who come to the workshops – all the men who take part are mestizo, Pacific Coast men who believe that racism does not exist in Nicaragua and we haven't made any effort as an organisation to incorporate men from the Coast. We have talked about it informally at times – *it would be interesting to know* the experience of Miskito men and black men from Bluefields and how their experience of growing up differs and is similar to the rest of Nicaraguan men. We haven't been able to do it.

Not only does Peter immediately interpret the words 'race' and racism as referring to divisions between Nicaraguan people, but he also creates distance by positioning himself as someone who has a legitimate curiosity in the 'experience' of the Miskito and black men but without declaring his own role in the situation. He continues:

> So in the workshops the 'race' issue has not been brought up. We have talked about it in the co-ordinating team – when we present the structure of the sex/gender relationship we can see the same relationship in terms of *white superiority over black people*. There are similarities. But Nicaraguan men haven't had that experience – most Nicaraguan men from the Pacific Coast would have prejudices against people on the Atlantic Coast – but their actual experience of inter-action with people on the Atlantic Coast is very limited, very minimal. So they have lots of pre-conceived ideas and prejudices against them.

Here, 'white' is being used to delineate the lighter skinned Pacific Coast (largely of Hispanic origin) people from the mostly darker skinned Atlantic Coast people. In the Nicaraguan context, such a use of the concept of whiteness may be entirely valid, but it is significant and characteristic that any sign of the presence of European/North American whiteness is completely omitted.

An illustrative article, written by Roger Lancaster (1991), gives a complex picture of how skin colour, race and racism operate in Nicaragua, and he points out how much anthropological work on race and ethnicity in Latin America generally has tended to focus on specifically Latin American mechanisms for ensuring subordination and elitism. Nicaragua is not a particularly racially polarised society, comments Lancaster, but he illustrates how everyday discourse amongst 'ordinary people in Managua' undermines the official line, that racism does not exist, espoused by politicians and the cultural elite. He argues that associations of backwardness and evil are made with darkness of skin colour, but that far from being solely applied to the 'others' of the Atlantic coast '[it] is but an extension of a much deeper seated pattern internal to mestizo culture, not external to it' (p342). One of Lancaster's interviewees observes that:

> 'in the land of the negros (sic), the moreno [brown-skinned person] shall be blanco' – something of this very issue – power, status, wealth – clings irrevocably to colour distribution and colour descriptions. Of poor barrios, it is sometimes said 'They're very black.' It seems there really is a loose correlation between darkness and poverty. Of wealthier neighbourhoods, it is also said 'They're whiter.' In this case there is a very clear connection between affluence, status, power and whiteness (p344).

Historically, the origins of this can be located in the ascent of whiteness that began with the Spanish conquest and which associated 'Indian' and 'black' with defeat and subsequent inferiority. Although Lancaster emphasises that this defeat is more than a legacy of the past, in the sense that it is played out and re-played over and over in myriad daily interactions, he omits to extract any links with current-day relations between Nicaraguans and their usually white foreign visitors. Thus acknowledged, indeed heavily dissected, racism is kept entirely within national borders, and any mention of the entanglement of whites from the North is relegated to the periphery of distant history.

1.5 IDENTITIES OF NOT BELONGING AND BEING MIXED UP

Concepts relating to the idea that individual human beings are increasingly, in these times of globalisation, the result of mixed input in terms of ethnic, including genetic, biological and cultural inheritance and that there is no such thing as a 'pure' British, North American or Nicaraguan identity, can be helpful in assisting avoidance of essentialist approaches to other peoples. However, there are hidden dangers in this approach. To argue, for example, that Western societies have been profoundly influenced by various strands of Latin American life and culture as a way of complicating the notion that influence consists only of one-way traffic is a reasonable corrective (see, for example, Quijano, 1995). The notion of hybridity is now quite fashionable in the West, though it has a quite different feel to it than the word 'mestizo' which still conjures up visions of imperial conquest and the imposition of one 'race' on another. The latter word carries heavy connotations of unequal power relations which the more benign-sounding idea of 'hybridity' seems to escape. However, I wonder if the difference is not simply that 'mestizo' is applied exclusively to 'Third World' peoples and is therefore a less acceptable term, whereas the latter refers to more trendy, culturally mixed urban life in the developed world. One could speak of a hybrid identity anywhere in the world, but the image of mestizo-ness is firmly fixed in a 'Third World' location. Similarly, the idea of 'not belonging' – as expressed by the following interviewee, is a perfectly acceptable notion, and we (the reader/listener) are invited to sympathise with her predicament. We may also, whilst recognising her distress about the situation, consider ourselves (as I did) relatively boring by ethnic comparison:

> I think the feeling of not quite belonging is a problem but frankly, I feel like I don't quite belong anywhere. And that's another issue. That's more to do with my personal history, but there is something about no matter how long you're here you're never quite Nica and so there's the thing about, you know, what does this mean if I want to take more action, for example, to be involved more actively in political activities. Most of us who came here in the 80s are people who want to be involved. So that is an issue. But, you know equally, when I go back to Britain, I don't feel like I really belong. I'm from a mixed cultural back-ground anyway because I'm second generation Greek and brought up very much in a kind of step-down Greek culture but in Wales. And so, I'm not quite Welsh, certainly not English, not quite Greek and not quite this. Do you know what I mean, it's quite different, I think from most people's experience. Talking to Jan, who's lived all over the place, I mean she also doesn't quite belong anywhere. Do you know what I mean? It's probably more frequent in this stage of the world ...

She clearly has a point in that the 'problem' of 'the feeling of not belonging' is 'probably more frequent in this stage of the world', but it is undoubtedly a Western luxury to wander the world and 'live all over the place' in this way as a response to a feeling of not belonging anywhere, for whatever reason. It is instructive to compare my sympa-thetic response to her situation with the response given, for example, to Nicaraguans who want to come to Britain. They too, as with many other refugees from all parts of the 'Third World', may feel they do not 'really belong' any more in their birth country. This does not mean they are in a position to make demands on their country of current residence. The question about feeling one has the right to undertake political activity in one's adopted country is highly contested in many European nations, where even the most basic demands of freedom of movement and the ability to work are regularly denied, as, for example, with asylum seekers in Britain.

I wonder whether the apparently general and universal application of the concepts of belonging (or lack of belonging), mobility and hybridity are only applicable in the West: and even then whether they might require problematisation in relation to signifiers of status and actual possession of resources. It is too easy to imagine a world where everything is apparently equalised in globalised rootless-ness and mixed-upness, and such a (Western) imaginary runs the danger of obscuring larger factors of discrimination and oppression as they affect the lives of those who live in the Southern hemisphere. This point is an important one in that there is no mention in the above quotation of anything to do with 'race', and I am certain that the interviewee had no conscious intention of making a statement with racialised connotations. Nonetheless, the ownership of a privilege (in this case that of being able to travel the world more or less as freely as one wishes) must raise the question of who it is that has access to that privilege, and whether such access is accorded on the basis of membership of a particular class or group. The ability to move relatively smoothly across international borders requires material resources, notably money and a valid passport, as well as a certain level of confidence, all of which are more readily available to 'First World' citizens. In addition, such movement is rendered considerably easier by the possession of a visible sign, such as whiteness of skin colour, or, failing that, a set of expensive luggage, to act as a mediating sign (see my earlier description of travel on the Omatepe ferry). The above interviewee may have a complex ethnic background, but I suggest that neither this nor her sense of not belonging negate her power position in a 'Third World' country as a result of her role as a Western development worker; nor do they affect her ability to obtain and exploit privileges which come her way thanks to her whiteness.

There are also occasions when such complexities of identity are used as ways of displacing a discussion and recognition of the concept and practice of white racism. Along with notions of hybridity, the issue of identity itself can also be used to side-step more difficult and challenging power relationships. Becky talks a great deal about how she perceives difference/s and complexities and, at first sight, this seems very reasonable – obvious even – and certainly a move away from the absolutist positions as she portrays them during the Sandinista Revolution. She argues that 'the discussion during the Revolution was, first and foremost, this is a class struggle and then all the rest comes after.' For Becky the over-riding issue now is one of identities, and she describes how she, and the other women with whom she works, incorporate ideas around identity into their work; she suggests that their practice preceded the absorption of a theoretical framework; 'I mean it was sort of what we stumbled upon (and) was what we used as the basis for our workshops, and later, much later, more recently, began to read much more about the whole issue of identities, and is there a dominant identity, and there's a whole theory which comes out of Marcela Lagarde (1998) about how there is a kind of archetypal masculine identity and feminine identity, as well as this issue of multiple identities.' Becky expands on what she means by 'multiple identities' and also problematises the idea of ascribing a particular 'race' or nationality to someone:

> In some ways we felt it was different being foreign, and being like Europeans or North American, and there was always that kind of colour difference, but actually because of the whole thing about nationalism and also I think Central America is very different from South America, from Latin America and South America in general and also there's all sorts of stuff about, you know, *what people here say about people from the Southern Cone – you know that they're arrogant and this, that and the next thing.* So I mean, it's not quite as straight forward as being Northern and Southern or white and black. It's much, much more complex than that, and to me it was a great salvation when we began to look at issues of identity, and that was later, and it was like, you're *not just one thing,* you're not just professional or working class, you're not just campesina or urban, and *you're not just in from the North,* you're not just lesbian or heterosexual – it was really important, I think, for all of us to begin to look at that – that it was actually much more complex ...

There are a number of important issues covered in this extract. Firstly, the restriction of such racism as exists to within specified boundaries. We saw in the previous section how this occurs within national (Nicaraguan) borders. Becky expands the geographical entity somewhat to cover the whole of Latin America, but the process still succeeds in defining who is implicated in the perpetuation of stereotypes and who is absolved. Her argument that it is more complex than 'being Northern or Southern, white or black', is true, but it is extraordinary how establishing complexity invariably seems to extract any Western engagement or responsibility.

Secondly, it is significant that, in order to give an example of simple difference becoming something more, a reductionist generalisation is proffered in relation to what Central Americans might say about people from the Southern Cone. This enhances the impression that the racism really is to be found within 'their' boundaries. Of course, such stereotyping may be a reality in particular situations, but to highlight this particular example in this context actually serves to evade or slip away from the central power issues which, as Becky is fully aware, are my main interest, focusing instead on the prejudiced attitudes of (othered) others. Furthermore, Becky talks in terms of being 'foreign', i.e. European or North American, as simply 'different' ('there was always that kind of colour difference'). Her lack of critical comment here stands in stark contrast to her forthcoming serious and detailed criticism of how Latin Americans treat each other. This can easily lead to the thought that any 'differences' between foreigners and Latin Americans are, at worst, neutral in their impact, whereas differences between Central and South Americans are more loaded.

The third point concerns her choice of power differentials in order to illustrate her interpretation of multiple identities, i.e. working class and professional, lesbian and heterosexual, campesina and urban. Here, I would argue that what is missing is also significant, and the lack of a similar dichotomy in relation to black and white is meaningful in its very absence. The words, 'and you're not just in from the North' are slipped into the list in a way which is almost defensive. I take her meaning to be that, even if from the North, one's identity has many other aspects, including sexuality etc, so that one is not identified as being aligned with a powerful group – or not exclusively so. But any acceptance of notions of complexity and diversity does not, as I stated earlier, negate power differentials, nor their very real impact on material lives. The use of the words 'in from' and 'just' make the listener/reader feel that this particular power differential is something trivial, particularly if one is oneself just in from the North (as, of course, I was); and again this militates against any serious exploration of the power issues involved. It is important to ensure that discussions of not just being 'one thing' do not obscure major power differentials.

1.6 IT'S THOSE NORTH AMERICANS ...

In the course of the interviews I ask a direct question about being white in Nicaragua. One respondent, Peter, discusses how visible this makes him feel and he tells me that the issue has come up around the workshops he runs because 'the men don't question as much the expertise of the workers because they're white' (I return to the issue of expertise in a later chapter). On further questioning, Peter avoids acknowledging any sense that he is in any way implicated – I ask if the issue of white co-operantes is discussed amongst themselves. Firstly, Peter tells me he has very little to do with the other development workers and does not 'participate much in the network of white workers'. He then tells me what he thinks of them, i.e. those workers who behave in a way which he considers to be unacceptable. He locates a great deal of this behaviour with North Americans working in Nicaragua, who can thereby shoulder the weight of whatever white racism is acknowledged to exist:

Peter For many workers who come out, the whole issue of culture is a very difficult one – they find it hard to be on a pedestal, find it hard – just because they're white and foreign (they think) that they're going to be more knowledgeable, or they come out and they are very arrogant, and they do believe they have more knowledge and expertise, and they want to get the project done as quickly as possible, their way. They get very frustrated, and issues of non-acceptance of culture, and whose way of doing things, explode into race issues, or at least the interpretation of Nicaraguans is that 'so and so is being racist'.

Me Can you give me any examples of what you mean?

Peter We had a North American couple came to work with us two years ago, both in organic agriculture – we have a small farm and bee-keeping project and we wanted to develop the organic side. This couple, from the start, it was very clear they had their own vision, what they wanted to do on the farm, and it didn't really coincide with the Nicaraguan organisation's vision. Because they were funded by a North American organisation which is a friend of the Nicaraguan organisation, not even an NGO, they had a certain power. We tried to negotiate with them to let them see what our vision was, but their attitude was very much 'we've only got a certain amount of time and we need to do that now'. We were glad when they left because the energy and resources we were putting into nursing them was more than it was worth. And basically it was because they came with their First World view of the needs and the methods. They were frustrated at the Nicaraguans not doing things properly – 'things don't work properly in this country, you can't do anything'. They found it very hard.

Me Would you describe that as not understanding about culture or as white racism?

Peter First of all it is a cultural intolerance, or a misunderstanding, or a lack of willingness to give yourself time to understand the culture. Most people who come from the States or from Europe perceive time in a very different way and would see that as a waste of time rather than a way of learning.

I don't think most people are consciously racist, they are products of a racist system and they assimilate the values and attitudes which they think are run-of-the-mill, and because they've never reflected upon it and never been confronted with it. And Nicaraguans perceive them as being racist, and that, for people like them, is such a blow, because they perceive themselves to be liberal and non-racist and prepared to come to Nicaragua.

Peter continues by telling me that there is no focus on anti-racist training for the co-operantes, and I ask him if what he has said maybe applies to all of us to some extent, and not just the Americans. It was beginning to occur to me that perhaps relations between the 'First' and 'Third Worlds' are so thoroughly racialised that it is not possible, as a Western visitor, to remain outside or unaffected by the power imbalances. I put it to Peter that it could all be seen as part of the idea that the West knows best, and asked if he thought that was unfair. Peter is unequivocal in his reply but his justification is interesting.

> Peter Yes, it is unfair. I don't know where else I would work if I wasn't here. The thing about popular education is that everyone knows something, everyone has something to learn. So I feel that's how it works, everyone believes it, not just at work but at home. There is a constant dialectic between life and work and home and teaching. *So I don't perceive that problem.* Sometimes *I feel it* when I'm out and *I see* groups of foreigners, North Americans especially and I think 'My God, is that the way *Nicaraguans who don't know me see me?*' I hate to think I had all this Western ... a certain naiveté but superiority and arrogance, if that's the way *Nicaraguans see me,* what does that say about me, how can I change that? How can I change the colour of my skin?
>
> Me Have you talked about this with Nicaraguans who you know?
>
> Peter Yes and they've said I'm not like that. Genuinely. A friend of mine said 'no way – even the way you comb your hair and the clothes you wear – you're obviously a foreigner but any Nicaraguan can tell you've been here a long time'. But it's not been conscious, the change – I've been here nine years now.

The first thing Peter does in this quote is to argue that he does not experience any contradictions – popular education, where he works, is based on the egalitarian principle that everyone has something to contribute and something to learn. No power differentials are being acknowledged here. And he applies these principles in all aspects of his life at home as well as at work. His belief in his own values, and in those of popular education, allows him not to 'perceive that problem'.

A further aspect of Peter's self defence against my line of questioning is his concern with his appearance and what Nicaraguans make of the way he looks. Though he does not see (perceive) the problem, it is, contradictorily, the visual aspects of the issue which he chooses to emphasise, and he does worry that Nicaraguans may see him as being like the other foreigners.[5] This could be a reflection of the extent to which the power of whiteness is inscribed simply through the presence of a white body and, as Peter says, there is nothing that can be physically done to alter that, as changing the colour of one's skin is not an available option. He responds positively to being told by a Nicaraguan friend that 'any Nicaraguan can tell you've been here a long time', but there is no recognition that this does not necessarily mean that the inherent power imbalances have somehow disappeared. He has changed the way he combs his hair and his clothes to become closer to his hosts, but appears not to be aware of the impact of the colour of his skin which cannot help but reveal him to be from a richer and more powerful country. I think it is possible that he is uncomfortably aware of these discrepancies at some level, because there appears to be a degree of pain apparent around the denials which would indicate something unspoken.

1.7 CLASS, MONEY AND WHITENESS

In this section, I want to explore the possibility that other power relations, such as class, can obscure and obfuscate a debate around whiteness. This enables those of us sympathetic to the position of the poor of the 'Third World' to target our feelings of anger or frustration at the elites or middle classes of the 'Third World' for not doing more to help. This entails ignoring the extent to which those middle class people are actually espousing values which are similar to those of many Western development and aid workers. The diversion assists the reluctance to examine our own values and how they might be impacting on the world's poor. I here illustrate the antipathy expressed towards middle-class Nicaraguans by three of my respondents, which, I would suggest, contradicts the way middle-classness when it is associated with whiteness, is accepted unquestioningly, and, indeed, is assumed.

The following dialogue concerns a conference to discuss 'democratic service provision' in Nicaragua, which is being organised in Britain. Jack explains to me that there are increasing moves towards privatisation in Nicaragua, and the purpose of the seminar is to look at the 'pros and cons', other possible forms of service provision and so on. He tells me this in a completely ahistorical way, as if the involvement of the West lies purely in terms of helping the Nicaraguans establish better democracy, omitting the critical role played by the West in not only urging privatisation but also in destroying democratic institutions, such as existed in Nicaragua and other Central American countries. He goes on to describe the seminar as 'two-way ... we can sort of tell *the white supremacists to get on their bike.*' The dialogue continues:

> Jack   We're working hard to get voices from the other side, but of course *some of them are white*, but then that's internal racism in the countries we're talking about.
>
> Me   What, you mean you'd get people coming, say, from a country like Nicaragua who are white?
>
> Jack   Well, we're not looking at the colour of their skin, we're interested *in their relationship with us.*

Me   Right, but who might they be? Because they wouldn't be Nicaraguan, presumably?

Jack You mean there aren't any white Nicaraguans *who are worth talking to* and are doing ...

Me   No, I didn't mean, I suppose it depends how you define, they're not very helpful words in a way ...

Jack Yes. *It's the class question* ...

Me   But I would ...

Jack It's not just the class question; it's more complicated than that ...

Me   So you would call – I certainly agree with you, and in my experience in Latin America generally there is a real issue about how the lighter-skinned you are then it goes with ... 'money whitens' is the phrase isn't it? That the higher up the hierarchy you go, it's not very often that you find someone who is either black or of indigenous descent who is in a position of real power in Latin America. So is that what you meant by 'some people coming from Nicaragua might be white', in the sense that they would be light-skinned Nicaraguans ...

Jack Yes, they would be white in the ethnic not in the political sense ...

Jack did not define exactly whom he meant by 'the white supremacists' and I failed to follow this up, but it is quite an interesting link with his next reference (within the same paragraph) to white people within Nicaragua and 'internal racism'. In retrospect, I am not surprised I became a little confused given this rather incongruous juxtaposition. Jack does, however, supply a number of interesting and important links between the meaning of 'white' in relation to other axes of power. Firstly, they are people of some status inasmuch as they have a 'relationship' with a British aid agency, and people whom Jack defines as 'worth talking to'. He establishes a connection with the class question and I then link this in with money. It would not be unusual if a kind of circular relationship were set up, whereby talking to and relating to the Western agencies in itself becomes one of the ways (if not the way) by which people are defined as whiter (both by Westerners and themselves). Though I found Jack confusing at the time, I now think he was onto something crucial whereby white as a signifier is far from just a skin colour, though, as we saw in the Introduction, that is very important. Status, wealth (especially money), class and, in this situation, having the links with Western agencies, have a kind of implied, if not literal, whiteness about them. Thus 'money whitens'. And perhaps whiteness can also be said to 'money'. And, once the links with the aid agencies have been established, this will further lubricate the relationship. This is a porous, not absolute and very slippery way of conceptualising whiteness, suggesting that rich folk (as individuals and countries) are to be considered whiter than poor people – almost, though not quite, regardless of 'racial' origin.

A number of other interviewees also brought up the issue of class in relation to whiteness within the Nicaraguan hierarchy. Jan tells me that, in her organisation, core workers are Nicaraguans, and she feels that this is a 'nice relief'. Nonetheless she describes them as 'very white Nicaraguans. Very rich, upper-class, pale skinned Nicaraguans – very Westernised in their outlook. They are quite separate from the rest of Nicaragua and could be seen to be quite imperialist'. Meg then introduces the element of professionalism into the equation, telling me that she dislikes 'professional Nicaraguans who have loads of money and go dancing'. Middle-classness on the part of Nicaraguans is less than acceptable to the majority of my interviewees and not infrequently the subject of critical discussion, whilst remaining a more or less inevitable component of the identity of Western development workers and researchers (see Bhabha).

Peter is also outspoken in his opinions; when telling me he does not associate with Westerners much, he also makes it clear that he does not like 'going to social gatherings where there are lots of twee middle-class Nicaraguans – I could just walk in because I'm white. I deliberately don't get involved in twee cultural circles in Managua just because I'm white'. An extract from my research diary illustrates how this can operate. My whiteness acts as a badge of entry and, I think, ensures my acceptance on a class basis:

20.4.98 – Should I go to the Olaf Palme Centre – the really flash, international conference centre – to see the presentation of Danilo's CD? He tells me a time and a place, I have no ticket but no-one doubts I will get in. The only topic of debate is what I should wear to stay warm in icy air-conditioned temperatures.

And so it is. I arrive as clean and smart as I can after a taxi journey through hot, dusty Managua – I only wish I'd cleaned my shoes. This centre – my first visit – is huge, spacious, tropical plantations everywhere. I explain at the door that I am here for the 'Italian Presentation' (I think I should have learnt the Spanish for CD ROM before leaving the house and then realise that of course it's CD ROM!) and am immediately escorted and shown where to go. The room I arrive in has a screen set up and a few Nicaraguan young men organising the presentation. The people in the audience are a combination of well-dressed Nicaraguans – including TV journalists – and some distinctly less well dressed *cheles*. Not quite fair as there is an older man in a suit who from his appearance and accent I think may be Italian (I later learn he is the Italian ambassador) and who talks to people whilst constantly scanning over their heads or shoulders, presumably on the look out for somebody more important.

I hadn't noticed the Italian and Nicaraguan flags in the corners but they suddenly become obvious as the presentation begins with both national anthems.

The Italian is the first to give a speech. The CD ROM is designed for children with special needs. 'For the Italian government, it is very important that children with special needs are given the same opportunities as other children' he says.

The CD itself is designed around a number of different learning concepts – visual memory, colours and shapes, for example. Each 'chapter' of the CD takes, as its visual theme, some figure of Nicaraguan folklore. It was hard not to see them as caricatures – the indigenous peoples of Masaya, campesinos, 'tropical' peoples – the stereotypes are scary and the lack of any relevance to city life either in Managua or elsewhere is also striking. The whole thing is accompanied by folkloric music.

This combination of new technology, traditional cultures and children with special needs may be seductive but the Emperor's Clothes come to mind. Especially when Danilo tells me later that the schools for special needs children do not possess the necessary equipment to use the CD ROMs. As with much development, it all appears to be a bit of a PR exercise, in this case for the Italian government.

Purely on the basis of my desire to attend this particular function, I am able to exercise a privileged right of entry. A privilege which is both created and demonstrated by whiteness, visible and instantly recognisable. In this situation I would argue that my whiteness is also acting as a communication about class and, to a lesser extent, about money. Both professional and personal status are also inter-twined here. My whiteness announces that I should be judged as possessing a particular standing and should consequently be treated in a certain way. Its visibility is crucial in quickly establishing all of this in order to render words unnecessary. Paradoxically, though, the absence of any verbal acknowledgement of such powerful visual communication, accepted and acted upon by all involved, somehow allows for a simultaneous denial to take place. White power in action is able to be denied in one framework of communication, the verbal, whilst another, the visual, is working overtime to ensure entrenchment and enactment of precisely that dynamic. Thus an invisibility can co-exist with a heightened awareness.

A major 'disadvantage' of being white, mentioned by a number of interviewees, was that of having money, or being perceived to be wealthy (of course this is actually one of the major privileges of whiteness, and a completely inextricable component of the situation, inasmuch as we would not be in Nicaragua in the first place were it not for our relative wealth). The cause of the problem once again is laid at the feet of Nicaraguans. For example, Paul says 'well, I mean the disadvantage of being white is people assume that you have money and the price goes up. You know, that's a form of racism at local, at personal level'. Sam refers to the frustration of 'this idea that because I'm white, I'm also incredibly affluent. It is terribly frustrating to think that everybody thinks that you can just put your hands on stacks of cash'. He clarifies, however, that he would not describe that as racism. Meg felt that the most difficult aspect of living in Nicaragua was money because:

> The average Nicaraguan can't afford to buy a drink and when you go out, it's always you who invites them or pays for the drink. I have the money, it's the *problem of dependency* which arises. And then somebody says, I need $100 for my roof. I don't miss the $100 but once you give it, you set up a process whereby you are expected to solve all their problems. That's difficult. Some people handle it very well. I have some friends who are very poor and *they don't ask for anything*. I've other friends and I've given them something and then *they give it back*. It's difficult, you're not going to see your companeros starve, *but where does it end?*

These are issues raised by Meg, which, as we shall see, parallel the debate within the field of development around dependency, how and by whom the state of dependency is defined. Also important in her narrative is the splitting of Nicaraguans into the 'goodies' – those who either don't ask or who pay back and, implicitly, the remaining 'baddies'. Once again, writing this triggered memories of my own similar interactions, and reflections as to when I was prepared to lend money and when I wasn't. I remember, whilst working at the Children's Centre, being asked by one of the Nicaraguan workers to loan her sufficient money to have her teeth done. There was no question that her teeth were in a terrible condition and apparently also very painful and the sum of money was not large. I agonised over what to do and in the end decided not to lend her the cash. In a different situation, with a more middle-class Nicaraguan friend who was doing some improvements to his house, I was not only happy to lend a sum of around $200 but I told him to take it as a gift. Now, what made the difference? Clearly an impartial assessment of need was not the basis for these decisions (medical necessity versus home improvements – the outcome should have been obvious); nor, indeed, was the sum of money an influential factor. No, I think, looking back, that the crucial determinant was actually a fear that because the woman at the Centre was poor, I might be opening some kind of uncontrollable floodgates and the demands for money would be unstoppable (both from her and from others, who, once they had heard about my generosity, would also come flocking around). My use of language is also significant here – flocking is an image of animalisation, raising visions of large numbers, of uncontrollable crowds massing together in order to demand all my spare change. This is a very frequent image in the West, depicting the 'Third World' and its 'hordes' of poverty stricken people knocking on the doors of Europe to demand ever more largesse. As Meg says above, 'you' don't want to see your friends starve, but the overwhelming fear is 'where does it end?'. My middle-class friend, on the other hand, was sufficiently Westernised to be trusted to stay within the limits of Western-defined reasonableness. I was not explicitly aware of these thoughts at the time but I can recall the feelings of fear and unease, which I now think were based on the preconceptions which I carried in my head.

It could be argued that the relatively well-off fearing the poor is an example of projection since it is actually the poor who have already lost out and are likely to continue to do so, since they are, because of lack of resources of all kinds, not in a position to exploit others. I recall a Nicaraguan friend telling me not to buy the cashew nuts which are sold in small plastic bags by, usually, women and often very young children, at road intersections, on the grounds that they were exploiting my Western sensibilities by appealing to my sense of charity whilst I was immobilised at traffic lights. He felt sure I was being overcharged and therefore exploited. I compared this situation to the selling of nuts in supermarkets and reflected that although prices there are marginally lower, the cost to the environment is greater (more packaging and probably more transport costs). Furthermore, it seems incontrovertible that more of the money which I spend on nuts at the cross-roads would go directly into the hands of the poor, thus helping in a small but direct way to alleviate poverty (after all, the overarching goal of development and aid workers). In subsequent discussion with my friend, we reflected on his concern that I would feel intimidated by the street-sellers and under pressure from them to buy something I did not really want. Again, I felt this was minimal compared to the pressures to buy exerted by supermarkets – pressures which are quite deliberate, based on market research and including aggressive advertising, the strategic use of displays and lighting and so on. What I felt was the underlying agenda here was my friend's anxiety that I would be unable to cope with the (unacceptable) behaviour and demands of the poor. And yet this is pure projection, for, as I have illustrated with the case of the supermarket, the exploitation of the poorer by the richer is much greater, more routine and more destructive.

In his book *White Racism*, Joel Kovel argues that the possession of money and wealth is intrinsically racially implicated:

> the infant seeks to master the agony of his individuation by displacing the rage of separation, first onto his parents, then to the self, then to the bodily self, and finally to his (expelled, hence separated) excrements ... self-hate and self-disgust – that is to say, guilt – becomes permanently

established within the personality and spurs it onward to further abstract definitions.

Such 'abstract definitions' gradually become transmogrified into money:

> Spurred by the repression of the sense of smell, the child shifts his attention first to street mud; thence as mud becomes objectionable, to sand (dried, deodorised and whitened); then to stones (hard as well); to artificial products like beads, marbles, buttons (no longer attached to the earth – indeed the first objects of exchange, and the first desirable possessions); and then to shining pieces of money, gold being the most desirable because it is the least concretely useful, the most abstractly mysterious of metals (p135).

As I have indicated, the issue of money does indeed raise extremely uncomfortable feelings for many development workers and such emotional responses do frequently seem to be resolved in some way through the process of feeling angry with, or blaming 'othered' Nicaraguans. Kovel emphasises the process of the abstraction of money in Western society, and how that process involves expelling or rejecting what is unacceptable; initially for the infant his/her faeces. This can be linked into theories of racism which stress the identification and subsequent expulsion of the unacceptable (black, poor), both at cognitive level and in lived reality.

1.8 PERSONAL REACTIONS

I was concerned during the interviews to establish how white development workers perceived the question of their whiteness at the more personal level of their relationships both in the work location and in their lives generally. I expected a degree of discomfort emanating from an awareness of power imbalances. However, the responses were highly indicative of the problematic nature of their/our positionality in that, as I suggested at the beginning of this chapter, the majority consistently represent our/themselves as occupying relatively powerless positions. Whilst individual comments are possibly a reflection of individual situated-ness at particular moments, the overall, accumulated impression of white powerlessness in Nicaragua is contradictory to global power relations.

Some interviewees acknowledged that the reaction to them from Nicaraguan people was at least partly based on skin colour and reflected my own experience of privilege described above in Section 1:6. Paul, for example, says:

> *Paul* On a personal level it's undoubtedly the case that I, as a white person, am probably given more respect, you know, I'm *automat-*

ically given respect before I've proved myself, whereas another person would have to prove themselves before they gained that. I mean that's true on a gender basis throughout the world and it applies to, *people make assumptions of white people*, you know that they're more capable or that they're *wealthier*, that they're *cleaner*. People make these assumptions.

Me   Nicaraguan people do you mean?

Paul   Well yes, I'm not sure about the last, that they're cleaner, because Nicaraguans realise that actually we're not by any stretch of the imagination, those that know us. I can get into the National Assembly just by holding a *camera or by being white*, whereas a Nicaraguan can't do it. During the General Strike or something I can walk through a police cordon, no problem, Nicaraguans can't. *Now that's racism applied by the recipients of it or applied by those who are disadvantaged by it.*

Even though Paul is describing some of the types of privileges accorded him purely on the basis of being white, he concludes with a definition of racism which implicates its recipient. He begins this quote by acknowledging the power differential, but rapidly disavows it by moving into allocating primary responsibility to the people who 'automatically' give him respect, the people who 'make these assumptions' i.e. Nicaraguan people. Once again, in a very subtle manner, the oppressed become the makers of their own oppression. In this context, it is the possession of a camera (with all its abilities to see, interpret and record) that adds significantly to the marker of being a white Westerner and to the role of gazing and judging, of which we are usually unaware. The all-encompassing 'English eye', as stressed by Stuart Hall (1991, p20), sees everything but itself, becoming 'coterminous with sight itself'. What Paul describes is very similar to my diary entry quoted in the previous section and, whilst it may not be due entirely to his (or my) agency that such events occur, it is nonetheless an inversion to deflect the racism onto those Nicaraguans who are treating him so deferentially. And, as with my gaining easy access to the Olaf Palme Centre, he takes advantage of his position. Our privilege or advantage goes unremarked, whilst the reaction of Nicaraguans involved is portrayed as 'racism'. Joanne, on the other hand, is more able to implicate herself in the attribution of racism, though the phrase 'a kind of' perhaps lessens its harshness, when she says:

(It's) a kind of racism in that as a European, I have been accorded a special place because of my race – I have been listened to more or respected more or given *a God-like status*, having a higher level of education. So from that point of view, it has been in operation, but to my advantage.

I suggest to Joanne that this is largely because of her whiteness and she agrees. Her phrase 'God-like status' is particularly resonant with the evolutionary implications of development, which are expanded upon in forthcoming chapters.

Peter associates privileges with being white, but is at some pains to tell me how he does not accept those privileges which are on offer to him, but which he implicitly accepts are on offer to others because of their particular skin colour. I ask him if he can push himself 'a little bit further' in relation to acknowledging white racism and his potential role in it and he says:

> I can't think what I would do. At work and at home I deliberately don't accept privileges like others do, like I could demand that the computer is mine, because it's funded by my organisation. On the personal issue, I don't ask for subsidies, I feel that I already get paid a higher salary and if I work outside the office, I just do it. I don't ask for extra money.

Similarly, Jenny responds to my question about her awareness of being white with a description of her denial of privileges which are clearly on offer to others: 'I did experience a lot of being very conscious of my being white, in terms of people being surprised that I ironed my clothes and did my own washing'. Typing this brought back the memories for me that I did have my washing and ironing done for me for very little payment (see introduction), but justified at the time by lower rates of pay and providing a Nicaraguan with much needed employment. The self-denials of privilege are, I think, important recognitions of the existence of power differentials; otherwise why should anyone feel bad enough about, say, employing a cleaner or earning more money, to address it as an important issue? However, refusal to accept one aspect of privilege cannot erase the enormous arenas in which those from the North still possess relative advantage. Our individual justifications notwithstanding, there is a repetition of the pattern of who employs whom to do low paid menial tasks which, as we shall see, echoes the servant/mistress relationships of earlier colonial epochs.

A different response to the question about whiteness and racism was to recount the perceived problems of being white – often in great detail and at length. In some cases this was not only explicitly described as racism but was presented to me in such a way as to emphasise its greater degree of significance relative to white-on-black racism. Maggie describes how her experiences in Nicaragua made her realise 'what it's like to be a minority group' and Joanne acquaints me with her experiences working in a situation where there was 'a certain amount of resentment because people think the workers should be Nicaraguan'. She continues:

I understand their viewpoint. So for the first time I'm experiencing racism which affects me negatively. It's been quite interesting. *I don't feel it in a personal way*, in many ways I feel they are justified in feeling like that. Although it hurts because I've tried my hardest not to be racist myself, not to display colonialist and imperialist attitudes, I've tried hard to listen and to learn and to think about the way that I act and modify that. So it hurts a bit when I find I'm being discriminated against or mistreated on a certain level simply because of my race. At the same time I can understand the historical perspective for that and I can understand the resentment that engenders.

This is clearly an honest and somewhat painful attempt to come to terms with some difficult personal issues, and Joanne's attempts to balance her emotional reaction of hurt with her understanding of where and why such reactions to her might originate, and her endeavour not to 'feel it in a personal way', elicit a degree of sympathy. However, it must be noted, that, in the interviews overall, more space and energy is devoted to an exposition of the suffering of white people at a personal level, as recipients of racism from Nicaraguans, than is afforded to the experience of being the more powerful party. This may be linked to the idea of the prevalence of underlying narcissism in the West, and the promotion of the feelings of the individual to the extent that their importance supersedes anything else.

A number of interview participants discussed their reactions at being called '*chele*' or 'whitey' by Nicaraguan people. Paul felt that being referred to as a *chele* was not a problem, but some interviewees did portray a more general unease at their identification by Nicaraguans as white. Vicky tells how she feels she has often been given the message on the street that her presence in Nicaragua is not welcome, and that 'the least little thing that happens and you get the fact that you're a gringa thrown in your face, or you're an imperialist. I mean during the Revolution, you know, anybody could say that to you. It didn't happen very often but it was there, and it was kind of lurking'. She feels that at some point, having been in Nicaragua for a lengthy period, 'you (should) stop being a foreigner in the eyes of those kinds of people with polarised views'. Again this illustrates how much easier it is to perceive oppression apparently directed at oneself than vice-versa; and in this case this identification is taking place even though 'it didn't happen very often'. Furthermore, it is interesting to speculate somewhat on what might be meant by 'stopping being a foreigner'. She cannot mean becoming ethnically Nicaraguan, so her desire must be to be accepted as of different ethnicity but equal – a position which certainly is not a possible option for many from the 'Third World' who live in England and seek equality. Furthermore, I would put this comment alongside my own, more limited experience of living in Nicaragua, when I was continually surprised that Nicaraguan people treat Westerners with such goodwill and respect, given the impact of centuries of unequal power relations and exploitation. And this was even the case during the Contra War – not once did I find a situation where North American individuals were reminded, let alone blamed, that their own 'highly developed' nation was waging a war against Nicaragua. My view is that it is the Western exploitation of the South which keeps 'us' foreigners.

To return to the issue of having one's whiteness publicly identified and commented upon; the interview with Sam was very informative in this regard, and I want to try and indicate here how his utterances on how he felt on being identified as a *chele* changed over the course of a nearly three-hour long interview. At the beginning of the interview he portrays how the young people with whom he is working regard him:

Me And what do they call you?

Sam 'Chele' or 'whitey' (we both laugh) or 'baldie'. So quite, you know, they do have immense respect – 'hey, baldie'.

But by the end of the interview it is clear that Sam's reactions are much more complex and he cannot simply laugh it off:

Me Last question then. What have you found most difficult about living and working in Nicaragua?

Sam The most difficult thing. I suppose it's a bit of a paradox – it's all about power relations again, and it's the paradox between being a foreign volunteer and all that that entails and then wanting to be taken completely seriously, wanting the best of both worlds, I guess. I'll explain that. Wanting the best of both worlds – volunteer status gives you certain privileges, it allows you to take holidays. I was saying, 'oh, I wish I had a holiday' and in fact, I've already had two months holiday, and that was fine, I wasn't leaving people in the lurch. But then at the same time I want the work I do to be taken completely seriously. Would you say that I expect it to be taken seriously because it's my work and because it's different to other people's work? It is certainly different to other people's work because, because of my status and because of my different approach. On the other side – I do find it difficult sometimes, like we were talking about at the beginning, to try and strike a balance and it kind of crosses gender, strike a balance between familiarity and distance, professionalism and friendship and finding it quite difficult sometimes – and it's just a term of endearment – I find 'whitey' or 'chele', I find it so hard to get through that and nobody ever calls me Sam or Samuel or whatever and I certainly ... Oh, I don't know. It is, I mean I'm not picked out.

Me Why is that so hard?

Sam Because I find it offensive, I think, and so I'm automatically on the defensive

Me Because you want to be seen as not …

Sam Yes.

Me Not white, or not just white.

Sam You know it depends, it's a day to day thing. Some days, yea, I mean this is all, not just to do with Nicaragua, it's also my personal experience in Cuba as well and my quite open rejection of Britain and British culture and Britishness when I go back and wanting to just leave that. So to be daily reminded of the fact that, you know and I know this, I know that I will never be Cuban – which is what I kind of wanted and it took a while to come to terms with that. But it does feel limiting in my relationship with the kids.

Me Have you ever talked to anybody who calls you that?

Sam Yea and they said 'well, I don't mind if you call me "negro"'. 'But I don't really want to call you "negro", I'd like to call you David or Bob or whatever your name is'. I didn't really get very far with that one. I said 'it's like being called gringo', which is an offensive term. Chele. And they said 'no, no, it's not, it's completely different – it's just because you are chele'. And I've never really had any experience with the nick-name thing before, I've never been called, I don't know, 'baldie' before.

Me Sam has a crew-cut.

Sam Skin-head (we both laugh).

Me A big softie skin-head.

Sam And in daily life I get bothered by the shouting thing and the greeting thing – the exuberant friendliness which I laud so much in Cuba, really gets on my nerves here. If somebody shouts out, I've no idea who they are and they're driving past in a car, somebody shouts 'chele palone' i.e. 'whitey baldie', out of a car and I get so angry, I want to throw nails on the road, and stop them, and say, 'well why do you feel you have the right to shout baldie, whitey at me from the car'. It just makes me so angry for the whole afternoon, and you can just drive away and you think ugh …

Me Why do you think they might be shouting at you?

Sam I don't know, it's just like, it's like goading. It's not like, it's certainly not, when somebody you don't know shouts something at you, it's certainly not just like 'oh, hello, I'm glad you're in my country and I appreciate the work', it's certainly not that. Because when you're walking, people wait until you've gone past them to say anything. I'm sure this is the *same as sexual harassment*, it's never a face to face. You know, it's never a face to face 'you're white, aren't you'. It's very under the breath, snide kind of poky, not aggressive but challenging. You know, are you going to say anything, do you know enough Spanish to say anything? And so,

you know, I often find myself slipping into lots of rude Spanish
words to show that I do and it leaves me feeling terribly silly and
kind of debased and lowered. Just smacks to me a little bit, I don't
know, of *kind of bullying of the white blackbird.*

Me Do you think that's the most difficult bit?

Sam Yea. I mean lots of jokes about there not being any Frosties or stuff
like that.

Me Sorry, Sam, that wasn't quite the last question. What's been the best
bit about living or working in Nicaragua – the most rewarding bit?

Sam Oh, good. Most rewarding thing. Oh, it was lovely to, in the work
context, it was absolutely lovely to get over that feeling of being a
poverty tourist, get over that feeling of just skimming over the
surface and touching down and just disturbing people and stirring.

I was very struck by the pain, anger and hurt experienced by a number
of my interviewees when their whiteness is commented upon by
Nicaraguans (though my understanding is that 'chele', unlike 'gringo',
is not perceived by Nicaraguans as a term of abuse, and Bonnett (2000
p52) informs us that it is a Mayan word meaning 'blue', denoting eye
colour); but, since these interviews were carried out, I have come across
a number of further examples of white development workers expressing similar feelings. Sam feels so strongly, for example, that he relates
the experience to that of being sexually harassed. Again, I wonder how
narcissistic is this degree of concentration on the pain *'they cause to us'*,
in contrast to our apparent inability to offer much evidence of a degree
of awareness or even discomfort around the impact of whiteness in
relation to the exercise of privilege. It seems clear, from the examples I
have offered from my own diary and the interviews, that whiteness
does (amongst other things) act as a marker, but the tendency in
conversation is to slip away from it as quickly and silently as possible,
except when it causes some discomfort to the white person. Then it can
be readily identified and the ramifications discussed at great length.

1.9 STEREOTYPES, SEX AND WHITENESS

A significant element in the stereotyping of others involves expressions
of desire and excitement, often connected with sex and sexuality (see
Kovel, 1988a and Rattansi, 1992). A look at some of the examples from
the research will illustrate this phenomenon. The following extracts
from two interviews illustrate the paradox that it is Nicaraguans,
specifically Nicaraguan women, who are here construed as sexually the
predatory party, a common stereotype in relation to black people
generally.

Me How about the issue of being white in Nicaragua?'

Tim First of all, I'm absolutely visible, being white and blue-eyed, in

Nicaragua – and it's uncomfortable sometimes walking down the street or in the market – there's always someone who makes a comment about the colour of my eyes or my skin. And women actually invite me home for sex. Just when they look at me. It gets annoying. It's tedious. I don't feel threatened – a woman who is insinuating she wants to have sex with me cannot rape me – no way – because although she's taken the initiative, I have the power because I'm male and because I'm white.

Another quote, this time from a woman, continues this theme:

Me   Are there situations, I mean by virtue of being marked by the colour of your skin, that you're treated differently?

Mandy Yes, there is – if you're out in the street or in a taxi you might meet somebody who is automatically anti-you because you're foreign, but most people here are not, because they think that what goes on in the North is better, and if you're from the North or look like you're from the North, then you are treated with more deference. And I suppose if you wanted to you could take advantage of it. And there's a whole other issue about being a white woman who's a professional and in relationship with men which you never know. I haven't been much in this situation but you just don't know, people say you just don't know how much this guy is interested in me or because I'm a passport to something else. And you don't know how much is really about whether they think you're sexy, or whether it is a way out, which is classic, and which is what *Nicaraguan women do all the time, latch on to white men.*

Thus the persona of the Nicaraguan woman, most frequently represented in development contexts (see the discussion of women and development later) as the least powerful group of all, suddenly seems to have acquired a great deal of power and agency, which is highly sexualised. The speakers do not accept any responsibility or agency for the unfolding of events. In a third interview, Sam tells me about his views of Cuba, and in so doing he identifies his own propensity to racially stereotype, for example that 'Cubans have an abundance of human warmth and human relationships are real and vital and spontaneous'. He recognises that this has historical roots:

Obviously, somewhere in my mind the roots of the idea may well be the kind of semi-naked Native American and the kind of sensuality and that kind of – linked with Mother Earth – and certainly I don't feel in contact with Mother Earth in Bethnal Green or in Sheffield. Maybe that's why, that's one attraction of trying to say it's not just an idea, a stereotype, I experience this – Cuban people are incredibly warm – just to justify this kind of all-encompassing idea that Latin people are sexy, warm folk and making it the antithesis of England, which it isn't, and making England the black to Cuba's white and vice versa, which they're not.

Me That's interesting. Putting it in terms of black and white, although you have changed it round, but using that kind of physical marker to describe those kind of stereotypes. It seems to me that is what comes into people's heads with those kinds of markers.

Sam Oh, yea. And it is completely ... When I was in England and was glorifying and fantasising Cuba I would use terms like this – it was whitewashing of England, it was excessive whiteness, it was pallid, it was insipid, it was just washed out, whereas Cuba has a darkness, a thickness – of course, it's so easy to use such trite images, so easy to get passionate about ...

I then asked Sam if he thought that stereotyping of this ilk would have an impact in practice, and he felt that, if he or anyone else wanted to make 'a serious investment in Cuba', then images of 'people dancing and jigging up and down ... shimmying in a Hawaiian shirt' would not be 'the sort of people I'd want' to be a partner with in a business venture.

On a more general level, it is also interesting to pursue the notion that people can be 'in love' with a country, or, as was the case with Nicaragua in the 1980s, a country and a revolution, and I would suggest that this is likely to be largely a Western phenomenon resonating with the unequal power relationship. Jenny talks about how she initially went to Nicaragua on a brigade 'and decided that I wanted to go back there. I sort of fell in love with the place – it's that very, very strong feeling of falling in love with a place.' I also, after my first visit to Nicaragua, described myself as having developed some kind of romantic attachment to the Nicaraguan land and its peoples. Perhaps it does not impact upon anyone except myself that particular types of music and literature, which left me unimpressed before the visit, now had the power to move me to tears. Suddenly all things Nicaraguan, from coffee mugs to the sacuan oche (the national flower), took on huge significance for me and I wanted to madly identify with it all. What matters in this, I think, is that Nicaragua and Nicaraguans become virtually irrelevant except when viewed through the rosy glow of my desires and my fantasies. From the perspective of being in love, injections of reality, particularly around the realities of lived power relationships, are best avoided as long as possible. I think frequent emotional reactions to the inevitable realisation that actual poverty is not romantic, and Nicaragua is not all Latino music, flowers and dedicated revolutionaries (who themselves may turn out to be more humanly fallible than their image could allow) – this realisation can lead to massive disappointment on our part. We may also begin to realise that our self-allocated role of enraptured bystander is, on closer investigation, a relationship constructed by and immersed in power inequalities, but, on the whole, I think we reject this way of thinking in favour of taking the easier path of blaming Nicaraguans for failing to live up to our expectations. And instead of being angry with ourselves for being so driven by our own needs to latch onto something, to lose ourselves in something remote from everyday Western life, no matter how ephemeral, we can easily become disillusioned and even angry with those who are in a less powerful position, in this case Nicaraguans.

A further consideration, though, is that defining and portraying such a relationship in this way can be used to give 'us' Westerners carte blanche to think that, because we empathise or are in love with Nicaragua, then we have, and can legitimately deploy, some kind of inherent authority within the relationship. Falling in love in itself may not necessarily imply an unequal relationship, but it certainly does nothing to counter power imbalances and may be used to justify them. Academics are not immune from this kind of analogy: McGee, in the middle of a discussion about the impact of development in Southeast Asia, inserts the following: 'Even in Malaysia, a country and its people with whom I had fallen in love, where ostensibly economic growth was occurring rapidly, poverty while being abated still continued' (1995, p200). The juxtaposition of an intensely personal feeling, i.e. that of being in love, with issues of structural inequality and poverty is, at best, patronising and affirms his superior power position. At worst, there is an underlying implication somehow that his feelings of being in love should actually have some kind of impact on the poverty levels. I have yet to hear a person from the South use such a construct to portray his/her feelings about a country in the North.

The following dialogue between myself and Ellen illustrates this further and indicates that perhaps the real importance is in terms of fulfilling our own projected needs.

Me Why do you think the effect of the Revolution was so powerful on people like you and me and lots of other people here and in other European and North American countries? I think you said something earlier that I think was really interesting, that there was a clarity that I think people kind of felt. I mean, it did have a huge impact on people, didn't it, emotionally as well as politically. I mean why do you think that was, why was it so powerful?

Ellen I think it was powerful partly because people, it was a very polarised situation, I mean looking back, I mean, maybe we were, we tended to *project our own hopes and visions.*

Me Because we'd just got Thatcher at the time and it was an interesting conjuncture of things.

Ellen Yes, I think that was certainly one factor that motivated quite a lot of people from here to go to Nicaragua, but I think it was partly the extremes of the Reagan administration which provoked extremes of outrage against it as well and quite rightly so. So that was a very powerful motivating force I think. Contrasting that with a political project in Nicaragua that was very committed to a very profound programme or transformation of social and economic justice for the poorer sectors of society, and I think obviously one huge motivating factor was people going to Nicaragua to see for themselves what was going on and that very personal contact with people and organisations there. The *sense of hope and great expectations for the future* that people could see for themselves when they were talking to people there and the sense of dignity of local people and I think that had a very profound impact on huge numbers of people who visited Nicaragua at the time.

Me Yes, I think that's right and people got, I can remember when I went, it was just so exciting and people talked about being in love with the revolution didn't they. It was almost like a kind of relationship thing as well as a political head thing that you knew was right and interesting and it was such a gut thing as well.

As Ellen points out, people were partly motivated by strong reactions to the actions of the Reagan government (many of which were indeed so 'extreme' as to be illegal in the eyes of the World Court), and the desire 'to go and fight for something' positive 'instead of always putting your energies into fighting against something' (Jenny); but we were also motivated by our own hopes and visions, many of which (certainly in Britain) had been effectively thwarted by the Thatcher administration. This process, though, of projecting our own hopes and expectations outwards, instead of dealing with them 'at home', can instigate a range of relationships, reactions and feelings which bear little relation to what, in this case, may have been reality for Nicaraguan people. Particularly dangerous is the tendency to project negative feelings onto Nicaragua when our own expectations and hopes are not fulfilled. Combined with the tendency, already noted, to disavow the impact of history and geo-political realities, this can emphasise greatly the sense of disillusionment when 'things go wrong', and encourage a relationship whereby Nicaraguans are consistently held entirely responsible for things not turning out well.

Being in love with a country can also, I would suggest, be closely linked with personal motivations and relationships for individual workers. The linking of the desire for sexual excitement and fulfilment is more explicit and obvious in connection to exotic holidays, but is a theme that can also be fruitfully explored in relation to those who choose to work 'abroad', as I indicated in the Introduction (particularly in relation to the VSO leaflet discussed in the Introduction). Nearly all of the white Western people whom I have known in Nicaragua over the years have had close involvements with Nicaraguan individuals, either of a sexual nature or, not infrequently, involving the adoption of a child, or, as in my case, both. In a regional newspaper (*Yorkshire Post*, 1999) I was quoted as saying, about my decision to sell up and go to Central America, that 'I had a vague plan that I might fall in love, sort out my life and live happily ever after'. I doubt I was conscious of this desire at the time, quite so explicitly, but I now think it sums up my subliminal goals, and certainly I had no conception of the power complexities that would be involved in my own relationships, both serious and casual. What is striking is that the issue of power and its connections to whiteness, within those relationships, is rarely acknowledged or discussed, in contrast to gender inequalities which come up much more frequently (especially in relation to other people's unsatisfactory relationships!). There are some exceptions, and, as I suggested above, some of my interviewees were willing to look at this aspect of their relationships – to some extent. Ellen pointed out how, in relation to the brigades, when visiting Western women have sexual relationships with 'local' men, this raised issues connected to whiteness or Western power, and these were discussed amongst the members of the brigade; I asked her in what ways issues of power and whiteness had come up on the brigades:

> *Ellen* I think it's come up in other contexts on a brigade when women in a brigade have got involved with local men, having sexual relationships with local men. It's come up as a huge issue within some brigades and caused quite a lot of divisions within the brigade.
>
> *Me* So how does it come up around that issue, I mean what's the issue?
>
> *Ellen* Well, the issue would be the impact it has on other and local women.
>
> *Me* And local men presumably, who would see white women in a particular kind of way?
>
> *Ellen* Yes.
>
> *Me* Does it get talked about openly on the brigades?
>
> *Ellen* Well, to my knowledge, a couple of brigades I know it has been, but in response always to a particular situation they've had to face.

In my experience, a number of Western women, and I include myself here, who would describe themselves as broadly feminist, are nonetheless prepared to engage in sexual relations with Nicaraguan men who are married and have children – this does not seem to be considered a feminist issue in the Nicaraguan context, at least not in open debate. It is almost as if, in this context, the Nicaraguan woman, of whom we hear so much elsewhere, is made to conveniently disappear.

Jenny was an unusual interviewee in that she did offer her views on the subject of personal relationships, and she offers an important insight:

> And then in my relationship with Pedro, the only Nicaraguan man I had a relationship with, and that was over a period of five years, which was full of ups and downs and contradictions and fights and battles – basically because I represented for him the imperialist West, and he at times hated himself for loving me. It was a really big contradiction – it was the biggest contradiction in his life because we were part of the destroyers of the world, of their world. And being white, and being different and being from the West did sort of influence the sort of strength of the emotion of all those relationships, I would say.

Me Both the love …

Jenny Both the love and the hate and the mixture of it and the resentment and the …

Me Anger?

Jenny Yes. And fun (laughs). Surprise that you could have fun together as well …

Me So, for you the whiteness came up mostly in your closest relationships? And were you conscious of that yourself or when Pedro brought it up?

Jenny Oh, he didn't keep that sort of thing to himself. That came up right from early on.

Me It was more his perception of the relationship than yours. It wasn't something you would have said about it yourself?

Jenny One of the things I learned very quickly was not to be the big white chief coming bearing gifts. I learned that in terms of visiting people that the most I should do was to at least take enough, a contribution to food, because I was going to be an extra mouth to feed, and that food might be fruits and vegetables that they hardly ever saw and couldn't afford to buy and were also incidentally things that I would like to be eating as well. But anything other than that was seen as over the top, resented, imperialist (said with a laugh). I once arrived with two stools that his mother had asked me to get and we had such a terrible blazing row over that and my only resource was to say it was his mother's and nothing to do with you. In that sort of trap, and the material difference, the wealth difference – they were quite poor – was very noticeable and definitely not wanted – you know what I mean. He did not want to be the beneficiary of my wealth and the only things that he accepted from me with good grace were books that he could not get hold of. So, yes, I did get my come-uppance.

Such an acknowledgement of power relations is exceptional, particularly in its direct linking with geo-politics and imperialist history.

1.10 CONCLUDING COMMENTS

Whiteness and its associated privilege as a form of political power is not on any existing development agenda and attempts to discuss its potential impact meet with a number of blocking mechanisms. This is clearly not true of all power relations, as the issue of gender, for example, is very definitely on the agenda of the majority of development and aid agencies. It is possible that it is easier to consider gender from a Western perspective because the responsibility can be exclusively allocated to 'Third World' men and thus any indictment of the West is avoided. A possible reason for the lacuna around racialised power relations is, in contrast to the issue of gender relations, the difficulty discussed in the Introduction of identifying power axes where one might be implicated as the oppressor oneself. No doubt these blocks are employed on a largely unconscious basis but they are nonetheless effective for that. As I have demonstrated above, such avoidance strategies include: focusing the discussion solely on racisms which can be identified within Nicaraguan boundaries; blaming other white people (North Americans) for any white racism which can be detected; sliding away from the subject; transferring the agency to the less powerful party (victim-blaming) e.g. Nicaraguan women. The latter seems to be particularly visible in relation to sex and money, where a number of interviewees expressed significant levels of emotion, including anger, which raises the question as to whether there is a degree of guilt, especially given the exploitative role played overall by white Westerners in relation to both sex and money (and, indeed, children). Guilt is then displaced onto Nicaraguan women who are, in contrast, in more theoretical constructs, invariably allocated the position of the most oppressed. Such potentially complex analyses, taking us into the arena of psychoanalysis, are beyond the scope of this book, but I would tentatively suggest that following up these issues would tell us a great deal about how individuals from the North relate to people perceived as generally inferior in the South, and it may be reasonable to extrapolate the usefulness of psychoanalytic concepts into global relations. Certainly, the content of these interviews would affirm the view that any automatic solidarity between white Western workers and Nicaraguans must be problematised. The polarised stereotypes of Nicaraguan women which are operational across the discourses of development, either of sexual predator or benighted beast of burden, recall similar tropes from colonial eras, utilised in relation to black women generally. They now, I would argue, contribute to constituting the South as an entity distinct in its various forms of inferiority from the more powerful North.

It is striking how acutely aware my interviewees were of their own difficulties in relation to their embodied whiteness, which at times marked them out as recipients of often difficult and hurtful responses from Nicaraguan people (as perceived by the interviewees), while neither they nor I sought to apply this knowledge and understanding to the vice-versa situation. This is possibly the ultimate in narcissistic self reflection; to the point where a superior power can only perceive its own pain at the slights and rejections delivered by the less powerful party, but cannot put that aside in order to conceive of how it might be for the less powerful and how their own associations and affiliations with the superior power might impact. I would now consider that analysis of my line of questioning implicates me fully in this process of virtually abjecting Nicaraguans, their feelings and reactions, to the edge of what matters.

The two final questions in the interviews were; 'what was the most difficult thing about living and working in Nicaragua?' and, secondly, 'what was most rewarding?' (see the interview with Sam quoted above as an example). It is only since writing this that I have become more aware of how very narcissistic those very questions are, and that, in order to answer, my respondents were obliged to perform in a similarly self-obsessed manner. The following excerpt is an example of a response:

> I'm not sure what's going to happen in the medium or long term in my life. Now you realise what it means to be in one of the poorest countries in Latin America, one of the poorest countries in the world. So what that means for the long term future, getting old in a country when you don't have a family network, I don't know. And it's very hard at a day to day level to cope with the poverty. What you come across in the street, it's really hard to cope with that. The stress of that, much more stressful for the people who are in dire poverty, but nevertheless, it's just, you can't get away from it, it's just very hard to be amongst. It's wearing. Now, I don't imagine that I could stay here permanently because I would find it really hard to live in a situation of luxury in comparison to, you know, three-quarters of the population.

So we end up focusing on the impact of other's poverty on ourselves. The implication of the last sentence is that it is easier to live in comparative luxury at a distance, and not when the comparison is immediate, more obvious and therefore more painful for the observer. This poses an interesting challenge to the notion that globalisation somehow brings everyone closer together, not only spatially but morally as well (see Corbridge, 1994 for a discussion).

The concerns expressed in the above quotation belong to those who can fly in and out, i.e. have the choice, and would make no difference to the situation from the perspective of poor Nicaraguans. It is interesting to note the extent to which the impact of looking at poverty can be portrayed as almost more of a problem for the onlooker. Sam said 'in the beginning I felt very uncomfortable in the streets, very shocked by all the horrible things I was seeing and shocked and repulsed', but that he did not want to be some kind of 'apology tourist', who would later be able to write letters saying 'you'll never guess what I saw today'. He articulates the ever-present potential for development work to overlap with the gaze of the tourist, only-here-to-look-and-experience, but in his determination to differentiate himself from the tourist paradoxically ensures that he tells us about the similarities. What is absent is any linkage of poverty in Nicaragua either with its history or with current geo-politics. Such an absence encourages an identification of the existence of poverty and its shocking-ness with poor Nicaraguans and, by extension, suggests that the responsibility for such levels of poverty also belongs within the borders of Nicaragua.

NOTES

1. As I stated in the introduction, all names of interviewees and some other details have been changed in order to preserve as much anonymity as possible. I have also altered the actual wording slightly and added punctuation to the interview quotes to allow for easier reading. I hope any changes to intended meaning are minimal. I do not give details regarding interviewees' jobs or any other aspect of their lives which might make their identification easier.

2. The interviews were semi-structured. I had a list of questions which I covered with all interviewees but I was also interested in encouraging discursive dialogues as this is the most effective way of exploring underlying attitudes.

3. See Ashok Ohri (1997) for a discussion of how black people are largely excluded from development education in Britain. And are therefore likely to be excluded from development work.

4. I use italics in quotes from interviews to indicate words and phrases which I subsequently analyse in detail. It allows for the reader to make quick reference back.

5. It is important here to note that the word 'perceive' carries the meaning to see visually but also implies an understanding of the mind. It is Peter who does the perceiving (seeing plus understanding as well as feeling), whilst the Nicaraguans are only credited with being able to 'see', particularly in relation to 'seeing Peter'.

2

THE EVIDENCE OF WHITE POWER

Travel, History, Culture, Economics ...

In this chapter, I seek to establish some surrounding contextualisation for the whiteness of power relationships and the discourses which support them, in order to demonstrate that racialised 'Third World' development and aid discourses do not exist in a vacuum. Both at conceptual and practical level, relationships within the sphere of development and aid are affected by discourses and imagery prevalent in other arenas of life; and, in turn, they will have an impact upon discourses employed in other settings. In this chapter I take a fairly random sample of material from a wide range of sources, all publicly available and some well-known, to show how persistent such power relationships are. It is important to show that the typologies of methods of dealing with whiteness and power apparent in the last chapter are not unique to development and aid workers: on the contrary, the reason such discourses can flourish in relation to 'Third World' development and aid is that they flourish in the general environment, where the same attitudes are part and parcel of everyday life. I illustrate this by choosing examples which are unconnected with 'Third World' development and aid, although I continue with the approach of selecting the quotations from writers and others who situate themselves as broadly sympathetic to Latin America.

2.1 TRAVEL BOOKS AND TRAVEL GUIDES
I have argued that the sorts of discourses I described in the previous chapter cannot be separated from discourses circulating generally, and I want to give three examples here which show significant affinities with the themes emerging from the study of my fieldwork data. The following examples were chosen to demonstrate to what extent similar themes to those discussed in the preceding chapter are also evident outside 'Third World' development and aid. Such discourses will inevitably both feed off

and into each other. The three examples are taken from travel literature, in line with my argument that there is a significant overlap between discourses of development and aid and those of travel and holidays in the 'Third World'. The first example is taken from a popular commentator and travel writer on Latin America, the second from a travel book I happened to purchase in a charity shop, and the third is from a widely available and used travel guide. I also refer briefly to another travel guide to illustrate how historical referents can be used in ways which are apparently neutral, but which can be shown to be heavy with meaning, with particularised interpretations of historical events. Again, as in the previous chapter, each individual example must be understood in its role as contributing to the creation of an overall power relationship. The examples may be perceived as separately unimportant but they must be placed and understood together with numerous similar expressions of the same discourse of white Western superiority. Again, the pattern gradually becomes incontrovertibly evident once each individual example is added to the accumulative picture.

In keeping with the overall approach of this book, the examples offered are from the sympathetic end of the spectrum. Yet using discourse analysis to unpack the formations of power behind the apparent objectivity of the words offers some important insights. Hugh O'Shaughnessy has been an influential commentator on Latin America for many years, and the Latin American correspondent for both the *Observer* and the *Financial Times*. His book, *Latin Americans* (1988), was produced as a Radio 4 series. His interest in Latin America cannot be doubted – he has been travelling there and writing for 25 years and he acknowledges how exciting, enthralling and thrilling he has found his explorations and meetings with Latin Americans. Nonetheless, he establishes very quickly in his 'preface of an enthusiast' (p15) that he is going to contribute to, rather than challenge in any way, the existing discourses around Latin America. The chapter titles provide an illustrative summary: though he does not want to buttress the view of 'most people', for whom 'the region and its inhabitants remain an exotic mystery' (back cover), the list of contents spells out precisely who O'Shaughnessy thinks the inhabitants are:

1 Who are they?
2 The Military
3 The Guerrillas
4 The Church
5 Indians and Blacks
6 Do they matter?

It is hard to imagine a Latin American (or, indeed a European) questioning whether an entire continent of Europeans matters. Many of his portraits of individual countries combine travel-guide type descriptions of the flora and fauna with some basic history, all spiced with personal experiences. His view of the European encounter is quite fundamental to all of his observations and comments: 'While it would be wrong to romanticise the circumstances in which greedy and triumphant Europeans landed on and seized the New World, the juxtaposition of familiar and exotic cultures which 'the Discovery of America' brought about has, for me, been at the centre of Latin America's fascination' (p17). In his, admittedly brief, historical overview O'Shaughnessy makes use of certain verb formations to convey a very particular view of power relations – of interest here is the way in which he portrays the inter-face between Nicaragua and the US. He talks in terms of how the Monroe Doctrine 'allowed Washington to take over a quarter or more of the territory of Mexico ... and, in the succeeding century (they) were to come to Mexico again and again, to annex Puerto Rico and to occupy Haiti, the Dominican Republic, Cuba, Panama, Nicaragua for spells' (pp34-5). Somehow, he manages to make all these invasions and occupations seem almost accidental and the effect of creating an active agent which is actually a city (and not, as in reality, armed forces) is to set up a benignly distancing and almost dream-like quality to these events, which are further reduced in significance by only lasting for 'spells' (a word, in terms of time, more commonly associated, at least in the UK, with the weather – 'a cold spell in April': a turn of work – 'a spell of woodwork': or taking a break or holiday (OED). The connection of the word with witchcraft adds a further level of potential meaning). The cumulative effect of the use of such language is to reduce the impact on the reader of such events, and thus to encourage an untroubled response, which helps to maintain existing power relations.

In the chapter called 'Indians and Blacks', O'Shaughnessy takes the reader rapidly through ancient civilisations, referring to the 'amazing' skills of the Maya (p119); and the 'truly horrifying affair' that is his view of the Aztec religion; and, finally, he informs us that 'an even greater and older civilisation awaited the Spaniards in the Andes'. He does rather make it appear as if the Incas did not really exist until their period of waiting was over and their lives became bound to that of their Spanish conquerors. Pizzaro, the Conquistador, 'who in 1532 brought the Incas low' (p121) is described by O'Shaughnessy as 'a ruffian and an adventurer', and this does have the effect of giving his mass killings and ravages a somewhat mischievous and not very serious air. This stands in stark contrast to the intricate details provided of an Aztec sacrifice (p120), utilising words such as 'gruesome', 'hideous', 'monstrous', and ending with the apparently neutral information that the 'mass executions were occasion for great rejoicing by the Aztec people'. The message conveyed here is that the interventions of Pizzaro and his ilk are really nothing to be concerned about. In this chapter, O'Shaughnessy also provides his insight into the slave trade from Africa to Latin America – a section which he opens with the comment 'workers had to be got from somewhere, especially when it was discovered that sugar could be grown easily and fetch high prices from Europe' (p122). No comment here about monstrous, or even ruffian-like behaviour: just an apparently objective comment that the 'trade was to grow and grow'. As if it grew on its own, without any human agency. He makes a direct link between the 'disappearance' of the Indian population with the arrival of the 'blacks', saying that 'as the blacks arrived from Africa so the Indian population withered. Some, like the Tainos, disappeared completely. Others all but vanished'. At this point any European culpability is entirely absent, and although European aggression does make an appearance later in the narrative, for the reader, it is likely that the cognitive links have already taken hold.

The second example is a book describing Patrick Marnham's journey to Central America, the title of which is *So Far From God* (1986), which the front cover assures us is not just marvellous but 'trustworthy'. It was also the winner of the Thomas Cook Travel Book Award for 1985.The front cover continues: 'Marnham travels through Mexico, Guatemala, El Salvador, Nicaragua, beautiful countries full of death and fear, their people religious, courteous and violent, befriending and observing across political and racial divisions ...'. In similar vein to O'Shaughnessy, Marnham deals with any potential impact on these countries of globally exploitative relations in a summary manner. Even though writing during the mid-1980s, at the height of the Contra War, Marnham totally reframes the contribution of the US:

> [there are] three small countries where all the trouble occurs. Guatemala, El Salvador and Nicaragua. These three had not disappointed me; I wanted to go back. They recalled the old Spanish curse 'May you live in interesting times'; three insignificant little places posing problems which not even the US could solve.

There are a number of important communications going on here which add up to conveying a subliminal message establishing and affirming the author's superiority (and his right not to be disappointed) and, by implication that of London and England (the only information we have about the author, apart from the gender suggested by his name, is that he writes in London and he arrives back in London airport at the end of his journey and book). Not only does Marnham, in the space of three lines, tell us twice that these countries are 'small' and 'little', he also slips in the pejorative 'insignificant', to ensure the reader gets the message. There is a referent, with 'curse', to evil and the supernatural, which takes us into the realm of the less than civilised, and then we have the final surety that it is these countries where 'all the trouble occurs' and which are 'posing problems'. Which, to cap it all, 'not even the US could solve'. The remainder of the book is a fairly predictable tale of crazy bus journeys, mixed up religions, Indian traditions, Latino music and lots of violence. Apparently all of the violence is entirely home-grown and there are no connections to forces outside the state – there is no mention of US financial and logistical support of particular political factions within each of these countries, for example.

The third example is taken from the Berkeley travel guide (marketed as 'the budget travellers handbook', and written by Berkeley students in 1993). Each chapter covers a different central American country, and the one on Nicaragua opens thus:

> A few weeks into my trip to Nicaragua, I had had it. I had seen enough hopeless disorganization, machismo, crippling strikes, heart-breaking poverty, pickpockets, obnoxious drunks, and plain and simple unfriend-liness ... I was no closer to getting to know Nicaragua's people than before my trip.

In this short excerpt, the writer, Gregory Smith, employs several of the stereotypes we find elsewhere in relation to Nicaraguan people in particular and 'Third World' peoples more generally: that they are macho, cannot organise themselves, are criminals who drink a lot, etc. Needless to say, the existence of poverty is not linked to global forces but is presented as one of a list of unpleasant national characteristics.

The short section at the front of the book (px) which purports to tell us something about the writers themselves rapidly degenerates into a repetition of the list of stereotypes:

> Gregory Smith graduated from U.C. Berkeley with a degree in law and Latin American studies, before realizing that he would hang himself if he had to be a lawyer. Fleeing his suicidal urges, he skipped out on his bar exam to write the Nicaraguan chapter. After a few weeks of fight-ing chronic diarrhoea, belligerent drunks, cold shoulders and post-apocalyptic disorganization, the bar exam started to sound like a lot of fun.

There is also a stereotype of bribery when Smith is described as 'having to bribe his way out of the country'. Significantly, the fact that this was '(something about an overstayed visa)' is mentioned as an unimportant aside; what must be stressed are the aspects which reinforce the writer's portrayal of Nicaraguan people. Inevitably, we learn little about Smith, apart from a (joking?) reference to his parlous mental health, and the reader is certainly not encouraged to consider whether this may have indeed contributed to his less than happy stay in Nicaragua.

I want here to explore the role of history and reflect on how it can be used to buttress a particular point of view. As illustrated above, travel guides, even more than travel books, are frequently viewed as offering a neutral commentary – on locations, the weather, local currencies and curiosities, the best places to eat and so on. However, given that their reason for existence involves encouraging the Western propensity to travel, any travel guide deemed 'political' is likely to be so only insofar as it is critical of the country of description, rather than of the intentions of the traveller or suitability of the travel itself. Whilst one would, therefore, not expect power relations to be under particular scrutiny in such a publication, it does seem reasonable to demand that they do not actually exacerbate existing power differentials.

Historical stories and sites are often part of the attractions of tourism, and I want use a particular illustration – this time from the portrayal of Mayan civilisation – which links to wider connections with discourses of tourism and travel. A highly effective and persistent process in the establishment and maintenance of power imbalances is the obliteration of significant segments of the historical perspective of dominated groups, frequently culminating in the disappearance of all traces of processes of domination. Such destruction can take a number of forms – outright vandalism, persistent ignoring, challenging on the basis of superior force or technology, or the insistence of the more powerful, hence official, version. As is apparent in relation to Central America, such processes continue in different forms but with similar outcomes across the centuries. This is not to argue that any one version of history, whether that told by the oppressors or the oppressed, is intrinsically more 'right' than another (each version rather represents a particular point of view); but, as a Foucauldian genealogical approach to history suggests, what is important is the attempt to uncover relations of power rather than to search in the past for some kind of unadulterated truth.

This obliteration of Mayan history began some time ago. As Eduardo Galeano (1987) describes, the deliberate and wholesale destruction of books was specifically designed to annihilate the containers and communicators of an indigenous sense of history and knowledge, and this contributed to the founding of a power hierarchy which subsequently held sway across the intervening centuries. It is the aspect of establishing a fundamental sense of superiority, and the linking of this, in this context, with the imposition of the Christian religion, which has later echoes in development discourse. To quote from Galeano (p137):

> Fray Diego de Landa throws into the flames, one after the other, the books of the Mayas.
> The inquisitor curses Satan, and the fire crackles and devours. Around the incinerator, heretics howl with their heads down. Hung by

the feet, flayed with whips, Indians are dowsed with boiling wax as the fire flares up and the books snap, as if complaining.

Tonight, eight centuries of Mayan literature turn to ashes. On these long sheets of bark paper, signs and images spoke: They told of work done and days spent, of the dreams and the wars of a people born before Christ. With hog-bristle brushes, the knowers of things had painted these illuminated, illuminating books so that the grandchildren's grandchildren should not be blind, should know how to see themselves and see the history of their folk, so they should know the movements of the stars, the frequency of eclipses and the prophesies of the gods and so they could call for rains and good corn harvests.

The year was 1562. Drawing on a personal anecdote (shortened from a lengthy diary entry made at the time), I want to illustrate how those events still resonate with current North/South power relations.

As a development worker on vacation, I took advantage of being in Central America and travelled widely, as did many of my colleagues. In 1995, I visited Chichen-Itza in Mexico, one of the major Mayan sites open to tourists. I take the liberty here of stepping outside Nicaraguan national borders as these are arbitrary impositions, not yet in place in 1562. The site is large and complex, and I attached myself to a party of around 30 North American tourists, whose guide was of Mayan descent. The tour included a trip around the impressive ball court, where a massive field is flanked by temples at either end and surrounded by high walls, with small stone rings cemented up high. There are a number of carvings along the walls, including some showing players who have been decapitated. Our guide explained that it is not known whether the captain of the losing team was sacrificed, or the captain of the winning team. The latter part of his commentary was all but ignored by the group, who preferred to joke raucously about how such treatment might improve the performance of their local football or baseball teams. My guide book – *Mexico–a Lonely Planet travel survival kit* – embellishes even further: 'It may be that during the Toltec period the losing captain, and perhaps his team-mates as well, were sacrificed' (Noble, 1995, p893). I would suggest that motivating such a description is the desire to arouse levels of excitement and anticipation in prospective (Western) visitors as there is no visible evidence that whole groups of people were killed and, in a private conversation with the guide, he explained how a different approach to death to that in the West renders it perfectly plausible that the winning captain would approach going to his death as an honour. Not a possibility most of us tourists even considered worth a second thought. The tour around Chichen-Itza continued, with any interest in Mayan abilities in architecture, astronomy or mathematics over-shadowed by a consuming fascination with the idea of sacrifice.

The further irony of this is that a great deal of what is 'known' today about Mayan society comes from a book, written in 1566, by the same Friar Diego de Landa. His English translator, William Gates, acknowledges that, in the Auto de Fe, he burned 'ninety-nine times as much knowledge of Maya history and sciences as he has given us in this book' (De Landa, undated, p10). Furthermore, this book, upon which we are so very dependent for our picture of Mayan civilisation, was written by Landa after he had been returned to Spain to stand trial before the Council of the Indies, on a charge of using particularly despotic methods over the Mayans. He composed it as a means of defending himself. Compare Landa's words with those of Galeano quoted above:

> After the people had been thus instructed in religion, and the youths benefited as we have said, they were perverted by their priests and chiefs to return to their idolatry; this they did, making sacrifices not only by incense, but also of human blood. Upon this the friars held an Inquisition – they held trials and celebrated an Auto, putting many on scaffolds, capped, shorn and beaten, and some in the penitential robes for a time. Some of the Indians out of grief, and deluded by the devil, hung themselves: but generally they all showed much repentance and readiness to be good Christians (p52).

It does not seem too fanciful to suggest that, given he is defending his own harsh treatment of the Mayan people (so harsh that other Spaniards sent him back to Spain to stand trial), Landa is likely to paint as unflattering a portrait of his subjects as possible, and that emphasising anything connected to idolatry and sacrifice would suit his purpose well. I do not wish to argue that human sacrifice did not exist, rather to suggest that this particular version of history ignites and rekindles current ideologies of North American and European superiority which serves to excite and arouse the tourist, whilst at the same time underpinning the very notion of the 'Third World' as an undeveloped and inferior sector of the globe.

One important aspect of power, then, is not simply the deployment of brute force, though this is still often used, in actuality or as a background threat; there is also the aspect evident in Landa's account – the fundamental assumption of manifest rightness which justifies whatever requires justification. We can see here how Landa postulates a higher cause (in this case the Christian religion) which demands whatever sacrifices those who dominate see fit to impose. Later higher causes have included the Western notion of civilisation (Fernandez-Armesto, 2000) and even the globalisation of market forces – all of which have been and are used as justifications for a particular configuration of forces of power, requiring the obliteration of the history of the dominated. These fundamental aspects of the operations of power are already evident in the time of Landa; he claims to know what is right for whom, and decides how those placed in the wrong should be treated, and upon whose shoulders the responsibility for perceived acts of barbarism should fall, as distinct from who attains the (unacknowledged) benefit. The crucial cognitive link with current day development is the pervasive idea that, as with Christianity, such actions are for the benefit of the recipient community, no matter how much the evidence, such as Landa's own description of Indians hanging on the scaffolds, may suggest the opposite conclusion. Furthermore, with the destruction of the abilities of the (in this case) Maya to represent their own cultural defence, the written words and language of the in-comer also dominate the power of representation.

2.2 TV AND FILM

In this section I discuss a TV documentary and a film, both chosen to illustrate similar and parallel discourses with those described in the previous chapter. It is important to recognise that it is not only in the written format that these discourses of superiority and inferiority are manifest; they occur regularly and can be unearthed in other forms of the media. Each example by itself may appear relatively insignificant, but when looked at together their accumulative impact becomes clear.

During 2001, on summer Friday evenings, BBC2 broadcast a series of programmes collectively entitled *Conquistadors*, which were written and presented by Michael Wood (there are also a book and audio cassette with the same title). The format of the programme reflects the Western obsession with travel, but this time with a difference. The historical connection is made quite explicit as Wood elects to travel around Latin America, tracing the footsteps of the Spanish conquistadors of the sixteenth century. Clearly this is a useful device for TV as it allows stunning images of the relevant country, its landscape and peoples to be shown whilst the historical tale unfolds, though, for the purposes of my argument, I wish to concentrate on the narrative element of the programme rather than its visual impact. In one of the episodes, as Wood recounts the story of Francisco Pizzaro's conquest of the Inca empire, he demonstrates great sensitivity to the culture of the Inca civilisation and he is clearly sympathetic to what he calls the 'Inca resistance'. He refers to the Spanish conquest as bringing about 'the end of sacred time and the beginning of profane time' and he leaves his audience in no doubt that he considers the sole motive of the Spanish in Peru – from Pizzaro's first incursion, when he promised his small band of men untold riches, to the gold rush that followed later – was profit. It is, however, apparent when one looks closely at Wood's choice of words, and perhaps even more at the type of words he does not use, to describe Pizzaro's incursions, that his narrative unwittingly underscores the points I have been making above. In the opening shots of the programme, he describes the conquest of the Incas as 'one of the most amazing events in history'. The word 'amazing' is important for, not only does it carry the relatively neutral meaning of surprising and extraordinary, it also has a current resonance with 'marvellous, fabulous, wonderful', even (according to OED) 'far-out'. He repeats the word 'amazing' later, when describing how, with only 62 soldiers on horseback and 102 foot soldiers, the Spanish, nonetheless, could defeat an enemy of some five million people. Wood explains this feat by saying that Pizzaro was 'a canny character', 'tough as old boots'; these descriptors have a similar feel – a bit rough, but basically acceptable – as those used by O'Shaughnessy (see above). Wood continues with telling us that Pizzaro is 'very, very clever because he understood the Incas were a civilisation at the level of the Bronze Age and with guns and Toledo swords, he could strike where it really hurt'. Later in the story we learn how the description 'really hurt' is perhaps something of an understatement, when Wood relates how and with what results Pizzaro employed his superior weaponry. On entering the town of Cajamarca, the Spaniards found it empty and they occupied one of the buildings on the main square. The Inca inhabitants then returned into their town, singing a 'lilting song' in welcome to the Spanish. A Spanish priest made a speech, inviting the Inca Emperor, Atahualpa, to change his religion. When this request was turned down, Wood states that Pizzaro had 'the moment he had been waiting for and he gave the order to attack':

> The Spaniards just opened fire on the masses of people crowded there. The Inca sticks and fans were no match for Spanish guns and steel. Some said 6,000 people died in that square. As the rain fell, the square ran red with blood.

This, continues Wood, 'is the moment on which his whole career had converged'. So, at a point of supreme cruelty and disregard for the lives of others, Wood offers us a comment on the life-path of the main protagonist. Absent is any hint of rhetoric of the 'savage, monstrous, barbarous' variety so often used to describe those peoples whom the Spaniards overran. It is noteworthy that deaths which occur as the result of the use of 'modern' weaponry seem to excite less outraged comment than those resulting from a killer using his/her bare hands in some way. Guns and their descendants kill at a distance (with distances today becoming ever greater), and the distancing seems to condition the degree of expressed reaction. Essentially, in describing the deaths of six thousand people in Cajamarca Square, Wood does not use the emotive and value-laden adjectives that are routinely deployed when representing historical deaths at the hands of those deemed inferior. Here it is the absence of language which is effective in establishing who (or what) is superior to whom. I would also suggest that the possession of a 'superior' form of weaponry seems to imply superiority in other respects (see Worsley 1967).

There are plenty of films with wide circulation which use the crudest of stereotyped imagery of the 'Third World' – one only has to glance at the James Bond or Indiana Jones movies to see how frequently the presence of a villain is rendered immediately obvious by the use of a Latino appearance (often signalling some form of involvement with drug smuggling), emphasised by the shrewd use of accent and other attributes such as disability (see Barnes, 1992), so that the villains carry with them a label of inferiority. For the purposes of this book, however, I wish to take an example which sets out to be generally supportive of the 'Third World'; and in the particular example I am going to discuss, the writer and director were intent on presenting a viewpoint sympathetic to Sandinista Nicaragua. Ken Loach is often perceived as one of the most left-wing of British directors, and he has made a number of films with a Hispanic connection. His film *Carla's Song* is a fictional story, but is set in the reality of the Nicaragua of 1987, two thirds of the way into the Sandinista interregnum and whilst the Contra War was still raging.

The story begins in Glasgow and the central character is George, a bus driver who breaks all his workplace rules with hilarious results, including hijacking his own bus and driving it out into the Scottish countryside of mountain and mist, in order to romance his new girlfriend. She is Carla, a traumatised but beautiful Nicaraguan refugee, who scrapes together a precarious living by singing and dancing (traditional Nicaraguan songs, naturally) on the streets of Glasgow. The film gets serious when George embarks on his rescue mission. To begin with, he takes Carla off the streets and out of unsatisfactory lodgings, continually overcoming Carla's verbal attempts to resist such interference in her life. She constantly protests that she wants to be left alone, but to no avail. The climax of the Glaswegian portion of the film is George's discovery of her in the bath, unconscious and with the copious blood and slashed wrists of a suicide attempt. Needless to say he rescues her.

At no point in the film is it explained how she was able to enter Britain even though it is precisely this issue which is central to the concerns of the vast majority of refugees, especially those originating from 'Third World' countries. But it does not warrant a mention in this film. The two fall in love, and at George's insistence, they travel to Nicaragua to search for the cause of her trauma. As he becomes aware of the background of torture and horrific violence which is the genesis of Carla's trauma, George announces that he has to 'go back': 'I can't take all this killing. It's fucking chaos. They're all fucking animals'. The 'they', the 'chaos' and 'animals' – even the 'fucking' – all refer to Nicaraguans and he does not need to be explicit for this message to be clearly communicated. His view that the causes of the war and its violent disorder are exclusively to be found within the borders of Nicaragua is, as I have indicated in previous sections, very common and ensures that that which is apparently deemed unacceptable by the West is firmly and consistently located in the 'Third World'. Unusually, Loach is aware of this, and he has the North American ex-CIA officer (now working for Witness for Peace) explain to George that the culpability is, largely, not Nicaraguan, but belongs rather with their northern neighbour, and he understands this because he was, until recently, a CIA officer, himself carrying out the dirtiest of war tasks. He shows George how the attacking Contra used satellite photos to guide them to the schools and health centres which were routinely targeted in their assaults: 'the CIA runs the whole show. There would be no Contra, no war without them'. George is shocked by this possibility and I would argue that a more in depth exploration of this kind of dilemma could have presented a valuable challenge to current global power relations. Instead, Loach chooses to finish the film with a scene which could have been taken straight out of Rambo. George and the CIA operative, on a crazy mission to find Carla in hostile and dangerous territory, commandeer a local bus and George uses his skills as a bus driver to maniacally but successfully negotiate the most inhospitable terrain (narrow, rutted roads; dust; boulders; no signposts), whilst his partner finds a rifle and single-handedly, courageously, though improbably, fends off attacking Contra forces. The use of the ex-CIA man as a cipher would, I feel, have been an effective tactic for Loach to try and communicate to his audience the role that global politics and power played at the heart of the Contra War, but the film finishes on a note of the two white boys arriving, in the nick of time, to perform the heroics and carry through the rescue. In the final shots of the film, we are shown the two white lads establishing their mutual bond as George leaves for Scotland.

In tune with his political credentials, Loach later returned to Nicaragua in order to show his film to 'the people who had made it all possible'. He was accompanied by Dan Glaister, a journalist who wrote it up for the *Guardian* newspaper. Throughout the article (*Guardian*, 8.11.96) there are references to the problems which beset such an enterprise; 'broken projectors, obstructive politicians and power cuts' – all of which have a Nicaraguan origin. Glaister describes a showing of the film at the University of Central America in Managua:

> There are more problems. The print to be used has been treated carelessly: someone has cut the blank leaders from the beginning of each spool. Tension rises in the packed classroom as 300 18-year olds begin to fidget. Someone is dispatched to buy Sellotape. Some Loachian improvisation is called for: 'Is there a faculty of politics here?' asks Loach. There isn't.

When the screening finally gets underway, the image does not fit on the classroom wall.

And so on. Nowhere is there a mention of how one of the poorest countries in the world might be expected to have some difficulty in providing the kinds of resources which could be taken for granted at a film showing in the UK. The sense of superiority is however apparent in all spheres of life, not just technical expertise. It might be expected that, give their direct experience, it would at least be a Nicaraguan who could best explain the politics and morality behind the film. Not so: Glaister continues:

> Loach and Laverty (the film's writer) are in turn ambushed at the university. 'What about the Soviets?' asks a student. 'In every war there are two sides. Did you try to get a Contra to explain their side?' Loach tells a story about the Venice festival. A Russian journalist had said to him: 'So, you're on the side of the KGB against the CIA.'
> 'I said that I was on the side of the people who build schools. I was on the side of the people who build hospitals. I was on the side of people who teach. And against the people who destroy hospitals, the people who destroy schools and the people who kill teachers.' His reply is met by silence.

One might agree with Loach's every word, and some of the responsibility for the overall message imparted here is clearly Glaister's – for example, the choice of the word 'ambushed', which would have powerful and traumatic resonance for many Nicaraguans and is therefore, I would argue, used here inappropriately. It is part of the overall pattern, that, on the one hand the West (specifically the US, but consistently backed by Britain) destroys Nicaraguan independence and then, on the other, it announces what the problems are and what the solution should be. It so often is the case that we have the scenario of the Western figure explaining to Nicaraguans (whether poor campesinos or, as in this situation, educated university students), not only geopolitics, but matters of a moral nature as well. We are not informed whether it was the eloquence of Loach's statement or his arrogance which led to the ensuing silence as a response, but I suspect, from the content and tone of his entire piece, that Glaister did not even consider the possibility of the latter as a factor.

2.3 ACADEMIA AND ECONOMICS

The first example in this section comes from a book, *Beyond Solitude* (Duncan & Karidis, 1995), whose subtitle is *Dialogues between Europe and Latin America*, and which emerged from a conference, entitled 'Perspectives on Gender, Ethnicity and Politics in Chicano and Latin

American Studies', held at the University of Birmingham in 1994. The Introduction to the book tells us that that, whilst the book is based on issues raised by the conference, the emphasis in the book is on 'an exploration of the relationship between Latin America and Europe' (Karidis, p1). The Introduction then proceeds to introduce relevant theoretical directions which are important throughout the various chapters of the book, which are authored by different people. The first major 'trend' to be considered is that of multi-culturalism and Karidis argues:

> Multiculturalism necessarily involves a dismantling of existing theories and ideologies. It poses a challenge to the monolithic and generalising oppositions, West versus East or West versus Third World. Culture is no longer regarded as fixed property, nor is it seen as pure ... Oppositions, divisions and barriers dissolve to be replaced by communication, conversation, and dialogue. Multiculturalism recognises interactions between cultures and encourages respect through knowledge ... it provides an ideal framework within which to read Latin America.
>
> To examine Latin America from a multicultural perspective we must first turn to the developments in postcolonial thought ... (p3)

It seems something of an insurmountable contradiction to suggest the dismantling of monolithic theories and then to establish the overall goal of the book as 'reading' and 'examining' Latin America. This seems rather less a dialogue than a one-way activity involving interpretation of meaning and, possibly literally, translation by the powerful subject, in this case, academics based at a British institution. The nature of the subject is not made clear, nor are the power relations explored beyond an assumption of equality. It is clear that the role of Latin America is to be the object of knowledge – to be read and examined. It is always instructive to imagine the power play the other way around: in this case, the reversal would involve a group of Latin American academics who would perceive barriers and divisions (all barriers, including immigration regulations? Or just those connected to culture?) as dissolved sufficiently to permit them to 'read' and 'examine' Europeans – this seems an unlikely eventuality. The project can only be phrased as it is because of the underlying assumptions of superiority, in spite of protestations to the contrary.

I wish to examine what I believe to be a further example of the Anglo-centric application of theoretical constructs in a way which is not only inappropriate but which also feeds into unequal power structures by reaffirming the view that 'we' know better than 'them' what is really going on; furthermore, in the example which follows there are comments on how 'they' could have done it better. In her article, 'Woman's Place/El Lugar de Mujeres' (subtitled 'Latin America and the politics of gender identity'), Sarah Radcliffe is concerned to discuss the response of Argentinean women to human rights abuses committed by the military governments during the 1970s. This was a time when political opponents of the government were routinely 'disappeared' and when one of the most famous resistance movements became the known as the Mothers of Plaza de Mayo (May Square). This movement consisted primarily of women who protested vigorously for the return of their relatives, particularly sons and daughters, who had been taken by the regime, with their whereabouts pronounced unknown. Often the police would deny all knowledge of their existence and so the Mothers would go from police station to police station in search of their loved ones. (Something of a similar trauma of those times was captured by the 1985 North American film *Missing*, though this film takes place in Chile and, inevitably, the central figure of concern is a missing North American journalist). Radcliffe begins her article with a moving quotation from one of the founder women of the group who said, 'the boots, the slaps and the kicks were necessary before we good housewives would finally go out and participate' (1993, p102). She is primarily concerned to challenge existing interpretations of the actions of this group, which have been portrayed as breaking down some of the traditional boundaries between public and private spaces in the lives of 'ordinary' women. The conclusion which she reaches is that, whilst there may have been a move for the women from the private to the public in terms of usage of spaces (from the indoors to the outside), this did not represent a transformation in relation to their gender identities, 'power relations, nationalism or violence' (p112). Thus their 'progressive transformative potential' (p113) was limited.

Radcliffe does acknowledge the fact that these women posed one of the most serious arenas of challenge and resistance to the Argentinean military, and that they were themselves subject to arrests, surveillance and intimidation. Nonetheless, they are judged in this piece according to criteria which could be seen as Western imposition. The Mothers' explicit goal was to exercise as much pressure as possible on the military junta in order to secure the release of their relatives and, by 1982, they were able to hold protests in Buenos Aires involving some 5,000 people. Given the climate of extreme repression within which these women were operating, this was no mean feat. I think it quite extraordinary that these women should be judged in early 1990s English academia to be found wanting because they apparently failed in some way to change the politics of gender identity. Only a cultural criticism which allocates unto itself the right to judge all others could use the criteria of 'gender identity' as applicable to the Mothers of the Disappeared in 1970s Argentina.

As a 'First World' academic discipline, geography has had a close relationship with the 'Third World' and has often taken up particular stances in relation to centuries of unequal power relations. Here, I will offer two examples of texts from British geography, both of which were written from a specifically feminist standpoint and therefore from a viewpoint supportive of the unravelling of power relationships, at least those based on gender differentials. It is important to recognise again that alertness to one form of domination does not imply, in this case, an awareness of those forms of control located in whiteness. Both texts portray themselves as taking an inherently sympathetic approach to 'Third World' women. The first is *Viva*, edited by Sarah Radcliffe and Sallie Westwood (1993), and sub-titled *Women and Popular Protest in Latin America*. The editors emphasise in their introduction that they are 'mindful of the critiques generated by black and minority women and by women of the South' (p5), and consequently see their task as deconstructing the homogenising, universalising account of Latin America, specifically in relation to the women. Instead they aim to give full attention to 'diversity and the specific ways in which racisms, gender and class relations are articulated in the different states of the Americas'. In spite, however, of an acknowledgement of Stuart Hall's work in relation to the impact of the European encounter and the subsequent 'otherization' of the peoples of Latin America, all further references to racism are limited to those operating within the borders of various Latin American states, for example those types of racism that intertwine with the fate of indigenous peoples, and there is a complete silence around white racism which might implicate themselves. So we have the rather extraordinary situation where reference to the white Eurocentric elite is only made within Brazilian, Venezuelan or Peruvian boundaries, and the editors themselves and the wider context, both historical and geopolitical, are presented yet again as neutral and non-affective. This seems to me to undermine their original argument and justification for the book.

The second book I wish to consider from the academic discipline of geography is Janet Townsend et al's *Women's Voices from the Rainforest* (1995). Townsend offers the reader a very full and complex picture of her own positionality and that of all of her co-researchers and co-authors. The book takes an explicitly feminist approach and goes into considerable detail regarding its research methodology, consistently attempting, quite self-consciously, to present a critical account of themselves in all aspects of their relationships with the women in the rainforest whose life stories they wish to relate. Though insistent on shared experiences as women and unequivocal that every aspect of the research work is to be carried out by women and with women, nonetheless their position of relative power is acknowledged on a number of occasions. Townsend et al indicate their awareness of the diverse ways in which their difference in respect of greater power is communicated to the women they are researching – being able to command a means of transport, for example, or the fact that 'we are well-fed and healthy so that even our bodies tell of power and prosperity', and they are always able to arrive in the selected village accompanied by effective introductions 'from a peasant league or a World Bank project ... from a Mexican university and local officials...' (p16). The researchers also present introductions of themselves to the reader which emphasise 'some of the reasons why we all represent the intractable outside world in these areas' ... 'colouring, accent, qualifications and childlessness. (Childless grown women who have no male partners with them are very strange indeed, blue eyes are quite strange, brown hair is unusual and fair hair almost unknown). Our personal characteristics, of course, coloured not only how we were seen but what we saw' (p12).

In practice, though, and according to the versions of the Mexican women's contributions, the latter were only ever encouraged to talk about themselves and their lives and nowhere are they recorded as having had feelings or views about the 'friendly strangers' who put them through the highly unusual experience of attending workshops and being asked to answer questions on their work, their childhood and such in-depth issues as puberty – which, as Townsend points out, 'used not to be discussed in Mexican families' (p88) – as well as physical violence within the household. The stated aim of the project (p4) was 'to develop with pioneer women some guidelines for women's grass roots organisations in areas of land settlement in Mexico, and perhaps some guidelines for the planners'. No where is it clear how discussions on puberty contributed to this aim, though it is perhaps more relevant to a re-formulation of the aim to be found later in the book: 'one of the aims of this book is to make the voices of the women who gave their life histories to the project accessible to a wide-ranging English speaking audience' (p139). In this context detailed group discussions of the sort outlined above begin to make more sense, as perhaps does the following comment: 'We wrote up all workshops and returned the originals to the groups, but we recognise that following these feminist precepts may be little more than 'feel-good' measures for us. We do not think that people gain enough from being interviewed or telling their life stories for these benefits to justify the process' (p16). Whatever happened to the guidelines?

Another important and well-used relationship between 'Third' and 'First' World women is the chronicling of the lives of the former with a determining input by the latter. I would argue this is valuable up to a point, useful for those of us with more privileged lives to be reminded of the hardships faced, resisted and frequently overcome by those who inhabit less privileged circumstances. However, the relationship is perhaps not always straightforward and the familiar power relationships often become apparent. Margaret Hooks (1991), for example, presents the lives of Guatemalan woman with herself very firmly located as the one who is producing, though she acknowledges the help and support she received from the women, and no-where is it clear what feedback the women received from the book. Rigoberta Menchu (1983) wrote her life story with the assistance of a French woman, and spent a week in Paris in order to do so. The editor of her recordings, Elisabeth Burgos-Debray, writes in her introduction: 'We established an excellent rapport immediately and, as the days passed and as she confided in me and told me the story of her life, her family and community, our relationship gradually became more intense.' Interestingly, there is no record of Rigoberta Menchu's views of the relationship but one can perhaps surmise that, in such a situation of dependence, it would have been extremely difficult for her to express any criticism.

The World in 2002 was the title of an edition of the *Economist* (Jan 2002) devoted to an assessment of how the year 2002 was likely to unfold, with a series of predictions, each relating to a specific country or world region. The editorial announced that it would be 'a year of convalescence', and thus we knew that the central focus would be America's war on terrorism. It is noticeable that forecasts on life in North America took up 10 of the chapters, and a similar number concerned what might happen in Britain. Latin America's future is covered in one chapter, significantly entitled 'Latin America's Bad Luck'. Whereas economic developments in Britain are attributed to an 'excellent economic performance' and a surprising degree of resilience in the economy (p26) and the potential problems for the US economy are discussed in terms of falling economic output, monetary and fiscal responses (p54), what happens in Latin America is portrayed as the consequence of luck. Serious economic language is suddenly lacking and we have instead the implication of events happening in an unplanned way, by chance or accidentally – and certainly unconnected with any attributes of the inhabitants. The message is once again located in unpredictable Latino territory with its 'maverick politicians' and 'many uncertainties'. Thus even in the 'globalised economy' of the twenty-first century, the *Economist* perceives different parts of the world as being affected by entirely divergent factors – and there is a persistent pattern in that those ingredients of a good economy are persistently associated with the North and they are invariably more weighty in tone, more likely to be the result of sensible economic decisions and superior performance. The article dealing with Africa covers less than a page (p78) and is entitled 'Winter in Africa'. The use of the metaphor of the coldest season of the year (in Britain) again suggests that the responsibility for the fate of the economy belongs with forces outside of human control, even though the view of the World Bank is quoted in the article – that aid to Africa will fall again (it fell from $18 billion in 1990 to $11 billion in 1998) and terms of trade will worsen again. The overall image communicated by this issue of the *Economist* is that the hardworking people of the Northern developed countries are responsible for their good fortune, whilst the negative forecasts for the south are somehow outside of any human agency. Furthermore, there is no discussion at all of those ways in which the North relates to the South (such as the examples it gives of deteriorating terms of trade), or the possible outcomes of such imbalanced relationships, particularly on assisting the economies of some regions at the expense of others.

2.4 BACK TO 'THIRD WORLD' DEVELOPMENT AND AID

In the penultimate section of this chapter, I return to illustrating these discourses of superiority and inferiority as they surface in debates around 'Third World' development and aid. The following quote provides an example of how ideas of Western progress and enlightenment are utilised in development discourse to establish the standard by which the 'Third World' is judged, and generally found wanting. As with the quotes in the sections above, it is from within the West that the problems of the 'Third World' are defined, both at practical and moral level, and the solution is invariably one which exculpates the West from any kind of involvement in causing the problem. Such an approach, as I shall show throughout the rest of the book, is identifiable at every level of 'Third World' development from individual operatives in the field to public pronouncements from the responsible government minister. I begin by quoting the views of Bowen Wells the Conservative MP (for Hertford and Stortford) who, in 1998, had an important role as the Chair of the International Development Select Committee. In his editorial, in the third issue of the Labour government's international development magazine, *Developments*, Wells bases his argument on 'classical human rights put forward in the American constitution – the right of life, liberty and the pursuit of happiness', thus ensuring that in his subsequent comments, on poverty and its causes, the US and its adherents remain strictly not-implicated. Indeed, the US is the model to admire and to follow. He continues:

> Human rights must always be coupled with human responsibilities. The right to food must be coupled with the responsibility of planting crops and watering and tending them so that the family can feed, house and clothe itself. The right to basic health care must be coupled with the responsibility of taking elementary steps to keep both body and living spaces healthy. The right to work must be coupled with a willingness to work hard, learn new skills and add value to the product.

He then insists:

Where rights are granted and responsibilities willingly embraced, growth and development can take place. Most human societies will respond positively in these conditions.

The writer's photograph is published alongside the article and shows him to be white, middle aged, dressed in a suit and tie, clean-shaven and smiling straight at the camera. His use of the discourse of rights and weighty reference to the American Constitution, re-articulates the West as the source of freedom, liberty and equality; thus all forms of Western madness, over-indulgence, cruelty and violence are banished, or 'explained away as alien presences, occlusions of historical progress, the ultimate mis-recogniton of man' (Bhabha, 1994, p43).

To focus on one of the rights enunciated by Wells: he is adamant that the right to food 'must be coupled' with the responsibility to plant, water and tend crops and, yet, it is very unlikely that such injunctions would apply to many Conservative MPs, or, for that matter, to very many of those of us inhabiting the West, where processed food is abundant and consumed unquestioningly. Many in the West now devour food without any understanding of the processes of production, transportation and marketing, and the costs of these processes are often expertly and deliberately hidden from public view and scrutiny. Certainly the notion that we only have a right to food if we take on the responsibility to produce it would be very far from the average Western mind. So, far from delivering the universal message that his language would signify, he is actually talking to and delivering a series of rulings to a particular part of the world, a part of the world which is also not designated to be his readership. And, somehow, I and presumably others easily work out for ourselves whom he really means to address at both levels.

By the time I as the reader reach the telling phrase 'where rights are granted', I am beginning to be very clear who is in a position to grant what to whom, and who, therefore, grants him/herself the apparently corresponding right to judge inputs and outcomes on a global scale – we are, after all, talking 'most human societies' here. The use of the word 'human' in this context is highly instructive. Which are those 'human societies' that will/may not respond positively in such circumstances, thus placing themselves outside of all that is human? The implication is clear enough – there are some 'Third World' countries that simply won't respond even when the West pulls out all the stops, thereby establishing themselves as somehow beyond the borders of the human. There is enormous resonance with the discourses of colonialism here.

On the surface, the implication is that poverty has nothing to do with the speaker/writer – or with myself as the complicit reader. And yet, this piece says more about white identity and its construction than about its apparent subjects. The affluent, white West is here powerfully present (emphasised visually through the photograph), though completely unacknowledged, except for its propensity to pass judgements on and grant rights to those designated as the Other. The oppositionality of those deemed to have rights and responsibilities is locked in a hermetically sealed vacuum, where they can be observed, commented upon, decided about, and judged to be invariably lacking, a discourse resonating with the colonial view of the 'native', who can only be rescued from his/her plight by a judicious amount of British/Western control and guidance. And when this is applied to Nicaragua as one of those countries suffering 'abject poverty' then it not only provides an effective smoke-screen, completely obscuring the role played by the US in exploiting and dominating Nicaragua, but it also serves to shift all of the responsibility onto the least powerful and the least able to achieve any real change in their lives.

2.5 CONCLUDING COMMENTS

An extract from my diary, written whilst travelling in Nicaragua:

> During a discussion with a North American traveller, he said: 'they could get jobs if they really wanted to. No-one has to stay in poverty. I mean, I was born in New York and life was hard'. Later, I overheard him say to Karen, a Dutch traveller, 'you have to live your dreams and not lick arse. I've left every job I've had because I couldn't stand being told what to do and I've even been fired for the same reason'.
>
> I don't point out to him that this is the essence of privilege – but I think of what he said earlier and I compare his own morality, applied to himself, of not wanting to 'lick arse', to his condemnation of people living in poverty in Nicaragua. I think of the people working in maquiladores, on banana plantations and how incredibly hard they work and for how little reward And if they refused to 'lick arse', the consequences would be such that they certainly would not have the resources to travel around a neighbouring continent!

The diary continues:

> The degree of self-absorption and narcissism amongst the majority of travellers whom I encounter is quite breathtaking. Close to 100% of the conversations I overhear (and I listen to quite a few) are about our/themselves and about 80% concern the prices of this or that. They are inevitably too high and we (us travellers) are inevitably being exploited in one way or another.
>
> This morning though outclassed the lot! Karen talked for the whole bus journey on the single subject of her lost walking boots. Fair enough, up to a point, but she somehow always managed to blame Nicaragua! We then met Amir, an Israeli, who also found loads to complain about.

Everything is wrong from 'the usual poor choice of drinks' to 'Nicas speak too quickly, they never move towards you to help'. At the ferry terminal: 'why do we have to wait two hours for the ferry? I don't suppose they have any life-rafts'. I mildly challenged him, to which he replied that he doesn't complain, most of the time he remains very calm!

Wherever one looks, from left-wing films to academic treatises, the underlying discourses impart a similar message – that Latin America is inferior in every respect, from the economy to the savagery of the history. The way in which power is exercised between different ethnic groups and between men and women is also deemed inferior to the way in which we apparently conduct such relations in the West. Informal conversations with Western travellers point up the same tendency, only perhaps more graphically and less elegantly phrased. The persistent application of double standards is apparent throughout, and I would argue that its deployment in one context reinforces the acceptability of its usage in another, different context. Whether subtle or overt, the message is consistent and adds up to a relationship which could be termed Latin Americanism. I take this idea from the work of Edward Said, who argues that the approach of the West towards that entity which has become defined as the Orient is a tenacious portrayal of inferiority in every respect, with profound impact. This is what he refers to as Orientalism.

Said explores how that which has become known as the 'Orient' has been created and maintained as an object of Western knowledge, and he shows how Western discourse constructed a 'knowledge' of the East and a body of power-knowledge relations articulated in the interests of the West (Said, 1991). I am arguing, from the evidence presented so far in this book, that the same process has occurred and is still occurring in terms of power relations between the West and Latin America. Said describes how the West has ascribed certain characteristics to what is termed 'the Orient', represented as generally inferior to the West, and how these subsequently stick like glue. This is particularly obvious in recent media treatment of Islam, which, for example, automatically qualifies for epithets such as 'fundamentalist' and 'fanatic'. This supposed inferiority then allows for all kinds of actions to take place, justified by the superior party inevitably 'knowing best'. 'Orientalism,' says Said:

> can be discussed and analysed as the corporate institution for dealing with the Orient – dealing with it by making statements about it, authorising views of it, describing it, by teaching it, settling it, ruling over it: in short, Orientalism is a Western style for dominating, restructuring, and having authority over the Orient … My contention is without examining Orientalism as a discourse one cannot possibly understand the enormously systematic discipline by which European culture was able to manage – and even produce – the Orient politically, sociologi-

cally, militarily, ideologically, scientifically, and imaginatively during the post-Enlightenment period ... it is the whole network of interests inevitably brought to bear on (and therefore always involved in) any occasion when that peculiar entity 'the Orient' is in question (Said, 1991, p3).

Thus Said argues that Orientalism is a kind of archive, consisting of a mass of texts which describe, explain, and mentally and physically characterise 'Oriental' peoples using a highly potent mixture of fantasy, myth, and stereotypical imagery. We have seen how the West also deals with Latin America by 'making statements about it, authorising views of it, describing it, by teaching it, settling it, ruling over it', and I have offered examples of all of these. Hence my use of the term 'Latin Americanism'. Similar processes can be identified in relation to Africa and I have also provided a small number of exemplars to illustrate this. It will become increasingly evident in forthcoming chapters, where I continue to present particular examples as well as general argument, that much development material, in addition to that supplied by the interviewees, can also be viewed as a collection of textual material, documenting people of the 'Third World' from a specifically Western standpoint. Thus becomes established the concept of the 'other', i.e. that which is not considered by those, who by definition have the power and authority to make and enact such pervasive decisions, to be the 'norm'; the 'other' can then be depicted as consistently and invariably inferior to those who have effectively set themselves as the standard against which all else shall be measured.[1]

This process of othering has been identified by Said as one of the most effective ways of creating and maintaining balances of power on a global basis, affecting the whole range of global interactions. It occurs at both individual and institutional levels and operates to establish regimes of truth, enframing whole regions of the world and portraying them as possessing certain qualities of inferiority and superiority; these are so embedded and encrypted in representations that the subconscious can take for granted the rightness of the imparted assumptions and fails to question them, or indeed place them in any historical or geopolitical context. We have seen in Chapter One how frequently this occurs in development discourse.

In the following chapter, I want to pursue the idea that the use of Latin Americanism, to signal the inferior other, accrues even greater resonance due to its racialisation. We have already seen how whiteness is equated with superiority, either directly or through its assumed equivalence with middle (or upper) class and superior wealth. I now want to explore the possibility that racialised inferiority is insistently identified with place – this has already been effectively argued in relation to place within Britain or the US (see Jackson, 1989), but it is not, as yet, a concept which is applied on a global scale. I suggest that both the terminology of the 'Third World' as a whole and referents to particular individualised countries, such as Nicaragua, become part of a racialised relationship by means of their very mention within Western discourse. The location of 'Third World' countries, within the Western imaginary, at one end of the superiority and inferiority binary, renders any more direct allocation of greater or lesser worth unnecessary. Thus we can speak of 'Third World' racism.

It is this 'Third World' racism, evident in discourses apparent in writings as diverse as those by O'Shaughnessy and Karidis, in film and TV, in travellers' dialogues and in discourses of development, which consistently sanction and underscore the actual expressions of Western power – the invasions, economic embargoes, establishment of unequal terms of trade, exploitation of cheap labour, and so on. Thus a web of power relations becomes established and legitimated which determines the big picture in North/South relations (though never ruling out the existence of local contradictions and ambivalences). For the West, the one sanctions the other – a mostly implicit racism sanctions everything from invasions to use of cheap labour, and the powerlessness and poverty of 'Third World' countries then marks and communicates their apparent inferiority. The role of discourse, through a myriad of means is to build up an accepted truth that establishes, historically and geopolitically, which regions of the world are to be perceived as inherently superior. Such a notion of superiority, with its corresponding attribution of inferiority, is likely to affect all aspects of life (economic, social, cultural, moral) and, I would submit, allows for and encourages the exploitation of othered, 'inferior' peoples, who can be represented as less developed (in all respects) so that the consequences of exploitation matter less. In circular, self-reinforcing fashion, such discursive formations are fed by the racialisation of the relationship.

NOTES

1. Said has certainly been critiqued for enhancing the binary divisions which he sets out to dismantle (see Young, 1992, p11); but my purpose is to explore to what extent the process of othering can be seen to be a contributory factor in determining power relations within the orbit of development and aid.

3

THE PLACE AND TIME OF 'RACE'

In this chapter I look at the theoretical work of writers whose work on 'race' seems particularly relevant to a discussion of development and aid, and attempt to bring some of their insights to bear on a discussion of the discourses deployed in the aid industry. Section 1 focuses mainly on location, looking at ways in which racialised attributes are mapped onto different parts of the world, while Section 2 looks at the continuing importance of attitudes derived from colonial history in shaping perceptions about the 'Third World'.

3.1 THE LOCATION OF 'RACE'

The previous two chapters concentrated on offering specific examples of those discourses which feed into a consistent portrayal of the 'First World' as superior in every respect. Thus inequalities in the material world are refracted through discourse, which then serves to both help create and subsequently buttress the existence of such inequalities. Put bluntly, it matters less if a 'Third World' country suffers extreme poverty, or if its nationals are bombed to protect Northern interests. It matters less because 'Third World' peoples are consistently portrayed as inferior technologically, economically, socially and morally. Such markers of inferiority are also given additional weight by their constant referencing to inferiorities based on racialised constructs. It is harder these days than it was in colonial times (though it is still not impossible) to express racist sentiments openly, but this does not lessen the effect of racialised ways of thinking on development practices and analysis. In this section, I wish to pursue in more detail the way in which the allocation of inferiority and superiority to particular places or locations is implicated in racial inequalities. The ways in which racialised place and spatiality operate on a global basis will be addressed, particularly in terms of relations between North and South. And I shall also indicate the ways in which the Western concept of time is closely linked to a process of marking and defining who and what is to be considered better than whom.

The following quote is from a development worker who said to me during an interview:

> I mean you've got that combination of rural and women and disabled and Nica and you think you're going to advance quickly? You're off your head.

Short and to the point, it encapsulates a number of important mechanisms establishing and consolidating an assertion of superiority and corresponding inferiority, incorporating their allocation on the basis of location. The imputation of 'advancing forwards' as invariably the best direction, together with the absolute necessity for as much 'speed' as possible, are themes oft repeated (as we saw in the Introduction and shall see further in later chapters) as signs of a superior state of being. Paul Gilroy (2000, p70) quotes W.E.B. Du Bois, who questions 'the meaning of progress, the meaning of swift and slow in human doing, and the limits of human perfectibility, which are veiled, unanswered sphinxes on the shores of science'. It is the 'swift' which is relentlessly and exclusively pursued in Western culture, and its attributes are elevated above those of the different possibilities suggested by Du Bois. Similarly, the theories and practices of development and aid work tend to emphasise that whatever is fast is equated with desirability, often explicitly linked with the concept of making progress. Doreen Massey has considered how certain sorts of time are inextricably bound up with notions of progress and change. She contrasts 'time internal to a closed system, where things may change without really changing' – including 'cyclical time, the times of reproduction, the way in which a peasantry represents to itself the unfolding of the cycle of the seasons, the turning of the earth' (1993, p144) – with concepts of linear time, which suggest the expectation of rapid, uni-directional (so-called forward) movement, coupled with lots of change (invariably, as I suggested earlier, linked with 'improvement'). This connects with the discussion of the 'road to development' (chapter 1.3), where I pointed out how the illustration is designed in such a way as to render travel 'forwards', both literally and metaphorically, the only way to go. Massey is here looking at links with gender and rurality, with women and peasants being associated with the more 'backward' ideas of time; her focus is not on the power dynamics of disability and nationality. However, the aid worker quoted above is using a more wide-ranging series of references (women, rural and disabled), as markers of a remoteness from modern temporality and a location in immovable spatiality. The usage of a number of binary markers of inferiority linked together compounds the overall effect – women, rural, disabled (with 'off your head' introducing an additional factor of mental ill health into the equation). The use of an abbreviated and impolite reference to nationality, already established as inferior by association, contributes a further element in case the listener/reader still retains any doubt. Significantly, 'race' is not mentioned overtly, but I would argue that it is conspicuously present by its very absence. The combination of other signifiers, particularly nationality, renders its overt use unnecessary; the message is nonetheless effectively communicated: I would argue that, effectively, 'Nica' in this context, tied together as it is with the long list of other markers of inferiority, is synonymous with black. The speaker, meanwhile, unintentionally confirms his own positionality from which he can define terms of inferiority and radiate superiority.

The racialisation of place ensures that immediate associations are made with the very mention of a geographical name. Think, for example, of the way much of the British tabloid press uses the words 'Brixton' or 'Moss Side' to convey instantly negative and stereotypical images of 'race' in a British context. This issue has been discussed by Peter Jackson (1989, p134; see also Kobayashi & Peake, 1997), but it is interesting that the location of this discussion to date has been largely confined within Western urban settings or within the national boundaries of Western nations. Clearly a similar dynamic is likely to be operating on a global scale. In his essay on the racialisation of space in British cities, David Sibley offers an important insight when he analyses the way white British people deal with their anxieties in relation to 'inner city' Britain by turning that location, in the imagination, into 'another country'. He argues that the people that make such identifications are often concerned about a loss of power; as a result they need 'simplified mappings' to make themselves feel more secure. They need:

> ... to locate imagined threats in particular places. So, 'inner city' becomes *another country*, a convenient depository for anxieties about mixing and merging, about the breaking down of the boundaries of the self and the group ... These imagined geographies, with their echoes of Empire and colonialism, are to some extent realised ... (Sibley, 1998, p127, my italics).

The process of how, or indeed why, 'another country' becomes 'another country' in the Western imagination is not specified and yet, without the need for such specificity, Sibley's readers will know that he is clearly not referring to France or Norway. Such anxieties are located in the 'other' countries of the 'Third World', countries associated with black – sometimes subliminally and sometimes explicitly. As Sibley stresses the threats and fears which are so powerful a part of the imagination are exactly that – imagined, but nonetheless powerful for that. Thus 'Third World' racism travels back and forth, not least in the rucksacks and minds of development workers and other travellers. White Westerners utilise ideas of 'Third World' inferiority to buttress and reinforce stereotypes of black people living within Britain. Think of the negativity conveyed by the insult 'Paki' and how that is connected to images and discourses of the 'Third World'. Similarly, our notions of the 'Third World' cannot remain untouched by the racism rampant within Western societies.

Thus I would argue that the process of echoing Empire and colonialism (see next section) is also applicable to current day relations between global regions, although the imposition of spacialised racial difference between nations and between blocks or camps of nations (a phrase used by Paul Gilroy, 2000) is still largely unexplored. The references to 'Nica' in the above quote are implicitly racialised and, moreover, are located very firmly in that part of the globe commonly referred to as the South, clearly differentiated from the North or the West. Michael Keith and Steve Pile assert that the West is 'a description of economic development but also an imagined locus of a particular form of rational enquiry ... symbolically at the heart of global power' (1993, p22). Although they do not explicitly point to the racialised aspects of this powerful position, their implication is that the non-West (or South) is not only under-developed, but inevitably irrational, chaotic, corrupt and so on. The most frequent and unquestioned images of the South to be found in the Western media are certainly those of chaos, backwardness, degradation, starvation levels of poverty, countries ruled by despotic and corrupt governments. The portrayal of Nicaragua fits well into this, and these themes are evident in a number of the interview quotations, including the one which opened this chapter.

Furthermore, it is clear that, at times, different 'Third World' countries are almost merged into one, and become indistinguishable from each other, as the power from the North which assesses, judges and invariably finds something wrong, also finds it difficult to differentiate between 'Third World' individuals and even nations. To illustrate the power of gaze from the North, I quote from my diary. I was travelling in Mexico, with my daughter and a friend, and we were visiting a town in the northern Yucatan. We were seated in the small market square, which was enclosed by shops and cafes on all four sides, having our breakfast.

> There were a few other travellers, but not many. Several people going about their business, it's obviously a popular place for cafes and places to sit and eat outside, away from what is quite a busy road. We sit in a café close to the entrance as it is a good place to sit and watch the world go by.
>
> Valladolid is on the route for day trips from Cancun. Cancun is a resort development, basically for the rich, who venture out now and again to get a view of 'real life' beyond the hotel foyers and swimming

pools. Without any warning, a luxury air-conditioned coach drew up blocking our view out of the square and a group of North Americans descended. Most of them wandered off towards the splendid cathedral building, but a small group, 3 or 4, came towards us. They stood in the entrance to the square and just stood and stared. I will never forget the look on one man's face as he caught sight of the man who, having no legs, used a skateboard for mobility, moving from tourist to tourist and asking, with an incredible smile, for any loose change. The expression of the North American's face changed from one of ogling with naked curiosity, bordering on outright rudeness, to an expression of sheer horror. The guy on the skateboard approached him with an even broader smile than usual and I think he actually laughed as the North American fled back to his coach. I don't think he got down again, even to see the cathedral.

I wanted Rob to take a photo of the North American guy's face as it seemed so expressive of the Western gaze in action! It was all too quick, though.

It is this look – this assumed and unquestioned right to gaze; to gaze without acknowledging that one is a part of what is happening; to stay apart and to judge; to judge and to invariably find something wrong or something lacking – it is this look which travels from North to South, and any reciprocation is roundly condemned. Neither the source nor the purpose of the gaze is openly acknowledged – it is, as it were, a look from no-where and, simultaneously, the look from everywhere which counts (see also Keith and Pile, 1993, p31).

The effects of such location-based power (or 'power geometry' as Massey calls it: 1991, p26) also operate at a personal level. As the adoptive mother of my Nicaraguan daughter, living in the UK, I have become aware of two quite different responses to her, both of which originate in perceptions of who she is that are based primarily on the colour of her skin. As a white mother, obviously I cannot directly experience what she goes through, but over the years I have learnt to interpret 'the look' and the evasions which signify that something untoward is happening. Firstly, there is the reaction of overt white-on-black racism, which was evident at her first secondary school. The most dangerous location for her was the playground, where she was regularly taunted and abused. To begin with, she pretended she did not hear what was being said, or that it wasn't really directed at her personally; but as she was the only black child in her class she eventually realised she could not escape the message. Somehow, she knew that words such as 'baboon', 'bogeyman', 'Paki', were designed to assault her very sense of being. 'Is that me? Is that a baboon?' she asked me on one occasion, pointing at a double-decker sized poster of a gorilla adorning the sides of buses to advertise a *King Kong* movie (see Briggs, 1999). It is significant, in the context of my overall argument, that many of these highly rejecting epithets utilise images frequently associated with under-development in the 'Third World'. 'Baboon' has evolutionary resonances and conjures up notions of living in the jungle, whilst one of the meanings of 'bogey' is 'an evil or mischievous spirit; a devil' (OED). 'Paki' is similar to the use of 'Nica' as I indicated above: a derogatory usage of nationality to denote inferiority. Thus does 'Third World' racism becomes incorporated into British society.[1]

The other reaction in Britain towards my daughter consists of comments along the lines of 'how lucky she is'. Sometimes the commentator cannot put into words the assumption that she has been fortunate to escape unspecified 'Third World-itis' and sometimes I do not challenge the response, allowing my sense of doing good to be stroked. At other times my sense of history and the role of geopolitics comes to the fore and feeds an angry retort: 'how can a child be lucky who, at the age of two, witnessed the massacre of her family by the US backed forces during the Contra War? Not to mention the devastating impact of the racism she has been subject to over here.' Gayatri Spivak requests that 'what goes on over here be defined in terms of what goes on over there' (quoted in Watts, 1997, p495), by which she means that those of us who inhabit the relatively affluent West cannot ignore the extent to which that affluence emanates from the exploitation of the 'Third World'. We would also do well to remember the part played by Western forces in determining conditions and events in the non-West or South. The fact that my daughter was adopted and brought to live in Britain by me cannot be seen simply as a result of calamities or prob-lems located within Nicaragua, which she is somehow 'lucky' to escape; her situation is actually a direct result of US power relations towards Nicaragua and other Central American countries which includes the regular and organised adoption of children.[2] 'The framing of time and the ordering of space' in the 'Third World' are indeed determined by an 'externally imposed logic' (Slater, 1999, p391). My particular interest is an exploration of the racialisation of that 'logic'.

At this juncture, I want to consider more closely the processes which contribute towards the racialisation of place and, by extension, the racialisation of a people. Numerous strands can be identified as contributing to such processes, and their patterned accumulation adds significant value to each as an individual component. Broadly, I intend to identify four processes under which to discuss racism: othering (already discussed above, particularly in relation to the work of Edward Said), assimilation, rejectionism and ambivalence. They are not distinct categories, rather overlapping and intertwining and reinforcing each other's impact and, again, it is important to stress the accumula-tive impact. However, some structure is helpful for the purposes of analysis and discussion.

In his consideration of the making and unmaking of strangers, Bauman (1997b, p48) refers to the strategy of assimilation: 'making the different similar; smothering cultural or linguistic traditions; forbidding all traditions and loyalties except those meant to encourage conformity to the new and all-embracing order; promoting and enforcing one, and only one, measure of conformity'. The quote from the development worker at the beginning of this chapter would indicate that those Nicaraguan women referred to are to be judged on their ability to 'advance quickly', and it is clear, though not explicit, that such advancement entails adhering to a particularly Western point of view. On the one hand they are 'othered' and represented as everything the speaker is not, but at the same time there is a desire to bring them into the Western fold via a process of assimilation. Western style development is construed and presented as essential everywhere on the globe (and furthermore it must be brought about through the essentially capitalist model as prescribed by the West).

This transposing of a supposedly superior way of life from one part of the globe to another echoes the aim of missionaries in colonial times, who tried to protect their converts from the worst excesses of the conquistadores and – with the best of intentions – encouraged approved forms of 'development'. However, their activities had massively destructive consequences for indigenous peoples across the whole continent. The missionaries were in practice often responsible for breaking down precisely those ethnic loyalties and traditions which they proclaimed worthy of saving, 'in the name of 'modernisation' and 'civilisation' (Wearne, 1996, p89). The activities of current-day development and aid workers can similarly be understood as breaking down those same communities and customs which they purport to be defending against the ravages of Western capitalism and free trade. The constant introduction of 'better ways of doing things'; of apparently superior technologies in everything from medicine to transport; the perceived need to learn the English language; all contribute to the message that the West is culturally superior and that 'Third World' countries and peoples will not 'advance forwards' unless these examples are followed. Thus, as in the age of the missionary, the desire to make countries and peoples conform to the value system of the West is apparent in the development and aid industry.

The motivation to assimilate requires definition of oneself – one's culture, one's economic system and so on – as superior (or why try and make others like oneself?), and the to-be-assimilated as correspondingly inferior. The processes of development are eminently suited for this task as the very notions of progress and development require classifications and orderings to be made and, once this process is underway, it becomes axiomatic to sort into good and bad, better and best, most developed, least developed and so on. The overarching process of classification into developed and undeveloped requires that other, contributory, technologies be put into place: the technologies of observing, enumerating, dissecting, analysing, evaluating – all essential components of development work. It is becoming clearer to what extent and how 'race' and 'race' typologies are thoroughly implicated in such practices and how such practices contribute to the formulation of white, Western countries as essentially developed and, therefore, good in all aspects. The other side of this process entails defining the black countries of the South as under-developed, together with all those attributes persistently associated with inferiority such as slowness and less technology.

As the opening quotation suggests, much racialised essentialism as currently expressed does not rely on the more overt biological and phrenological justifications of colonial eras. Instead we have – often unconscious – responses of rejection of those perceived as other – what Bonnett (1993, p14) refers to as 'rejectionism'.[3] He argues that rejectionism is the rationality underlying exclusion and inclusion, often operating at a subliminal level, and maintained by boundaries both cartographic and in the mind. This question of boundaries is crucial in establishing modern day insiders and outsiders, and the potent invoking of national and regional borders to connote degrees of assumed superiority is a major feature of the interviews, as previous chapters have demonstrated.

There are also links with the classification process discussed above. Gilroy (2000, p31) suggests that the concept of 'race' as currently employed is a modern construct which emerged when 'once confused and unsystematic race-thinking' became 'something more coherent, rational, and authoritative'. He argues that this threshold is important because it identifies the junction point of 'race' with both rationality and nationality. Gilroy talks about nations as 'camps' (p68), deliberately emphasising their territorial, hierarchical and militaristic qualities as well as their fiercely inclusive and exclusive attributes. The image of a Western or Northern camp of nations has a particular resonance, with borders which are rendered increasingly impenetrable to those from the South, and with the imposition of ever fiercer immigration controls and ever more rejectionist attitudes towards the most desperate. It is interesting to note how borders are collapsing in relation to the globalised movement of capital flows, but becoming more rigid in preventing the movement of labour and people, particularly the poor.

The need to not appear rejectionist, whilst actually imposing limits and borders, can result in some bizarre contradictions. The following is the story of a border full of contradictory tensions. It is the story of a border intended to look benign, whilst the harshness of its purpose, especially from the perspective of the less powerful, remains undiminished. At the end of 1997, construction workers were putting the finishing touches to a 14ft high wall, designed to add a further barrier to those already in existence between the USA and Mexico. Its ambivalence, not to say hypocrisy, is revealed in the design specification; the barrier had to be strong enough to resist 'repeated physical assault by means such as welding torches, chisels, hammers, firearms, climbing over or penetration with vehicles.' But, given that the USA and Mexico are bound together in the North American Free Trade Agreement (NAFTA), the USA has to at least maintain an appearance of friendly neighbourliness and, accordingly, orders were also issued to the contractors that the wall should be as friendly-looking as possible. As a result: 'The concrete is steel-reinforced, but it is also salmon-coloured and inlaid with multicoloured stone chips and tiles that may be decorated with children's art. It has large, blue-trimmed openings built into it, covered with steel grating that has small holes, through which people can look across the border or talk to each other' (*Guardian*, 10.12.97, p16). US officials are apparently delighted with the result; a customs officer commented 'It works. It really did come out very pleasing as far as the colour and texture are concerned'. *The Guardian* reports that their Mexican counterparts are less thrilled.

At a subliminal level, as well as in the actual sense, very secure boundaries are erected in the minds of Westerners between those who can claim the right to control and dictate and the pre-determined other who is controlled; and it is important to stress that the creation of actual borders must be preceded by the existence of borders in the mind. Such borders are created to try and keep out that which is considered undesirable, and this takes constant effort and repetition to oneself and others of that which is to be deemed unacceptable. Julia Kristeva (quoted in Sibley, 1997, p8) maintains that the impure can in reality never be entirely removed: 'abjection is above all ambiguity ... while releasing a hold, it does not radically cut off the subject from what is threatening it – on the contrary, abjection acknowledges it to be in perpetual danger'. So, no matter how hard we may try to expel or keep at bay that which we consider unwanted (or even 'evil' to echo George Bush's refrain), we can never be entirely successful. The relatively well-off in the affluent, white world can never live entirely free from some level of awareness of those exploitative threads which bind us to those in the less well-off portions of the globe. Such uncertainty and ambivalence makes the creation and enforcement of stronger barriers, both imagined and real, all the more urgent and critical. Whilst physically within Nicaragua as individuals, development workers and indeed researchers nonetheless carry within us the boundaries in our minds formulated in and by our experiences of Western culture. In that sense, they/we are inescapably of the West and are likely to re-enact at least some of the mechanisms associated with inclusion and exclusion. There may be a degree of modification, dependent on the level of awareness and the willingness to confront and challenge the persistence of such boundaries, but travelling across 'real' borders does not necessarily entail erasing those in the mind.

The idea of the coding of stereotypes (Winant, 1994), or the use of enthymematic statements (i.e. those not stated in full: Reeves, 1983, p3) is important here. They allow the walls to be built without the need to express openly and fully what the purpose of the wall is. The rejection can be expressed but dressed up in an acceptable way which forecloses any possibility of challenge. Everyone learns to understand the coded messages which are often based upon assumed homogeneous national or ethnic groupings. Racisms, then, are epistemological practices that rely on the construction, dissemination, recognition and attribution of differences which are represented in a particular way as signifying inferiority, and which carry weight when presented, even in the most subtle of forms, by the more powerful party, represented as correspondingly superior. National or ethnic differences are represented in such a way as to suggest apparent innocence, and racism can thus be explicitly disavowed; but they are often simultaneously loaded with referent meaning, with a 'negative attribution given to culture, ethnic identity, personality as well as "racial stock"' (Anthias & Yuval-Davis, 1993, p12). The question of relative power is central to the effectiveness of these judgements. The assumed differences not only acquire their own degree of significance, but also become 'anchorage for larger and larger conceptual, models of human existence' (Reeves, 1983, p172). I have offered some examples already of how it is possible to attribute both negative and positive characteristics on the basis of Nicaraguan nationality, and sometimes to a wider, more nebulous but equally homogeneous concept of 'Latin American-ness', and forthcoming chapters will provide yet more exemplars. The effective employing of codes will be analysed, including the references to Nicaraguans as children and other evolutionary (or developmental) referents which have clear resonances with the more overt expressions of racism of colonial times.

Joel Kovel (1988a) presents a very interesting argument, exploring possible psychodynamic reasons for the impulse towards white rejectionism; I have already indicated, in Chapter 1:7, how he perceives the use of money as a means of exchange as being intricately linked in with the impulse of rejection. In *White Racism*, he briefly addresses the issue of development and aid, suggesting that 'solutions' employed in development discourse and practice are not created because of their relevance or suitability to the recipient community, but owe more to the nature of the rejectionist impulses of the powerful white nations. Kovel is primarily concerned to discuss white racism in the North American context, but much of his thesis is relevant throughout the Western hemisphere. He describes how the North American belief in its own rightness, and in its prerogative to go in to clean out what is not required, or is considered polluting in some way, has had a major impact on US foreign policy. From 'Manifest Destiny' in the 1840s to Vietnam in the 1960s, Kovel hears a similar, contradictory call:

> to clean house, purify and expunge the evil ... and get on to virtuous (ergo, white) conquests. The action should be peaceful if possible; but if not – if others, usually of darker colour, should resist – then the 'terrible swift sword' of American armed justice would clear the way. Moralism became ... the necessary accoutrement of American power (p29).

The US applied such tactics in Nicaragua, portraying those judged as needing to be expunged – the democratically elected Sandanista government – as unacceptable communists. The resort to moralism is very evident in the American war against terrorism following the events of 11 September 2001, with anyone who in any way questions the ethics of, for example, bombing Afghanistan, immediately denounced as a traitor and as existing outside the 'civilised' world.

This emphasis on American right, in tandem with the use of American might, is frequently communicated in US popular media. The box-office success *Black Hawk Down* (2002), for example, rewrites the events which occurred in Somalia in the early 1990s, and offers a picture in which the US becomes both the world's victim and the world's saviour. The relentless use of stereotypes in the film proclaims all Somalis as sinister, deceitful and inscrutable, and therefore as thoroughly deserving the retribution delivered by the 'terrible swift sword' that passes for American global justice; meanwhile the Americans are invariably innocent of any wrongdoing, engaged only in trying to do good. In the context of the war against terrorism, this representation of America 'as a sacrificial messiah, on a mission to deliver the world from evil' (Monbiot, *Guardian*, 29.1.02) is clearly extremely dangerous, as the rejectionist form of global racism takes on ever more powerful military forms, even whilst they are coded in the language of the US as victim and saviour.

The emotional response which many in the rejectionist tendency in the West exhibit towards the countries and peoples of the 'Third World' is thus a complex mixture of anxiety, fear and anger. These feelings are projections. It is actually the 'Third World' which is consistently threatened and exploited by the West, not the other way around. And this suggests that emotional reactions which would more appropriately be focused on the actions of the West itself – both historically and currently – are being displaced on to that part of the world which in actuality is habitually allocated the aggressor role. Such displacement is made easier and rendered more effective by the consistently racialised portrayals of 'Third World' countries and peoples.

To explore the possibility that much of the interaction between the regions of the North and the South is determined by forces such as Western narcissism, or the projection of feelings from the more powerful onto the less powerful, would require an application of the constructs of psychoanalytic theory from the level of the individual to the level of international relations. Sibley (1997), whilst noting that psychoanalysis in general has largely failed to address the issue of racism, feels that it does have some useful constructs to offer in trying to understand what happens when we reject something or someone. It may be that such forces not only operate at the person-to-person level, but also impact upon the interactions of nations and regions. Sibley argues that when an infant begins the process of differentiation of self from others, s/he also absorbs the notions of a symbolic order which has a much wider frame of references – and boundaries. He thus begins to establish a linkage between the individual psyche and forces operating on a broader basis:

> Associations are made between faeces, dirt, soil, ugliness and imperfection, but these are particularly puritanical, western obsessions. This initial sense of border in the infant in western societies becomes the basis for distancing from 'others', but the question of otherness can only be discussed meaningfully in a cultural context, for example, in relation to racism or to a 'colonial other' (p7).

Bauman also draws on the notion of a rejectionist tendency in his work on strangers referred to earlier (1997b, p47); the other is associated with dirt, excrement and all that is to be thrown away to the edges, or vomited out as strange and unwelcome. In this schema, the strange is bad; in contrast, whiteness is created and maintained as a potent symbol of all that is clean, pure and therefore to be welcomed within the boundaries, whether of the body, the 'home', urban space, the nation or the region of the so-called globalised world.

To attempt to unravel some of the threads of unconscious racism is a complex task, but the links with a sexualised view of the world would seem an important area to investigate. The ambivalence often apparent in racialised relationships is evident in some of my interview material. To quote Ali Rattansi:

> the operations of splitting, desire, fantasy, pleasure and paranoia ... are deeply implicated in racist discourses and ... may inherently produce dualities and ambivalences in racialized encounters between selves and others (Rattansi, 1992, p38).

In considering what he terms the psychohistory of white racism, Kovel (1988a) reveals how the materiality of racism is rooted in emotions, and is always expressed in highly emotive language. There is nothing 'rational' here, though the language used may sound very reasonable. Furthermore, the 'object' of racism is always a complexly structured one, not simply a rejected, belittled other. There is frequently an element of idealisation involved: hence what are apparently positive images – often closely connected to aspects of sexuality and sexual prowess – can be interpreted as incorporating the envy of desire. The role of fantasy is crucial here and Kovel is talking not in a purely personal sense, but of fantasies which become cornerstones of the dominant culture and therefore of magnified import. As with stereotyping in general, those which exist in the sexualised realms of racialised fantasy are extremely contradictory, and exist at extreme ends of a supposedly 'normal' spectrum of sexuality. Within Britain, for example, there are numerous images of the black Caribbean male's sexual prowess, whilst Asian women are often depicted as passive and totally subjugated by their menfolk.

Such ambivalent messages illustrate continuities from the times of imperial conquest and colonial rule; and they can be discerned in present day narratives and pronouncements in the development sphere. On the one hand there is the apparent desire to assimilate the 'Third World' – as evidenced by the very existence of 'Third World' development agencies and workers; on the other, we have continued messages of rejection, frequently linked with questions of borders and boundaries. This kind of ambivalence emerges in a number of ways in the material quoted in this book. As will be demonstrated in later chapters, assimilationist and rejectionist approaches can be deployed almost simultaneously; and this perhaps suggests an impetus to maintain existing power relations whilst also expressing a degree of guilt, which is manifest in the urge to try and do something to improve the situation. Such ambivalence may re-enforce the bond linking oppressed and oppressor, but it in no way negates the very real dis-similarity of effects on each of the inequalities of global power; these individual relationships must be understood as taking place within a much broader context of power relations.

A central argument of this book is that the power dynamics of development and aid work do not exist in a discursive vacuum; they are part and parcel of global patterns of power. There may be no absolute standard against which racism can be measured: black is 'black in relation to the white man' (Fanon, 1991, p110); but this does not mean that there is no violence – whether implicit or explicit – in power relations based on 'race'. Fanon continues: 'the black man has no ontological resistance in the eyes of the white man'. Bhabha (1994, p42) picks up on Fanon's use of the metaphor of vision, and argues that it is 'complicit with a Western metaphysic of Man', in which the 'white man's eyes break up the black man's body'. This metaphor of vision, together with the subsumed violence of its impact, resurfaces in the discourse of development. The mutual relativity of the concepts of blackness and whiteness does not mean that the relative power of the one does not have very real material as well as metaphysical effects on both the relatively powerless and the relatively powerful

In the next section, I will pursue these themes in an exploration of the colonial era, and show how powerful are the continuities linking the more explicit racism of earlier epochs with the more hidden varieties of current day discourses.

3.2 COLONIAL CONNECTIONS

The connections between the racism of colonial and imperial times and current day imagery and discourses in the field of 'Third World' development and aid have been neatly summarised thus: 'where colonialism left off, development took over' (Kothari, 1988, p143). Beginning with the missionaries, there has always been a strand of colonial thinking and action which has taken on board the idea that conquerors and settlers should exhibit some concern for the welfare of peoples who have been conquered and settled. This could take place alongside the continuing economic exploitation and establishment of cultural dominance, which would use any means – including extreme violence – necessary to ensure that Western power was enforced. Ideas of a 'civilising mission' became transmuted into theories of imperial development (Cowen & Shenton, 1995). Such theories of development became very useful indeed, for they enabled the colonists to proclaim a degree of genuine concern for the welfare of their subjects – which could be worn and paraded as a badge of honour – while pursuing changes driven by economic expedients, designed first and foremost to serve the interests of the colonists and settlers. Esteva illustrates this in his discussion of various instances of colonial concern with the well-being of the subordinate, for example the transformation of the British Law of Development of the Colonies into the Law of Development and *Welfare* of the Colonies in 1939; this was evidence of the dual mandate approach: 'the conqueror should be capable of economically developing the conquered region at the same time accepting the responsibility of caring for the well-being of the natives' (Esteva 1992, p10). Central to a concern for the 'caring' aspect of the relationship with the 'natives' was the imperial concept of trusteeship, which incorporated a promise of reliability and a sense of obligation on the part of the trustee – a view which is now, at least in theory, rejected (Cowen & Shenton, p4). It is certainly the case that the contemporary language of development tends to refer to concepts of co-operation and partnerships rather than trusteeship, evoking a sense of sharing on a joint basis and thus implying a greater degree of equality than in the past. However, as I shall argue in later chapters, the language may have altered more significantly than current development discourse and practice. This is not to suggest that discourses of development are merely updated versions of justifications for colonial and imperial conquests, nor that the one can be readily mapped against the other. However, there is a history of transition from one to the other (the discourses and practices of imperialism did not at some point in time simply disappear), with historical continuities evident in both discourse and practices.

What I aim to do here is to explore the main discourses apparent during the colonial era in order to assess their re-occurrence within development discourse. This will provide an essential basis for my contention that much development discourse and therefore practice is fundamentally racialised. Homi Bhabha's articulation of colonial discourse as an 'apparatus that turns on the recognition and disavowal of racial/cultural/historical differences' (1994, p70) is useful here, as it emphasises the importance of addressing the fixity and rigidity of both positive and negative stereotypes whilst also acknowledging the ambivalence of the process of stereotyping. It is, he argues, precisely the force of ambivalence that gives the colonial stereotype its currency, as it 'ensures its repeatability in changing historical and discursive junctures' (p66). I will indicate how certain stereotypes are repeated over and over in development discourse (as in other racialised exchanges), but each time with the suggestion that something new is being propounded.

The continuities evident between the concepts of trusteeship and its descendent, partnership, are often coded and made harder to distinguish by the element of ambiguity. Nonetheless, some of the cruder caricatures which were predominant in colonial times can still be discerned today, and – perhaps most importantly – so too can the powerful mechanism of projection employed by colonisers to provide psychological cover for what they were doing. I am concerned then to establish overall patterns of power in 'Third World' development through the process of unearthing ways in which significant tropes can be identified which build into (and must be read as part of) 'a pattern of repetition' (Spurr, 1994, p8); these tropes combine together to ensure the legitimation of domination. One source of such legitimation was the classification into developed and under-developed, which was applied to nations as well as individuals, and involved a process of identifying difference and solidifying a hierarchy based on internal characteristics. This, says Spurr, 'has consequences for the classification of human races in the Western mind and ultimately for the analysis of Third World societies' (p63). Such processes of classification are employed constantly in development, as we shall see, and they invariably seem to buttress each other in relation to the overall picture of who has power and authority, and who is ultimately subject to it.

A number of writers concerned about the discourses and impact of colonialism have written about the part occupied by overt expressions of white racism and the ways in which it affects both recipient and oppressor. Bhabha describes skin as the key signifier in establishing racial and cultural differences, as it is 'the most visible of fetishes' (1994, p78). The use of a range of physical markers to delineate groups as 'others' has a lengthy history in Europe pre-dating colonialism (Nederveen, 1992, p18); and images equating blackness with evil, dirt and ugliness were already circulating in Medieval times, linked with religious ideas of Europe as the cradle of Christianity. Such ideas bolstered emerging Latin Americanism (see chapter 2) during the period of conquest, and reinforced emerging discourses of superiority established during the first encounter between Europe and the indigenous peoples of what was to become Latin America. Hugh Honour has studied European images of America since that time, and he comments on the prevalence of the European tendency to project their own feelings and fears on to those whom they were in the process of subjugating. He says: 'Europeans increasingly tended to see in America an idealised or distorted image of their own countries, on to which they could portray their own aspirations and fears, their self-confidence and … guilty despair' (quoted in Hall & Gieben, 1992, p308).

The constitution of Latin America and its peoples as a distinct 'other', firstly to Europe and later to North America, has an extensive pedigree, and there are many examples of visual imagery used to configure and buttress Eurocentric ideas of (Latin) America, Africa and Asia (see Nederveen, 1992). One example given by Nederveen is from the frontispiece of an English book, probably dating from the late eighteenth century, in which the continent of Europe is portrayed by the figure of a fair-haired woman, seated in a throne-like chair. She is surrounded by the trappings of 'European' culture: a globe, a transcript, a Greek building and statue, an open book – all items readily associated with 'European civilisation', and signifying science, progress, learning and world domination, and powerfully, albeit subliminally, linked with her whiteness. She is holding one hand aloft in a way which signifies her rule over the other female figures, who represent the continents of America, Asia and Africa; these are either seated on the ground – rather than on an impressive dais – or standing behind the figure of Europe. The body language is one of dominion and subjugation, and fortifies the message of superiority and inferiority. Furthermore, each non-European continent is associated with an animal – a horse, an elephant, a camel and a beaver. The figure representing America is holding tobacco leaves, an Arab woman is flanked by a fragrant vat of incense, and the African woman, a palm tree by her side, holds ivory and a slave chain – all, of course, symbols of European extraction and exploitation. The caption underneath the picture is as follows:

> Europe by Commerce, Arts and Arms obtains
> The Gold of Afric and her sons enchains.
> She rules luxurious Asia's fertile Shores,
> Wears her bright Gems, and gains her richest Stores;
> While from America thro' Seas she brings
> The Wealth of Mines and various useful things.

The words and image act together to create an impression not only of the unquestionable rightness of Europe's actions in terms of its own interests, but of their rightness in relation to those on the receiving end. The accoutrements of the black women, as described above, are in clear contrast to those of the white woman, and establish a power relation of domination and subordination, with Europe at the world's centre; these images contribute to the establishment of power relations in an embodied form, through use of the mechanism of animalising people. The associations of women and animals as closer to 'nature' reinforces the supposed superiority of European culture. There are important links with gender issues here, with a number of signifiers of inferiority coalescing – non-European, animals and nature, as well as women. As Nederveen comments: 'This architecture of power echoes throughout the imagery of White on Black as a set of iconographic codes recurring in the depiction of slavery, missions, colonialism, and up to contemporary advertising' (p23). It is worth remembering that most of us are exposed to such messages, particularly as disseminated through advertising, and it is therefore likely that development workers are also vulnerable to their potential impact; unless explicitly challenged, the effects of this would be carried by them, and transmitted through them, on their travels and into their work.

Early records of the European encounter with the peoples who lived in Admiral Colon's 'new world' provide a distinct parallel to such visual representations. A reading of Admiral Colon's journal (quoted in Sale, 1991) offers a number of stereotypes and images which became very much a part of the Eurocentric view of Latin America, and indeed the remainder of the world. Between 1492-3, Colon took possession of a number of islands and explored others, including Cuba and Española (now known as Haiti and the Dominican Republic), donating a cross as well as a Spanish name at each place of visit, though he was well aware of existing names (Sale, p92). Colon's descriptions of the people he encountered reflect his view of them as naturally inferior beings. For example, he recorded in his journal:

> They all go around naked as their mothers bore them – It appeared to me that these people were very poor in everything – they have no iron ...
>   They ought to be good servants and of good intelligence – I believe they would easily be made Christians, because it seemed to me they had

no religion. Our Lord pleasing, I will carry off six of them at my depar-
ture to Your Highnesses, in order that they may learn to speak (cited in
Sale).

From nakedness and not possessing iron to an implicit justification of
enforced conversion and slavery in under four sentences! And, ignoring the existence of their own language, they will also be taught 'to
speak', a construction which implies that only the European mode of
communication counts as legitimate, a theme which is ubiquitous in
development discourse and practice as we shall see. (The importance
attached to a lack of iron also prefigures the current obsession with
measuring the level of development in terms of the degree of technological hardware.) Iain Chambers comments that such 'power to name,
identify, classify, domesticate and contain ... simultaneously doubles as
the power to obliterate, silence and negate' (Chambers, 1996, p48).
Portraits such as that offered by Colon also often illustrate the ambivalence with which the first European arrivals viewed those they
conquered: on the one hand, they were monstrous and demonic Wild
Men and Women and, on the other, there were perceptions of fascinat-
ing and alluring sexual appetites and powers. 'What we see here', says
Rattansi, 'is the foreshadowing of the ambiguity of the "noble savage"
soon to be discovered and represented in other continents' (Rattansi
and Westwood, 1994, p43). Also foreshadowed is the exoticisation of
'other' lands, a vital component of most travel and tourist literature.
    In the late 1700s and early 1800s, something more was needed to
justify the enforced transport of between twenty and sixty million
African people across the Atlantic in the most oppressive and inhuman
conditions imaginable. A 'scientific' approach to demonstrating the
inherent and indelible attributes of 'race' manifested itself, in justification of slavery. In 1774, Edward Long produced his *History of Jamaica*,
writing (quoted in Fryer, 1991, pp58-9): 'I think there are extremely
potent reasons for believing that the White and the Negroe are two
distinct species.' Long proffers examples of ways in which the 'Negroe'
is self-evidently inferior; for example, instead of hair black people had
'a covering of wool, like the bestial fleece', and they 'were possessed of
a bestial or fetid smell' (see also Hall, 1997c, p239). Studies of difference in skull size were linked with unequal intellectual, and indeed
moral, abilities and contributed to an increasingly firmly established
myth of white superiority, with the brain of the white man positioned
at the top of the ladder of evolution, and increasingly of material and
spiritual achievement. The belief in such pseudo-scientific racial attributes has certainly declined over the intervening centuries, though it has
not disappeared entirely.[4]
    It is my contention that the forms in which such racism can still be
demonstrated to persist must be unearthed from current obscurity, and

squarely confronted, with the links to colonial discourse exposed. Furthermore, the overall effect of development discourse remains much the same as those operating in colonial times, and I shall demonstrate (particularly in chapters 4 and 5) a number of significant affinities and continuities, through analysis of the interview and other textual materials. Interestingly, Edward Long prefigures some of the later configurations of racism to be found in development discourse when he continues his litany of inferiorities: 'their roads ... are mere sheeppaths, twice as long as they need be, and almost impassable'. This motif of lack of transport, of lack of easy mobility and its imputation of inferiority is, as we have already encountered in previous chapters, a recurrent theme in development and aid discourse today.

Fryer quotes many such examples, illustrating that it is not just the overt imperialist adventurers who defined and justified racism, but that it was to be found in the writings of the most distinguished philosophers of the time. For example, the *Universal History*, published in the mid-eighteenth century – part of what Fryer (p153) calls 'a lot of muck (which) oozed its way into print' – is interesting from the perspective of this research, inasmuch as it again prefigures many of the referents of development discourse:

> If we ... take a cursory view of their manufactures and mechanic arts ... we shall find the spirit of indolence running through them ...
>
> If we look into those few manufactures and handicrafts that are amongst them, we shall find them carried on with the same ... tedious stupidity.

Two centuries later, we have Lord Lugard's defence of British rule in Africa, published in 1922, in which he asserts:

> The African negro ... lacks power of organisation, and is conspicuously deficient in the management and control alike of men or of business ... it is extremely difficult to find educated African youths who are by character and temperament suited to posts in which they may rise to positions of high administrative authority (quoted in Fryer, p186).

Current day descriptions of the capabilities of 'Third World' peoples may (or may not) be expressed in a more polite manner, but the sentiment is often exactly the same. In early 2002, as part of a series of television programmes entitled *No Going Back* (BBC, 30.1.02), one programme featured three young people, all white, who had decided to give up their lucrative but apparently monotonous careers in the City of London, sell their flats and go to Zambia, with the aim of building their own house and setting up a safari visitor centre. As I have noted before in analogous situations, there is a complete contrast between the totally unquestioned assumption that these three have every right to decide in which country they prefer to improve their quality of life and the treatment of people from the 'Third World' who attempt to make the equivalent decision to come to Britain. This issue is absolutely absent from the TV programme. Once in Africa, the stereotypical portrayal and treatment of Zambians begins. The three complain vociferously about Zambian bureaucracy, again with the underlying implication that it is their indisputable right that the necessary certificates should be issued as a priority. At one point, the commentator informs us that the three will soon be having financial problems if they do not get the requisite paperwork sorted. Sympathy for the three is completely assumed, though it would not, of course, be available for three young Zambians trying to establish themselves in Britain. The stereotyping goes beyond generalisations about the nature of the Zambian authorities. A number of Zambians are employed to do the building work, as carpenters and so on. The commentary from the three is replete with comments about laziness and slowness: 'it looks like the bed won't be ready for another month at least'. They frequently have the workers line up to be told off like children. The one worker who appears content with his lot, inasmuch as he smiles frequently, is chastised for talking too much. At one point, several of the workers are treated to a lecture on their dirty habits in not flushing the toilet properly. The negativities are all associated with African-ness and are redolent of the kinds of images more readily associated with earlier epochs.

Albert Memmi (1990) analyses a number of such themes, drawing a portrait of the 'other' as described by the coloniser. Memmi indicates that what is occurring is complex, involving projection and displacement on the part of the coloniser, who wishes to portray the colonised as everything the coloniser is concerned to present him/herself not to be. Negative qualities are unfailingly projected onto the weaker party in order to strengthen the identity and self-esteem of the more powerful. I shall explore this attribution of negative qualities, making some tentative links with psychoanalytic suggestions that the process is fundamentally one of psychological projection. Memmi offers a vivid example of the relentless ascription of inherent characteristics:

> the existence of the colonizer requires that an image of the colonized be suggested ... Nothing could better justify the colonizer's privileged position than his industry, and nothing could better justify the colonized's destitution than his indolence. The mythical portrait of the colonized therefore includes an unbelievable laziness, and that of the colonizer a virtuous taste for action ... thereby authorising his (the colonized's) unreasonable wages ... It is more advantageous to use three of the colonized than one European. Every firm needs specialists, of course, but only a minimum of them, and the colonizer imports or recruits experts

among his own kind. In addition, there is the matter of the special attention and legal protection required by a European worker. The colonized
is only asked for his muscles (Memmi, 1990, p146).

The issue of experts and their justification is particularly germane to
development work, and I shall return to it in some detail. Memmi goes
on to illustrate how the coloniser is not necessarily displeased with the
so-called laziness – on the contrary: 'He talks of it with amused affa-
bility, he jokes about it ... he becomes lyrical about it, in a negative
way' (p146). Other innate features are similarly ascribed by the more
powerful to the less powerful, including 'lack of desires, an ineptitude
for comfort, science, progress and an astonishing familiarity with
poverty' (p148). We shall, in the next chapter, see how far Memmi's
characterisation of a perceived persistent lack in the lives of the less
powerful resonates with power relations in development and aid.

Development discourse and practice is racialised in a number of
ways, but the connections and resonances with the more overtly racist
discourses of colonial times form an important constitutive part of this
process – though they are often expressed in more coded form. As we
shall see, a number of 'rhetorical modes' apparent in colonial discourse
(Spurr, 1994, p3) can be discerned in present day discourses of development and aid; and I argue that a referencing back to earlier times
often renders overt statements of racism less necessary.

The following chapter gives a number of examples from the interviews that illustrate the way in which the conjunction of colonial time
and places 'over there' acts as a communication of inferiority; this does
not have to be explicit because of the pre-existence of these powerful
resonances, readily understood and translated into implicitly racialised
relationships. Specifically, I explore the use of essentialist images to
convey the sense of dominance and subservience.

NOTES

1. Sometimes it would just be the usual daily name-calling but sometimes it
   would be a really bad day and, for example, my daughter would have to
   somehow respond to the question from an older white girl whilst eating a
   mini chocolate Swiss roll, which I had put in her sandwich box, 'why are
   you eating a black man's dick?' Again, the sexualisation of white-on black
   racism is a theme which I identified in a number of the interviews (see
   Chapter 2). One form of abuse seems to spill over into others; my daughter
   was also subject to physical assaults, which included a group of older boys
   running past her and throwing a punch to her stomach, or, alternatively,
   'touching my fanny'. Another boy would trap her as often as he could on
   coming out of the girls' toilets, shoving his hand either down her knickers
   or up her jersey. The only way of escape was to move to a different school.

2. I was once crossing a car park, accompanied by my daughter who would then have been about four years old, in Texas. A voice shouted out 'How much did yours cost?' At first, I did not realise that he was addressing us. But he then followed up with 'I paid $5000 last year for ours from Guatemala. Worth every cent. We're going back this year to get another one'. See also, for one woman's description of a narcissistic demand to have the kind of baby she wants, 'I saw people with adorable Asian babies, like dolls. That's what I wanted', by 'best-selling American author' Tama Janovitz (*The Independent* 24.10.99).

3. There are many other forms as illustrated above in the example of my daughter – not least, sexism, disablism and heterosexism – as well as racism.

4. Paul Gilroy argues that the impact of the current biotechnical revolution, with the increasing manipulation of human genetic material, demands that we 'reconceptualize our relationship to ourselves, our species, our nature, and the idea of life. We need to ask, for example, whether there should be any place in this new paradigm of life for the idea of specifically *racial* differences' (2000, p20, Gilroy's emphasis). As an aspiration for the future I would concur with Gilroy, but I also think that the remnants of such beliefs, together with their transmutations, will not spontaneously disappear and will continue to have material impact.

4

THE ROLE OF NATION
AND GENDER

This chapter explores in more detail the central mechanisms for creating and maintaining hierarchies fundamentally based on exclusionary criteria. It focuses particularly on two very strong themes in development discourse and imagery – firstly, that of nationality, with particular characteristics routinely allocated on the basis of nationality. I have already indicated how this apparently neutral attribution is actually loaded with racialised referents, with Nicaragua fixed in its spatial position as part of the South, and in its temporal location as vastly 'behind' in attempts to modernise and Westernise.

Secondly, I wish to look at the theme of gender and the ways in which a notion of an almost automatic axis of solidarity between women has been assumed throughout colonial and imperial times, ignoring the imbalances of power between different groups of women – an idea which still occupies a relatively unproblematised position in today's discourses of development and aid.

4.1 ESSENTIALIST IMAGES OF NATIONALITY

Essentialist portrayals depend upon positing a notion of ultimate essence, something which transcends the historical and the particular, to establish that a person, a culture, a nation, can always be expected to think, feel and behave in a certain and predictable kind of a way. Thus the way in which yuppies in Zambia in the previous chapter portrayed their workers has power, and needs no explanation, precisely because it fits into an already well-established imagery and discourse about African peoples. Such imagery depends upon the constant communication and repetition of what is signified as the essence. It is important to consider how essentialism is used: 'in and of itself, essentialism is neither good nor bad ... The question we should be asking ... [is] if this text is essentialist, *what motivates its deployment?*' (Fuss, 1989, p xi, original emphasis). I am concerned to investigate when and how essentialism is employed to create or maintain particular configurations of power. This section presents examples of essentialism from the interview material and my diary, both of a negative stereotypical nature, and (section 4.2) of an apparently more positive variety, in order to unpack the motivation behind its use. It is important to have regard to who is formulating – both formulating and uttering – the supposedly neutral and objective descriptions, and to note how the formulation of 'others' as presented in the dialogues actually serves to position 'them' consistently in the position of inferiority, whilst assuring the speaker and his/her culture of being in an inevitable place of superiority. This position continually reinforces the progress hierarchy, which then justifies the development approach and its constituent discourses and actions.

An interviewee says:

> Looking at *any Nicaraguan NGO* without any kind of *outside influence* in terms of co-operantes, there is a general lack of trust between people, a very hierarchical way of working ... a lack of praise and encouragement. I was reading an article the other day, written by this guy, a Nicaraguan, who said Nicaraguans often get caught up, particularly those in positions of responsibility or power, get caught up in the importance of themselves, you know, and they don't do, they don't do very simple things like make sure they keep their appointments, answer messages because they're too important ... *It's obvious to us, and obvious to many Nicaraguans as well,* the more you share information within an organisation, the stronger that organisation will be ... And I think people can see that, Nicaraguans can see that on a logical level but actually trying to implement it, you come across this lack of trust and it's like, I'm going to look *after my own corner* ...
>
> It is frustrating when you come out and you believe you have something to offer and you want it to be taken up and you want to be used and you want to be a part of making things better, you know, improving conditions in general and you come across all these problems, I think it does turn into a kind of sub-conscious racism and you find yourself saying 'oh well, that's just Nicaraguans for you' ... it's something cultural, it's not something to do with the person's race, you know. So you need to be very careful about the way you talk about this kind of problem.

This interview excerpt highlights a number of strategies which are effectively employed to create and maintain an essentialist view of Nicaraguans, and which increase their effectiveness by linking with wider discourses of how organisations and bureaucracies work in the 'Third World'. It occurs to me that this interviewee would have been most unlikely to have spoken quite as she did with a non-white person, or at least a non-Western person. To that extent my very presence as a willing audience is part of my complicity, heightened by the lack of any challenge.

The strategies establishing superiority in this quotation depend on a specific construction of what it means to be 'Nicaraguan'.[1] The communication of negativity does not have to be explicit, but it is clear, from the first mention of nationality, that the imputation is replete with negative connotations. I shall attempt to unpack the strategies in some detail as they recur with some frequency in other material. Firstly, the reductionism of the reference to 'any Nicaraguan NGO' implies that all Nicaraguan NGOs are essentially the same, especially in terms of the particular features which Joanne is about to outline. The stereotypes feed off (and into) one of the West's favourite images of the 'Third World', of bureaucracies which are inefficient, self-important, perhaps bordering on the corrupt. As we saw in the previous chapter, this discourse has been around since imperial and colonial times. This contrasts with the intervention of 'any kind of outside influence', which carries an automatic assumption of positive benefits (though unspecified). The critical and judicious positioning of the word 'logical' ensures that this is set in opposition to the practice of the Nicaraguans, and associated with what can only be appreciated thanks to the contribution of 'us' in the West. However, this raises again the possibility of projection – during a number of feedback sessions where I have shared this quote with other development workers, they have been struck by how true these comments would be of Western organisations and bureaucracies. Further considerations must include – by whom and under whose auspices were Nicaraguan NGOs set up in the first place? And on whose organisational theory and practice were they modelled? I do not have the answers to these questions but the rest of my evidence would suggest that it is unlikely that any Nicaraguan NGO could have been set up in a way which would entail its possession of a complete and separate Nicaraguan-ness – which this interviewee implies is possible. Furthermore, the recent history and geo-politics of Nicaragua as a country would hardly suggest a people, or indeed a conglomeration of NGOs, which is adept at 'looking after my own corner'. Finally, the use of the views of an accordant Nicaraguan constitutes a common tactic, one which exploits the internalisation of inferiority that has taken hold during the historical contingencies of the past five centuries (Fanon, 1991).

A number of interviewees used stereotypical representations of Nicaraguans during their interviews, and they were all images with which I am familiar from the representation of the 'Third World' within the West – through the media, advertising (including advertising for funds and personnel for agencies working in the 'Third World'), the way geography is taught in schools, literature and so on. Maggie also has strong views about 'dealing with the painful slowness of Nicaraguan bureaucracy', which she expresses when asked by me to describe the most difficult part of her life and work in Nicaragua. Avtah Brah suggests (Brah, 1996, p95) that it can be very difficult to decide at what point and in what ways the specificity of a particular social experience becomes a sign of essentialism. Clearly, when Maggie is telling me of her particular experiences with a particular immigration official, then her use of phrases such as 'one of the most frustrating experiences in the whole world' may seem somewhat exaggerated but not necessarily essentialist. But her use of the phrase 'an alien process' is a more worrying choice of vocabulary, given the resonance this would have for Nicaraguans and other 'Third World' people, who would truly be regarded as alien by British and other 'First World' immigration officials, should they attempt a vice-versa entry (another example of projection?). Finally, she makes a comment which is clearly essentialist, in that all involved with Nicaraguan bureaucracy are summed up thus: 'It was me against Nicaraguan bureaucracy'. This also has the important side-effect of setting up Maggie as the relatively power-less individual battling against tremendous odds – a theme oft recounted in tales of colonial adventurers taking on a variety of potentially over-powering but nonetheless-somehow-eventually-vanquished forces in the 'Third World'. Other fairly commonly used stereotypes include those involving lack of organisation, lack of punctuality, lack of routine and lack of work discipline, all of which are present in colonial discourse (see chapter 3).

A quotation from my own research diary, written in December 1997, also displays some interesting processes:

> Sitting in the garden of Theresa's house [a family I have known for 10 years], with my daughter, who is very much at home playing with Theresa's grandson, Renato, and me being treated – as usual – like the British treat their Royals. Within an hour of arriving, *I find I have* consumed frescos, coffee, agreed to a lunch and a weekend visit to some relatives in the countryside. Consuming is the operative word – I also realise I am busy consuming huge amounts of generosity, an unconditional love and affection and *I don't refuse the offer* to chill out in the hammock whilst being brought large, juicy mangoes straight from the neighbour's tree. They appeared (needless to say, not through any effort on my part) but because Danilo remembers my taste for them and had gone round to his neighbours with a special request.
>
> This all happened in the context of my turning up completely unannounced, having been away for nearly two years and not so much as an Xmas card during that time. But somehow, I always feel I can show up and be instantly treated as the long lost – what? – long lost foreigner perhaps?
>
> The other side of this is that, whilst I am here I stay with other British people, and I am reluctant to tell my Nicaraguan friends where I live, in

case they – guess what? – turn up unexpectedly. This does not have anything to do with Mary, who I stay with, as I realise I operated in exactly the same way on previous occasions when I rented our own house.

The contents of my diary jottings are signal enough of double standards in operation, but what is possibly of even greater concern is that, even whilst consciously in reflective mode (and well into the process of consciously thinking about these issues), I still adopt a number of distancing mechanisms. It is as if this 'habit' of 'finding' myself doing, thinking or saying something is an accident over which I have no control and which emerges even at the reflexive level. I would portray my relationships with Theresa's family as being close and of long duration, but it is clear that power relationships are deeply implicated in my personal relationships – no matter how close or how 'wonderful' I would describe them as being – and my physical position, stretched out in the hammock, being constantly served both bodily and emotionally, is very redolent of the power relationships between white and nonwhite in a more overtly colonial era. Another distancing mechanism evident in the piece above is the tendency to utilise double negatives, and again it is significant that this is occurring at a reflexive level of thought and action. To say 'I don't refuse' instead of 'I accept' implies that I am doing them a favour by not refusing, and it also suggests again that I am not actually doing anything pro-active, and therefore cannot be held responsible for the fact that I am lying around consuming whist others are actively meeting my every whim. The responsibility is actually Theresa's and Danilo's for offering such tempting delights! I will return later to the role of the positive stereotype, but would note here that a very common one in relation to this type of scenario is the 'wonderful hospitality' of 'these people' which, amongst other things, can serve to mask problematic relationships and block any serious attempt to explore the imbalances of power and their effects. The use of the vocabulary of the activity of consumption is also highly indicative, in this case of an approach which is hedonistic and unappreciative in my largely unthinking use of resources, and it is highly evocative of the nature of the relationship between the West and its use of both people and produce as resources to serve its own needs.

An expansion on my apparently trivial admission of a lack of communication whilst in England is important here, because it is a question of more than simply not being a very good letter writer. There have been a number of other situations where I have made promises which I have not kept (I shall resist the temptation to write 'which I failed to keep').

One such situation, for example, involved a school which I visited with a worker from the US who was delivering a financial donation from a North American group. The school was situated in a barrio in

Masaya, where the largest urban concentration of indigenous people are living. At that time, the school was trying to keep 'traditional' music and dance alive by teaching it both to the children and, after school hours, to interested adults in the community. A group of supporters in the US had raised funds for this initiative and Barbara and I were delivering it, though I went along primarily for the ride and an interesting day out. When we got to the school, we were received with an appropriate and enjoyable show of music and dance, and we presented the money, together with various caveats designed to ensure it was spent on the purpose for which it was donated. On the tour around the school, it became clear that several of the rooms were unusable due to recent severe storm damage; this could well make it impossible to put on the dance and music classes. Nonetheless the dollars could not be used to mend the roof as they were specifically designated to buy tape machines and musical instruments and could not be used for anything else. It was explained to me that the basis of this decision was that the use of the money had to be carefully specified beforehand as those receiving it could not be trusted to spend it properly. I told the head-teacher of the school that I would see what I could do on returning to England. I forgot all about it until writing this chapter disturbed the memory. What was of little consequence in my life had potential outcomes within the school which are to this day unknown to me. One such outcome would be the way in which the head-teacher, who had organised the day for us, would construe such a lack of response, and where she would place the responsibility. Whilst not wishing to make a direct comment on the actions of others in this regard, I would suggest that the lack of reciprocity, and the tendency for promises to be lightly made and equally lightly broken on the part of us 'foreigners', is probably fairly endemic, particularly in matters of sex and money. Certainly there is much anecdotal evidence to support this view and I would suggest that this bolsters the tentative idea that narcissism is a potent ingredient in North/South relations.

4.2 POSITIVE ESSENTIALISM

There has been a debate about whether or not using positive imagery to portray black people is an improvement on the kind of negative stereotyping illustrated above (see especially Donald & Rattansi, 1992). Interestingly, many of the more positive examples from my research are very closely bound in with personal issues of the interviewee – often, as we shall see, deeply connected with motivational issues, especially the motivation for living and working in Nicaragua in the first place.

The positive connotations of more 'community spirit' are mentioned by a number of interviewees in answer to the question

'What have you found most rewarding about living and working here?', but Jane gives the most detailed account of what it means to her:

> I was supposed to go back in 1995, but I've made lots of Nicaraguan friends. I consider I've got 3 adoptive families here who all look after me ... I feel much more cared for, much more appreciated, more loved than in Britain. I feel like I'm more of a part of a community – and I have more to offer. I feel more relaxed. My life is harder – but at the end of the day, I wasn't really happy, none of it satisfied me. Here, I get up at 5.30, wash my clothes by hand, go to work on a horribly over-crowded, mechanically frightening bus, work 10 hours a day and the pay is nothing.

Jane sums this up as being far more 'spiritually and emotionally rewarding' and she contrasts favourably the closeness of families in Nicaragua with those in Britain: 'I like the way people help each other, I like being a part of that and at the same time I've learnt how to receive help'. Jan also likes the sense of community, though for her it is more about the relative degree of political organisation – she says Nicaragua is 'the most politicised country I have ever been in. Compared to the average Briton, people are so much less apathetic. Being around people who stand up for their rights, it's been a real political education – an education in community spirit'. Jan portrays this as 'the antithesis to British individualism'. She gives a vivid example:

> they just get up and do it, organise themselves and get things done. Get the electricity put in or whatever – whether it's legal or not, build houses. They live for the moment and they deal with problems afterwards – so you don't think about property law when you need a roof over your head.

Another worker comments that, in spite of having more material problems, 'people here still have values which we lost some time in the last 30/40 years. There is too much materialism [in Britain], not enough thinking about friends and family'. This is a theme which is picked up in several other interviews. Paul comments that, for him, the most rewarding thing about living in Nicaragua is 'the contact with sanity, if you like, contact with real people. In a sense, people are more real or more themselves here than they are in Britain'. I asked him to expand on this and he continued; 'I think that the closer you live to the edge, the more human you are. Now, I'm not sure if that's what most Nicaraguans would want, you know. Of course not. But there is a sort of community spirit here for example that doesn't exist in Britain.'

The issue of belonging, or wanting to belong, is also a recurring motif and Maggie comments on how it is the optimism of Nicaraguan people which she finds rewarding: I ask her whether it is a different kind of optimism from that in Britain and she answers:

It's a more *simple kind of optimism*. People aren't expecting big complicated sorts of changes – it's short-term, looking for tomorrow or the next week. It's an ability, even if they're deeply pained or suffering from their social conditions, to be happy, they appear to be genuinely happy people. It's uplifting to see.

The kinds of things people worry about in Britain are different, it's a commercial society ... something which would drive you up the wall in a developed country is not going to be present in a developing country. Maybe it's the lack of those kinds of concerns which I find uplifting and refreshing. People are discussing real issues such as the price of beans and ... they are not worrying about buying a second car.

The kind of absolute contrast here between the one and the 'other' is striking – the one is all that the 'other' is not. And even though these are all examples of a definite preference for the 'ways' of Nicaraguans, evidenced by the fact that a number of those quoted above have lived in Nicaragua for upwards of a decade and several have bought houses, the positive description is somehow nearly always phrased by means of what is lacking in comparison to British society. The 'simple' is presented in implicit contrast to the sophisticated. The positing of this kind of contrast, whether 'good' or 'bad', also tends to obscure any analysis of the relationship between them – i.e. the possibility that the material lack in Nicaragua exists precisely because of the material overindulgence of Britain and other developed nations.

It is also possible to argue that the very presence of white, Western development workers in Nicaragua must, according to its own internal logic, set about destroying the very lack of materialism and sense of community that so many of the interviewees said they appreciated most. Paul comes closest to highlighting the contradiction; he knows he cannot argue that Nicaraguans should stay living closer to the margins or the 'edge' in order to stay 'human' and yet that is precisely what appeals to him most. The contradiction is also clear in Joanne's use of the word 'adoptive families' – her work in Nicaragua entails her constructing Nicaraguans to be in need of her (or her organisation's) expertise and yet when more personal themes are explored, it is clear who is receiving in this context and who is giving. The fact that so much of the traffic is from the 'Third World' to the West at an emotional level perhaps parallels what happens in terms of economic exploitation, and is similarly unacknowledged. It is a striking thought that those of us who adopted children in the 'Third World' are nearly always presented as 'giving them a good life which they wouldn't otherwise have had'. An alternative view is that our emotional needs, even at the level of our desire for children, are increasingly being met by the 'Third World' – yet another unacknowledged form of extraction.

4.3 THE ROLE OF GENDER

The genesis of this book came from the observation that, within development and aid discourse, a great deal of attention seems to be paid to selected power relations, notably those involving gender; whilst that of white power was completely absent. There was a contrast between the attention paid to issues of gender in development discourses and practice and the silence around issues of 'race' and racism, specifically white racism. It is interesting in this respect to consider whether there are any appropriate parallels to be drawn with colonial history. There is a tendency within development circles to assume a solidarity based on gender, which frequently eschews all other axes of oppression. In their studies of white women and imperialism, Vron Ware (1992) and Anne McClintock (1995) offer useful insights into this. Clearly the language has changed somewhat, but the image of women in the colonial era sallying forth on their peculiarly womanly mission to educate and civilise was underpinned by a discourse of women's affinity with other women; and Ware shows how the condition of slavery was likened in a number of pamphlets to the state of subjection of the average British married woman, and how this was meant literally not metaphorically. One such leaflet tried to prove that British women were actually worse off than slaves, arguing that a female slave was not required to submit 'to a second state of individual domestic slavery to the male slaves' (p103). Ware shows that the abolitionist movement and early feminist publications were deeply influenced by imperialism, and frequently exhibited deeply held racialised attitudes. Many of the most radical women nonetheless kept black women as servants, failing to apply their analysis of unequal power relations to their own situation – a phenomenon which I have also explored in relation to present day development workers, including myself (see Introduction). Breaking away from a conventional lifestyle in Britain was a common motive for female imperial adventurers, but after a while feelings of disillusionment and frustration were usually experienced, often blamed on the non-co-operativeness of the recipient community. Ware quotes from the diaries of one Englishwoman who concluded that her efforts to educate Indian women were continually thwarted by Indian men, towards whom she developed a deep and lasting hostility (p147). McClintock discusses the writings of Olive Schreiner at length, observing how she exhibits a resentment of African women, which 'would throw radically into question Schreiner's monistic longing for a humanist unity, then later, a universal, feminist solidarity' (1995, p267). Ware (p120) summarises the 'Englishwoman abroad' as a 'many faceted figure':

> from an intrepid adventuress defying racial and sexual boundaries to heroic mother responsible for the preservation of the white 'race'; from

the devoted missionary overseeing black souls to the guardian of white morals; from determined pioneer and companion to the white man to a vulnerable defenceless piece of his property ...

I would suggest that aspects of these roles have become bound together with the specialist, expert position now occupied by 'First World' women who still, though perhaps with less obvious missionary zeal, undertake their travels with very similar motives, glimpsing in development and aid instead of empire 'the radiant promise of escape' (McClintock, 1995, p260); and they often seems to conclude with similar feelings of hopelessness and disillusion. The contradiction and tensions of white women's relationships with 'Third World' women also demonstrate significant continuities, as I illustrated in the interview material and through personal reflection in chapter 1.2.

4.4 WHITE FEMINISM AND RACISM

In Nicaragua we cannot conduct a struggle of a Western feminist kind. This is alien to our reality. It doesn't make sense to separate the women's struggle from that of overcoming poverty, exploitation and reaction. We want to promote women's interests within the context of the wider struggle.

Nora Astega, quoted in Momsen & Townsend, 1987, p22

bell hooks (1989, 1990a, 1990b and 1996), Audre Lorde (1996) and Gloria Anzaldua (1987) are amongst those black women in the US who have challenged the hegemony of white, Western feminism. Many of their arguments are paralleled by writers from the 'Third World', who raise objections to the notion that all women, wherever or whoever they may be, share the same kind of experiences as women, and therefore an automatic kind of solidarity. Avtar Brah places the debate in the British context and problematises the notion of global sisterhood (1996, p102: see also Hirshman in Marchand & Parpart, 1995, p47). Such a sentiment of solidarity based solely on identification as women can be fractured along a number of lines. Firstly, there is the line of 'race' or, more particularly, racism. bell hooks points out that, historically;

> Few, if any, white women liberationists are willing to acknowledge that the women's movement was consciously and deliberately structured to exclude black and other non-white women and to serve primarily the interests of middle and upper class college educated white women seeking social equality with middle and upper class white men ... it is precisely the racism and classism of exponents of feminist ideology that has caused a large majority of black women to suspect their motives, and to reject active participation in any effort to organise a women's movement (hooks, 1990a, p147).

Audre Lorde identifies the anger that is her response to racism, challenging white women to respond to the anger, not to retreat in fear, but emphasising that responding to racism must also mean responding to 'the anger of exclusion, of unquestioned privilege, of racial distortions, of silence, ill-use, stereotyping, defensiveness, misnaming, betrayal, and co-optation' (1996 p172). Such strictures could also be usefully applied to power relations within the remit of development.

A number of women whose primary interests lie in the interaction between the forces of feminism and those of post-modernism have also contributed positively to these debates; Nicholson (1990) and Butler & Scott (1992), for example, illustrate how white, western women who would criticise much theory and scholarship on the basis of its universalising tendencies, nonetheless set about establishing a unified category of women which, securely based in the edifices of white, middle-class European and North American academia, is in turn reflected in much of the gender and development literature quoted above. The assumption of a particular standpoint, such as that of feminism, may well challenge the dominance of masculinist approaches, but it runs the risk of establishing instead the dominance of a particular group of women, who have the power and the confidence not only to speak, but to speak loudly enough to be heard and be assured of their audience.

Relations between women across the imperial divide, or between North and South, have also come under critical scrutiny (I discussed some of the colonial connections earlier in this chapter[2]). As Vron Ware points out: 'there would not be much point in understanding how the category of white femininity was constructed through history if this information was not used to engage with contemporary ideologies of domination' (1992, p43). Attempts to create a category of 'woman' which transcends all other barriers, as were reflected in the interviews cited above, are often thwarted by differences of class or 'race', and by the ability of the Northern/white woman to exercise powers and obtain knowledges in ways only made possible by the history of imperialism and the current-day operations of globalisation Thus there cannot be a basis for automatic solidarity or identification on the basis of gender. As Chandra Talpade Mohanty argues (1992, p79): 'The assertion that women constitute a potential world political force is suggestive: however, Big Brother is *not exactly the same* even in, say, the US and Latin America'. It may well be the case that women are suffering disproportionately more as exploited 'Third World' labour in relation to men, but the situation is more complex and there are a number of other exploitative dimensions also at work:

> The Mexican government and wealthy growers are in partnership with such American conglomerates as American Motors, IT & T, and Du Pont which own factories called maquiladores. One-fourth of all

Mexicans work at maquiladores, most are young women. Next to oil, maquiladores are Mexico's second greatest source of US dollars. Working eight to twelve hours a day to wire in the backup lights of US autos or solder minuscule wires in TV sets is not the Mexican way. While the women are in the maquiladores, the children are left on their own. Many roam the street, become part of cholo gangs. The infusion of the values of white culture is changing the Mexican way of life (Anzaldua, 1987, p10).

It is not necessary to subscribe wholeheartedly to this somewhat essentialist notion of the Mexican way of life to posit that US and European consumers, as well as those profiting from the choice of location for production of TVs and cars (whether manufactured in Mexico or elsewhere in maquiladores in the 'Third World' – their number is also on the increase in Nicaragua – see Richards, 1998 and CAWN), carry some responsibility for this particular dynamic of oppression – men and women. And to some extent this must undermine the possibilities for solidarity. Furthermore, women within the 'Third World' do not form a homogenous block, as Mohanty demonstrates in her classic text *Under Western Eyes: Feminist Scholarship and Colonial Discourses* (1988, p66); she argues that a sizeable amount of western feminist work on women in the 'Third World' is driven by 'assumptions of privilege and ethnocentric universality on the one hand, and inadequate self-consciousness about the effect of western scholarship on the "third world" in the context of a world system dominated by the west on the other'.

Jane Parpart, investigating WID (Women in Development) and GAD (Gender and Development) literature, comments that much of it has represented 'Third World' women as more or less uniformly benighted, overburdened beasts of labour who are totally repressed by their menfolk: 'the poor Third World woman remains truly "other" to her development expert sisters' (Parpart, 1995, p254). The answer to the challenges faced by 'Third World' women is often portrayed as being to allow 'Third World' peoples a degree of autonomy, or facilitating their empowerment in relation to their developmental needs. Parpart, for example, is in favour of what she terms a postmodern feminist focus (p262), which would 'encourage development planners to pay more attention to the concrete circumstances of Third World and minority women's lives'. She feels that a search for 'previously silenced women's voices' and an attempt to ensure that the goals and aspirations of 'Third World' women are 'discovered rather than assumed' would provide 'a more subtle understanding of "Third World" women's lives' and this would ensure that development theory and practice is more grounded in the lived experiences of 'Third World' women. I would suggest that this will result in a different approach in practice only to the extent that white power and racialisation are also taken into account.

As Spivak (1988, p28) points out, it is only in the context of colonial production that the subaltern has no history and cannot speak; and it is a challenge to those of us operating largely in that context to hear and to act upon what is said. Domitila Barrios de Chungara, for example, in her book *Let Me Speak!*, describes her visit to an international women's conference thus:

> some women stood up and said: men are the enemy – men create wars, men create nuclear weapons, men beat women – for me it was a really rude shock. We spoke very different languages, no? – for us the first and main task isn't to fight against our companeros, but with them to change the system we live in for another, in which men and women will have the right to live, to work, to organize ... The day the women spoke out against imperialism, I spoke too. And I said how we live totally dependent on foreigners for everything, how they impose what they want on us, economically as well as culturally (Barrios de Chungara, 1978, p198).

This echoes the quote from Nora Astega, the Nicaraguan Vice-Minister of Foreign Affairs during the Sandinista government, reproduced at the beginning of this section. It seems naive, then, to expect Barrios de Chungara or Astega to wholeheartedly embrace Western feminism, especially as their view of the necessity of a wider struggle, incorporating the impact of class, imperialism and racialisation together with gender, seems to be widely ignored in Western, white feminist writing.[3]

4.5 CONCLUDING COMMENTS

The apparent motivation, evidenced in the quotations above, that drives the concern of Western women and men in relation to the position of 'Third World' women is, as I have pointed out, often expressed in terms of solidarity and a sense of common interest between women across the globe. I have tried to problematise this, not in order to argue that gender inequalities in the 'Third World' (and, indeed, in the 'First World') do not exist or are unimportant, but in order to suggest that gender issues cannot be treated in isolation from other affective power relations. To reiterate the quote from Nora Astega, it is necessary to emphasise the wider struggle and to continually take other power relationships, including economic exploitation, into account. To consider the impact of the racialisation of the relationship between the 'First' and the 'Third World' would contribute to a greater understanding of how labour and materials of 'Third World' peoples can be exploited and yet, at the same time, be positioned as the needing-to-be-developed and therefore as the inferior. Currently, I would suggest, the role of 'First World' women in this process is critical, for not only does it contain its own seeds of paternalism, but it also overlays and obfuscates other power relationships which may serve the interests of Western women at the expense of their 'Third World' sisters.

It is important, therefore, to attempt to move on from a relatively constricted view of Western women in the position of offering help or solidarity to their 'Third World sisters', based on a uni-dimensional definition of power relations. We require, I would argue, less chroni-cling of the lives of othered women, no matter how inspiring, and considerably more analysis of how power relations of gender interact, reinforce or undermine those of class and racism. This might involve Western women acknowledging uncomfortable aspects of their own power in praxis.

The examples given so far throughout this book indicate a number of highly effective stratagems in operation, which utilise a range of different kinds of power, and which draw on both gender relations and nationhood as ways of feeding into existing power inequalities: the power of the gaze of the West, which carries with it the abrogated right to survey both land and peoples and to then pass judgement – judge-ments which usually find a lack or deficiency in some way; the power to appropriate – to decide simply what belongs to whom and for how long; the power to classify, both nations and individuals into developed and undeveloped; the power to patronise by pronouncing something (sometimes a whole country) as beautiful, acceptable or hospitable; the power to summarise whole nations and peoples as 'this or that' and to act accordingly; the power to negate – to treat people as if they are not a part of what is happening and are unaffected by decisions made in geographically distant lands; and the power to judge that some power relations are important, worthy of study and comment, whilst other power relations must remain hidden and unexplored.

The next chapter continues to explore these issues specifically in relation to discourses and practices of 'Third World' development and aid.

NOTES

1. By 'strategies' I do not intend to imply intentionality.
2. See Chaudhuri & Strobel, 1992 for a further account of Western women and their role in the imperial project located mainly in India and Africa.
3. See Hazel Johnson for an alternative view, where she presents arguments supporting the view that feminism was not imposed by Western feminist women but came about through a process of gradual empowerment (1992 p.170).

5

'THIRD WORLD' DEVELOPMENT – DISCOURSE AND PRACTICE

> To understand development as a discourse, one must look not at the elements themselves but at the system of relations established among them. It is this system that allows the systematic creation of objects, concepts, and strategies; it determines what can be thought and said. These relations – established between institutions, socio-economic processes, forms of knowledge, technological factors and so on – define the conditions under which objects, concepts, theories, and strategies can be incorporated into the discourse. In sum, the system of relations establishes a discursive practice that sets the rules of the game; who can speak, from what points of view, with what authority, and according to what criteria of expertise; it sets the rules that must be followed for this or that problem, theory or object to emerge to be named, analyzed, and eventually turned into a policy or plan.
>
> Escobar, 1995a, p40

Thus far in this book I have tried to unpack some of the relations which globally establish the 'system of relations' which determine what can and cannot be said, what can and cannot be criticised, what can and cannot be done under the remit of development and aid. It is, I hope, clear by now that development theories and practices do not evolve solely with the best interests of the recipients in mind. On the contrary, the impact of historical power relations and current day geopolitics are crucial and mutually affective. Furthermore, development discourse and imagery are shaped by racialised processes of othering, and a complex and ambivalent interweaving of assimilationist tendencies and rejectionism; these form the bedrock of the attitudes forged in the West towards those who live in the South. This chapter looks more closely at development discourse, as well as imagery frequently associated with 'developing' countries, and suggests that it has come to be accepted as an unchallenged regime of truth, and that this contributes to maintaining existing racialised formations of global power.

It is important to note how very wide is the reach of the discourses of othering in general and development discourse in particular – no aspect of life (at least in the South) is to be left untouched by the ramifications. The spreading of the remit of development to take into its ambit every aspect of the lives of those deemed in need of such attention is clearly visible, for example, in Claire Short's first speech as Secretary of State for International Development (May 1997). She made it clear that it is not only poverty, the spread of disease, unrest and war, migration, population growth, environmental degradation and the exploitation of children in plantations and sweat shops that are the legitimate targets of Western attention; basic values too must reflect the priorities of the Labour Party (Short, 1997, p2): 'modernity is everywhere ... we now live in a global society, with unprecedented flows between nations and peoples of knowledge, information and values. In the UK context the Prime Minister has spoken of "traditional values in a modern setting". Those same values are important for developing countries' (ibid, p7; and see Giddens, 1998, for the 'Third Way' approach to sustainable development). Thus virtually any kind of intervention in 'developing countries' can be justified. The problems listed by Short are nearly always portrayed as being of non-western origin, with the causes located within the boundaries of a particular 'Third World' country or region, with the impact of history and geopolitics entirely ignored. The presence of civil war and the absence of democracy within 'Third World' countries have become very common reasons for allocating complete responsibility for perceived lack of development to within the borders of those countries. For example, in July 2001 Kevin Watkins, head of policy at Oxfam, commented on a United Nations report which argued that much of the developing world was showing good signs of progress: 'Development aid plays an important part in some countries ... but ultimately it is down to national efforts, and governments being committed to reducing poverty' (*Observer*, 8.7.01). By 'national' he means 'Third World' governments. It is clear, from all of the arguments presented so far, that this perspective neglects to take any account of the system of power relations within which such governments must operate – the impact, for example, of IMF strictures on 'Third World' governments is completely omitted from this kind of analysis. It is also somewhat contradictory in that, increasingly, agencies such as Oxfam are actually by-passing those very same 'national governments' if they do not like them in order to intervene where and how the agency itself defines it to be necessary.

Alongside the discourses of development, there are fairly consistent visual images which tend to portray the 'Third World' in highly stereotypical ways. Esteva (1992) argues that development is essentially a metaphor and, whether used to refer to a historical process which unfolds according to laws of nature, or to human action to assist certain changes, it has acquired 'a violent colonising power' (p9). Some would argue that visual representations of mass starvation, sad-eyed children, women portrayed as beasts of burden, perpetuate a kind of violence. Escobar (1995a) argues that the violence enshrined in development discourse is symbolised by the bodies used to portray such relations. For example:

> ... the lethargic South American child to be 'adopted' for $16 a month portrayed in the advertisements ... is the most striking symbol of the power of the First World over the Third. A whole economy of discourse and unequal power relations is encoded in that body. We may say ... that there is violence of representation at play here ... It is thus that we come to consume hunger in the West ... (pp103-104).

In recent years this kind of portrayal has been modified somewhat, often to be replaced with pictures of smiling, colourfully dressed women and children. These too remain essentialist portrayals. Why are the women and children invariably smiling? Is it because they are genuinely happy, because they have been told to smile for the camera, or because they are grateful for what the aid agency has done to help and are hopeful of more to come? Whatever the reason, the images have become so ubiquitous that they detract from the individuality of 'Third World' people and create an additional stereotype in the Western imagination. A more realistic image, now used in some contexts, could be that of Western extravagance at the expense of 'Third World' resources and people.

This chapter aims to illustrate a number of the processes of power operational in development discourse and feeding through into practice. This includes the processes of categorising and classifying at all levels, from labelling people as peasants or as 'Third World' women, for example, to making decisions about an individual family's needs; this categorisation and labelling contributes to the building up of a hegemony of power relations, defining the less developed, the 'other', the 'abnormal', the 'savage' on an international scale. The basics of development work are also implicated, as apparently innocuous documentary and recording processes translate events and objects into textual form: 'the organisation's perception and ordering of events is preordained by its discursive scheme and the locally historical is greatly determined by nonlocal practices of institutions' (Escobar, 1995a, p108). Escobar is referring to here to the way a Western organisation will interpret and react to an event or situation in the 'Third World' according to its own organisational principles and practices, which often precludes listening to or understanding the nature of the local forces. We tend not to see or hear that which is outside of our own (or our organisation's) frame of reference, particularly if our own misuse of power may be implicated. Some six years after Escobar was writing, it can be argued that the impact of computers and other forms of communication technology has been to exacerbate these tendencies, by making it even easier to judge and assess from a distance. The processes of planning can be shown to be particularly critical in disseminating the power plays of development discourse, as they involve labelling targeted groups of people, describing a reality in terms chosen by the planners, and defining the problem and its solutions, as well as the means by which they are to be implemented and evaluated. The concept of the 'project', hugely popular in development theory and practice, is also, as we shall see, very problematic. The role of the expert is absolutely fundamental to assuring that these processes are regulated in ways preordained by Western definition and decision. Escobar stresses that planners and other experts are consistently 'uninfluenced' by their own relation (p121) to the reality which they describe as objective truth, rarely considering that they might (as individuals or as inhabitants of the North) be contributors to a differently defined set of problems. In his personal account of the process of becoming a development category, Nanda Shrestha (1995, p277) utilises the term 'Westernised development fetishism', thus turning on its head the usual application of the word 'fetish' to 'Third World' beliefs and practices.

This chapter includes analysis of two major discourses which weave through development writings and, as we shall see, the beliefs and views of its practitioners. I argue that both discourses, and the way they are employed, raise important questions about the racialised nature of development and its role in overall North/South relations. Firstly, there is the idea of progress, which links inevitably with evolutionary notions of development and thus with the more overt racism of earlier epochs. Then there is the notion of dependency, and its utilisation in development discourse to refer to a one-way street, with the 'Third World' portrayed as invariably dependent on the 'First'. I suggest that this is far from being the case, and obscures more complex relations, involving levels of exploitation which might induce guilt and shame were they to be openly acknowledged. Throughout, I point to the ambivalence of the racism which is expressed. Finally, I take a look at some of the possible implications for the practice of development.

5.1 PROGRESS AND MODERNISATION

The Enlightenment is generally seen as emerging and crystallising in eighteenth century Europe. Enlightenment ideas stressed the centrality of Man as opposed to God, his essential, ahistorical qualities, his sovereignty and his control of his own destiny. Declarations of the 'Rights of Man' were made, with their application assumed to be universal. Also of paramount importance was the insistence that reason and rational thought, empiricism and science, would lead inevitably to an increase in progress, that other central tenet. However, many contemporary commentators (e.g. Shanin, 1997) have argued that the idea of progress came about as a response to the need to make some sense of, to order and categorise, the new peoples, lands and experiences being 'discovered' by the European travellers and conquerors from the sixteenth century onwards. The duality of the civilised versus the barbarian fed into the notion of progress and was a crucial constituent of its definition, thus forming the basis for the essential categories of development and aid.

Such tenets are still very much in evidence, not least in many of the theoretical frameworks of aid and development. The language has changed: it is no longer acceptable, certainly in development circles, to refer overtly to rationality or to scientific approaches as being superior to other forms of thinking. Instead, reference is made to the virtues of democracy, of education, of institutional strengthening, of capacity building, of civil society; these have become some of the current talismans of efforts towards the ultimate goal of modernisation. References are still made to civilisation and progress as proceeding exclusively along Western lines, as the following quotations will illustrate.

In the following example, a development worker associates treating 'them' in a civilised sort of way with 'us', who, though admittedly not angels, nonetheless can lay claim to the description of civilised. Moreover, this claim, based on centuries-old forms of categorisation, is left unexplained, as it is unchallenged by me, the listener. It remains, I argue, a fundamental construct of Western ways of thinking about the 'Third World'. Carrie says ...

> I don't think we're considered to be angels because in all parts of the world things have gone on before, haven't they? Well, I mean people, because you come from a humanitarian organisation, yes people do have some expectations of your integrity or your honesty or your trustworthiness. But you have to earn that trust as well, I'm sure, it doesn't come just, just ... but I find you'll go to places where the people in authority don't go and people see you in that way. They see you've come to their village, you've talked to them, *you've treated them as equals* or however you've treated them (laughs – I think at her own assumption of equality] in a *civilised sort of way*
>
> Me   But on the whole people are very welcomed, aren't they ...
> Carrie Yes.
> Me   In my experience, whatever the history has been ...
> Carrie Yes, because you represent, you represent to them, yeah, because *you're coming with your money bags*, aren't you. There's an opportunity there for the people. So they're going to give you the benefit of the doubt, because they know that probably you've come with a bag of money which you've got to

spend in some way and if you don't spend it on their village, you're going to spend it on the next village.

The sense that 'we' are the ones in possession of the quality of civilisation is reinforced by the linking of the values represented by the people of the villages with caring primarily about 'money bags' and their desire to see it spent on themselves rather than someone else. Carrie offers an implicit contrast with civilised values which are somehow different and better than this 'bags of money' priority. It would seem that, whilst not 'angels', we are certainly closer to them than 'they' are, with connotations of being nearer to God and light and therefore further up the evolutionary scale. Her awareness that her use of the concept of equality is highly problematic in this context recalls Serge Latouch's comment that 'the civilizing impulse clashed with the insoluble contradiction that one cannot be both master and equal' (1996, p28). She struggles with the available language and I think her laughter indicates her discomfort at what, at one level, she knows she is saying.

Another worker, in discussing issues around the importance of education, and the impact 'bad education' can have upon self esteem, suggests that this will prevent 'them' from getting 'very far in life'. I did not ask him to elucidate further what he meant by this as, during the process of the interview, we would both have had a sense of what this implied in terms of – again unquestioned – bettering oneself or succeeding within the Western paradigm. He continues:

> You live in the *back of beyond* in places that people who've got money and power don't seem interested in, never go to, never want to go to. So you've got all that stacked up against you and, until you start, though you can work on people's self-esteem without changing their physical conditions, unless you start making *some movement and changing* the physical conditions of people, I don't just mean that from the outside, from the outside and the inside ... then you're not going to get very far improving their self-esteem because it still remains all stacked against them and anybody can say *'they're blinded with science'* so it's going to be *slow*.

Phrases like 'back of beyond' reassert the primacy of a forward direction to a place closer and more included in what is happening of importance; a place without 'movement' or 'change' is deemed automatically deleterious to people's sense of self esteem. As well as places being compared in this way, Massey (1999, p31) describes how differences in the stage of progress reached are also alluded to as being differences in temporal location. Thus, the word 'back' links with 'backward' and the West is understood to be more advanced, relative to those parts of the world deemed backward. Furthermore, the (Western) speaker/listener is assumed to be in possession of the key to improving such identified lacks and gaps and getting the necessary movement underway. The suggestion that 'they' are 'blinded by science' links with those colonial discourses referred to in Chapter 3 which consistently degrade the abilities of colonised peoples, though I think the speaker was being careful not to say this himself but to impute it to 'anybody'. And we have the repetition of the importance of speed with the use of the word 'slow'.

The presence of advanced technology and possession of material goods are frequently coupled with the idea of making progress and entering a world which is not only scientifically more advanced but also inherently superior in its cultural and even moral aspects. Peter Worsley (1967, p30) was one of the first commentators to point out that 'the technological superiority of ships, typewriters, money, and machine-guns, and White organisational superiority, seemed expressive of the overwhelming total superiority of the Western "rational spirit"'. Paul's feelings about the lack of telephone provision (quoted on p61) is one example of this, and the following example from a different worker makes a direct connection with whiteness:

> So that's the other thing. *The thing of being white.* Whether you like it or not *you're on top of a ladder* and you're working with people … you show up on a plane, a machine that may be anywhere up to a $60m machine and it's parked in front of a … it always used to crack me up when I was in Mozambique, we would fly into N, *the back end of the system*, it is so far away, you can fly for 3 hours in a jet and still be in Mozambique and land the machine, this Airbus 320, something like that, and pulled up at this terminal building which, at a push, cost $5000. This clash of, just so impoverished, *clash of two parts of the world* which have a hard time communicating with one another. Everything about that plane was *go-ahead* and everything else, everything about the terminal building is just *unreal* (says this very quietly)

Me   The opposite of go-ahead

Chris   Absolutely. I remember going outside of N, there was a little shed near the road, that shed was leaning and you could barely see the paint from about 20 years ago. This was a little school, which they had the walls up and the roof was just straw but they couldn't get a blackboard …

The notion of being in 'the back of beyond' is repeated here only, even more explicitly, we are at 'the back end of the system' and 'so far away'. The question of which system is not addressed, nor is it explicit what N is far away from, but the listener can infer that the system is the Western way of life from whence 'go-ahead' things like aeroplanes and telephones emanate. The description of the school resembles that of the Masai school children in the Introduction (see 1.2).

Furthermore, the aeronautical references resonate with the development theorist Walter Rostow's metaphor for countries 'taking off' into modernity. Rostow articulated his linear and evolutionist model of modernisation in the 1950s, and its quite overt links with colonialism are today much criticised. But, as Gilbert Rist remarks, 'it is always easy to marvel at the past while claiming that it is over and done with' (1997a, p93). Rostow provides a summary of his general thesis: 'It is possible to identify all societies ... as lying within one of five categories; the traditional society, the preconditions for take-off, the take-off, the drive to maturity and the age of high mass-consumption' (quoted in Rist, p94). Clearly such categories remain integral to Western views of the 'Third World'; the 'drive to maturity' conjures up yet again the emphasis on superior technology, now represented by the metaphor of driving, again linked with the resonant image of the car (see Introduction). Progress and modernisation, in present day rationales, are frequently linked to the forces of globalisation, with much emphasis given to its positive effects and inevitability. Tony Blair articulated this view in his Labour Party Conference speech of 1999 when he said: 'These forces driving the future don't stop at national boundaries. Don't respect tradition. They wait for no one and no nation. They are universal' (quoted in Bunting, 1999). Whatever else may change, we are all still driving apparently!

The need for societies to move from one stage to the next also justified colonialism in Rostow's view. He argues:

> Colonies were often established initially not to execute a major objective of national policy, nor even to exclude a rival economic power, but to fill a vacuum; that is, to organise a traditional society incapable of self-organisation (or unwilling to organise itself) for modern import and export activity ... (quoted in Rist, p96).

It is worth stressing here Rist's assertion that it is not Rostow's intentions which are at fault; on the contrary he refers to Rostow's 'marvellous fresco of humanity marching towards greater happiness' (p98). However Rostow's good intentions are full of such contradictions. Importantly, as I hope I am beginning to demonstrate, these contradictions are still very much present in current day ideas of progress and modernisation and the ways these are applied to the 'Third World'. It is rarely the intentions of development workers or agencies which are at fault; it is rather the system of relations within which they and we operate.

The metaphor of the ladder and its affiliation with evolutionary racism is very significant; if someone is at the top, then who is at the bottom? It also links with the previous use by the interviewee of the term 'angels', who are bound to be at the top of the ladder, carrying the imprint of whiteness; and I wonder whether the image of aeroplanes flying across the sky does not also feed into this. Such judgements and categorisations do not restrict themselves to descriptions of physical or material differences; they increasingly carry inferences of cultural and moral superiority, and corresponding inferiority, which are, in turn, linked with positions on the scale of development and progress. Jorge Larrain posits that such polarisation also operates on an emotional level, suggesting that the world outside the West is conceived therein 'as the world of unhappiness' (1994, p141). Indeed, the worker quoted above goes so far as to ascribe 'unreality' (for whom?) to the situation. We can also begin to see how very similar metaphors are ascribed to very different parts of the world (in the above quotes, Nicaragua and Mozambique), which nevertheless share in common their positionality in the 'Third World'.

The role of order and the need for security are significant components of discourses of progress and modernisation. A rapidly and constantly changing modernity, which implies massive movement, as indicated above, is also characterised by persistent attempts to impose order. Zygmunt Bauman stresses this, drawing on Freud to argue that order and security must come from controlling or renouncing instinct: 'Security from the triple threat hidden in the frail body, the untamed world and aggressive neighbours called for the sacrifice of freedom: first and foremost, the individual's freedom to seek pleasure' (Bauman, 1997a, p2).

Carrie continues,

> we aim to work at the interface between emergency work and develop-
> ment – *our fore mothers and fore fathers had the belief* that when
> emergency work finished people's problems weren't over and that
> development work could begin in *more unstable areas,* where we've been
> proving this right or wrong and so on and so forth for the last 15 years,
> tending to focus on countries which have had recent history of conflict,
> and of course many countries now are *characterised by being unstable,*
> there are still some elements of civil conflict. For example, in Peru the
> Sendero Luminoso is not dead, the Khmer Rouge is nearly dead, and in,
> for example, X (in Nicaragua) there is still a lot of *lawlessness*; in
> Cambodia there is still a lot of lawlessness.

No explanation is offered, and I did not request one, as to why or how development work provides a solution to conflict or lawlessness; it is taken as axiomatic, and based on the 'belief of our fore mothers and fore fathers'. I would argue that the characterisation of places as unstable (the West inevitably imposing this characterisation on 'others' in the first place) is ultimately about imposing Western models –

economic, political and cultural – in all parts of the globe. The causes of such lawlessness are unexplored, but the overriding assumption is that lawlessness is an intra-country affair, only relevant *within* the boundaries of Peru, Cambodia and so on – though the diagnosis and solution inevitably come from outside.

Another instance of a subliminal linking to issues of order and security is the frequent resort when discussing 'Third World' people to metaphors related to animals, and to images connected with large, uncontrollable numbers. So we have the deployment of words such as 'swarming', with its echoes of hordes or floods of people who will overrun and infest (as famously used by Margaret Thatcher to denote unacceptable levels of immigration). A development worker makes a similar comparison when he says:

> If you go to Nicaragua, you know an organisation will look you up, whatever. Especially, it must be even easier, *nightmarish* for the bigger agencies, Oxfam, making a visit to wherever and you know, they would be like *bees around a honey pot*. Because they know that you've got money and it's legitimate.

In spite of the statement of legitimacy, it is hard not to be left with the resonance of more overt racism. Bees, after all, are well known for their swarming tendencies. A metaphor which is backed up with the terrifying and evil invocation of nightmares.

5.2 THE EXAMPLE OF DEPENDENCY

The notion of dependency is often invoked in development discourse, and it is a good example of the tendency to use a key word in a particular way, as signifying particular characteristics, usually in relation to some designation of inferiority on the part of the 'Third World' countries. The layers of meaning behind the usage of such a word are rarely acknowledged; nor are the implications explored to any depth (other examples of words which are similarly employed could include participation and empowerment). In this case, there is an unchallenged assumption that we are referring to a level of dependency which the less developed countries have on the West (for assistance of all kinds), and which is often perceived as unacceptable. Let us look in some detail at how the concept arises in dialogue with a London based development worker:

> *Me* How do you think you would know if people were becoming dependent on you?
>
> *Mary* Well, I guess that they would assume that the project was going to continue next year *rather than work on what they were actually doing*. I've never actually thought of it, I've never been asked that

question before ... You've got to get it right between extending the project to do useful work and people just becoming dependent on you and that's ... which we don't believe in as an organisation and that's *a very strong value*, I guess, *it's one of those strong values of the organisation that people don't become dependent on us* ... Well, we would know if we ever got to the stage where we were providing curative services, ourselves, and people were relying on those rather than the Nicaraguan Health Ministry or whatever. Then, I think that certainly would ring bells, I know that's working in a different way than what we say we're working but that sort of thing is, we would see as dependency and not something which, because you would have to stop that work at some stage and then people would be in the same situation as they were before ... and then you leave people without anything afterwards. So you've got a very strong message that we're actually going to leave something if we had to leave tomorrow but, on the other hand there is a feeling 'well, we don't know when we're leaving', that's part of the problem because we're not very clear when we're going to leave and I don't think people ever believe that we are going to.

Me   No, quite.

Mary   They say 'oh, yes, yes you're going to leave next year' and then it's a surprise when we leave. So this does cause problems, the whole, the whole sustainability thing is very problematical. For example in El Salvador, we started paying our promoters and now they won't work because they're not being paid. The project's come to an end and they're not getting money and *no-body, no-body thought about it.* I'm sure they did think about it and then, but we didn't, and if we were going to ...

Me   They're the people who have been trained to do the preventive health care ...

Mary   Yes ...

Me   So there might be that problem in X as well?

Mary   No, we don't pay health workers, we don't pay our community health workers ... so that particular problem will not ...

Me   They just get paid when they do the training, do they?

Mary   Yes, that's right, but *there is a problem even with just paying expenses because people feel the money is income and I mean that's a problem,* and also people are motivated to work because of the charisma and the support that our project style gives them, I think. And we help in little ways, for example in Guatemala we provide transport for people to get to meetings – now, no transport, no meetings. And people feel supported. In Peru, you see the sense of solidarity and, *we're like elder brothers or uncles to the village people* and they see us coming and they see us as a big support to their community. And it's something very genuine and I think very

human as well. That's what people ... so no wonder they're going
to, no wonder they're going to be enthusiastic about what we do.
There must be a connection between those two things.

Me   Exactly. And it's so interesting, it seems to me, that we produce a
discourse about support, I've just thought of this listening to what
you're saying, you might think it's a load of old rubbish, when we
want to say its good and it's necessary ... It has a very positive ring
about it, and you hopefully get support from your manager or
management committee or whatever. And then when want to
distance ourselves from it in some way, then we bring in the
discourse of dependency. So, like, it's OK to expect and want
support while we can give it but when we need to pull out then we
have to reframe it and say 'sorry, but you're not going to become
too dependent on us'. It's quite interesting.

Mary Oh, it's certainly one of the things that makes this support that
we give, this friendship or this outside face, not necessarily white
or whatever ...

Me   But a kind of stamp of encouragement, of approval and all those
things that go with that.

Mary And you see that, I mean that becomes very important and it
becomes, for example, in Cambodia ...

Clearly this interchange illustrates some of the contradictions and
dilemmas in confronting judgements around the notion of dependency.
Mary states unequivocally that people not becoming dependent is a
strong value held by her organisation, but it becomes much more problematic and confusing, not least for her, when she offers examples of
what she means. When discussing the work in Nicaragua, where the
preventive health workers are not (unlike in neighbouring El Salvador)
paid to do the work but are given expenses, Mary acknowledges that
people are likely to perceive the money as income. She suggests that
this is a problem, but for the organisation rather than for the health
workers, who are presumably expected to function without such an
income at the point the organisation decides to leave. This practice of
leaving people without an income in this way is an interesting counter-
point to the earlier comment that 'village' people are the ones
concerned about 'money bags'. The proposition at the beginning of
this extract, that dependency is signalled by people assuming the
project will carry on rather than concentrating on what they're doing
now, also has important implications. It is instructive to try and imagine such strictures being placed on the Western-based development
workers themselves, or indeed any of us who take for granted the
exchange of some level of income for a day's work. The idea that one's
paid task will continue into the future does not seem so unreasonable
from a Western perspective (and there is much public debate when this

expectation is threatened) and yet Nicaraguan health workers are deemed unacceptably dependent if such considerations form part of their consciousness. My critical approach to Mary as an individual must be tempered with her statement that neither she, nor her organisation, have thought about this as an important issue – even though it's a 'strong value'. It is also hard to square this avoidance of dependency with her later comment: 'we're like elder brothers or uncles to the village people and they see us coming and they see us as a big support to their community. And it's something very genuine and I think very human as well'. This definition of genuineness and humanity separates out the need for an income, relegating it to an unreasonable demand or sign that 'people become dependent on us'; and this in turn raises the issue of Western development agencies regarding people in the 'Third World' as being inferior human beings to 'ourselves' – we of course are deemed worthy of being paid for what we do. It is also worth noting that such separation of 'humanity' and 'support' from the need to have a reliable income as part of the support system enables the aid agencies to remain in complete control of the definition of dependency: they can define an input as positive support, and then subsequently redefine the same thing as negative dependency. I suggested this to Mary, but the discussion becomes too uncomfortable for both of us and we move rapidly on to safer territory.

The notion of dependency is also important in that it has a presence in development theory. The shortcomings of modernisation theory (the sort propounded by Rostow, quoted above, amongst others) were challenged in Latin America by the *dependentistas*, who argued that the very development of the West was and still is both dependent on, and responsible for, the underdevelopment in the rest of the world. Thus, it is not a question of the 'Third World' being able to catch up in a linear fashion with the 'First World', because the power imbalances are such as to render this completely impossible, and the actions of the West tend to ensure the continuation of this situation. This book is not concerned to elaborate particular theoretical approaches in any detail[1] but I wish to borrow the broad concept of the centre versus the periphery from the *dependentistas* (without, of course, employing it to explain everything). Cardoso & Faletto, writing in 1979, are explicit when they argue: 'Latin American societies have been built as a consequence of European and American capitalism ... imperialism turns into an active and metaphysical principle which traces out the paths of history on the sensitive but passive skin of dependent countries.' Thus we have a central metropolis which expands its industrial and commercial base, but always at the expense of the more rural-based, primary-goods producing periphery. This then posits a view of development not as a one-way path to economic, social, even cultural, progress, but as a relation in which there is a successfully progressing (according to its own criteria) part and a dominated, dependent part. To accept this analysis does not necessarily imply total passivity on the part of the dominated, but it does imply that the power relations between centre and periphery are entirely unequal.

I wish to suggest that it is possible to perceive the issue of dependency from a somewhat different perspective, although it owes its genesis to the work of the *dependentistas*. I think it is possible to borrow the notion of dependency, but to look at its applicability in a mutual sense: i.e., the 'First World' has been and still is extremely dependent on the 'Third World', and simultaneously the 'Third World' is dependent in some respects on the 'First World'. Mutuality does not of course imply equality and it is clear that the 'senior partner' regards the junior with a great deal of contempt, not even recognising how strong the ties of dependence are. A glance at the *Oxford English Dictionary* is quite illuminating. Used as an adjective, the word 'dependent' can simply mean 'subordinate', in which case the sense in which the word is employed by the *dependentistas* is appropriate. However, 'dependence' as a noun is a different matter entirely – one of the proffered definitions is 'the state of being dependent, *especially on financial or other support*' (my italics). This is potentially much more complex. Although the 'Third World' is usually *represented* in the West (for example, in the dialogue between myself and Mary quoted above) as always being the financial recipient, there are alternative statistics which show the massive amounts flowing from South to North, especially in relation to the amount paid on debt interest. Other forms of support can also be shown to be highly significant, especially cheap labour in the manufacture of fashion clothes, shoes and sportswear, and the continued supply of raw materials. Currently, Western consumerism is highly concerned, above all else, to consistently be seen to be driving prices down. Not to mention our increasing dependence in the West on 'affordable' but exotic holidays!

I think it would be useful here to bring to bear some of the insights available from psychoanalytic theory, and to question the extent to which the representations of development and aid recipients as dependent are projections of the inability of the North to recognise the extent of its dependence and reliance on the South. Projection as exercised by individuals is described by Claire Pajaczkowska and Lola Young as leaving:

> ... white, middle-class, male identity as one of safety, power, control, independence and contentment, perhaps smug or self-righteous. Yet this is an illusory identity because it is actually highly dependent on its others to shore up its sense of security, to reflect back the disowned parts of itself as inferior, contemptible, dependent, frightened or threat-

ening, perhaps excremental. The illusory identity needs narratives to reaffirm its fictitious identity (Pajaczkowska & Young, 1992, p204).

Whether such processes can also be applied to nations, or camps of nations, must at this stage remain speculative, but I would suggest that the narratives of dependency as employed in development discourse do contribute significantly to the West's being able to hold on to features of national and regional identity similar to those portrayed by Pajaczkowska and Young.

So, far from rejecting the notion of dependency, perhaps we should be developing and complicating it, and trying to apply it to the status of the 'developed' world. Such a process would require a closer scrutiny of how practice, discourse and power are interwoven and lead to this kind of representation, where a particular feature (in this case the dependency of the West) can remain virtually ignored.

5.3 DEVELOPMENT PRACTICE – FROM BUYING A DESK TO NICARAGUAN MASCULINITY

Almost any old activity is equivalent to 'doing' development work.

Rist, 1997b, p83

The purpose of this section is to illustrate how the remit of aid and development has expanded, to encompass not only issues of potential material benefit to recipients but also, increasingly, the non-material aspects of life – in which it is also assumed that the 'Third World' is largely lacking. Almost any aspect of the lives of people in the South can be defined as lacking in progress from a Western perspective, and as therefore subject to being portrayed as inferior.

I begin with Jack, who talks about the outcomes of development work in very broad terms:

> *Some influence, some change* – yes, insofar as women are doing things and taking kinds of roles which personally they wouldn't have imagined, a lot of people around them wouldn't have imagined a relatively short time ago and I'm talking years not decades. And I suppose in some cases, even *the disabled woman who basically just hung around the house* and did what she could, now goes to regular meetings of a local group and next month is going to learn to do something or other and there's a possibility that she'll sort of receive some training so in the future she can become a leader of the group. In a small way that's real change.

So the goal or desired change need not be connected to any material improvement in people's lives – it seems sufficient here that the object of this discussion, 'the disabled woman', may receive some (unspecified) training and may become the leader of a group (the purpose of which is not clear). It seems unlikely however that she would have defined herself as someone who 'just hung around the house', and the impression is given that her imaginings of how life is or could be are deemed too insignificant to consider. The positive connotations to some form of change, no matter how indeterminate or unspecified, which is equated with also unspecified 'influence', are assumed and possibly given greater credence within this dialogue because of the current emphasis on gender issues.

A number of my interviewees refer to their role as being concerned with building self-esteem and working on identity issues, either at a personal level or in terms of institutional capacity building or strengthening. Increasingly, international NGOs are also working in ways which they perceive as contributing to the building of democratic and civil society within countries such as Nicaragua, where these aspects are considered to be weak and ineffective. Pam describes what institutional capacity building can involve in relation to working with municipal government in Nicaragua:

> So institutional capacity building, for instance, in the local council ... will mean a whole packet of *co-operantes*, of financing, doing things from very basic things like buying office furniture, I mean people just don't even have enough desks to sit at so *obviously you can't work at your most efficient* if you haven't got a desk. Buying furniture, infrastructure, building up the infra-structure, on a physical level to looking at training for people, helping to, helping them to be able to do their jobs better, to looking at things like recruitment practices because people aren't recruited on the basis of, you know, who's best for the job, people are recruited on the basis of who does the mayor know. They may need a secretary so rather than recruiting for a secretary to see who's the best skilled or the most experienced he, you know, gets his sister-in-law to do it because she needs a job. So all kinds of things like that, you know things that *we might take for granted really*, that you would do in a local council which don't get done here which means that the local council doesn't work very effectively in order to provide the people who voted for it with the benefits they need in terms of infra-structure or income creation, jobs creation, things like that ...

This quote moves almost seamlessly from articulating assistance with the basics, like buying furniture, which seem (to both speaker and listener) obvious in their necessity, to making value judgements, both on a general level (it is impossible to be efficient without a desk and that efficiency is incontestably positive) and on an individual level in relation to the personal operations of the mayor. As Pam says, 'all things that we might take for granted really'. Thus 'institutional capacity building' can be seen as a current discourse which updates the coloniser's disbelief that the colonised could be proficient at administration, and inscribes the 'without us, without our intervention ... these indigenous populations would still be ...' approach (quoted in Spurr, 1994, p77).

Recent 'alternative' texts on development ensure further additions to the development agenda – not least, the issues of gender (see chapter 4) and the environment. A quote from Tessa illustrates how widely the idea of 'environment' can be applied. It's not just about the practicalities of cleaning up or 'greening' the locality; the process also involves transmission of unspecified (and unquestioned) values.

> we're trying to inculcate *a few basic values* such as not throwing rubbish, cleaning up the barrio. It is a serious problem as it affects the *cauces* (drainage system). We're not just talking about looking pretty. We plant trees but it's more than that. We're taking a lead from UNESCO, there is no point teaching people what is wrong with the environment if you don't also train them to be able to do something about it. So we work on self-esteem and gender – it's all part of the environmental agenda.

Elsewhere in the interview, Tessa talks uncompromisingly about how she perceives the whole edifice of development and aid as being intrinsically racist, but her critical stance is undermined by her expressed belief that 'we' are in a position, and have the right, to 'instil a few basic values'. It is very clear that the people who live in the barrios are considered to be in need of being taught, and not as potential contributors to working out the solution. I did not request a break down of the components of the value system being invoked; again, both speaker and listener, at the time of the interview, shared a common assumption of mutual understanding. Eduardo Gudynas (1993, p171) argues that the views held in the North of the South's environmental problems rely on 'distorted images' and a highly reductionist approach, which simplifies the issues, and in so doing ensures the location of causality firmly in the South, with the necessary expertise for the solutions being located with Northern organisations and individuals (and their Southern allies). The intentions, he says, are 'usually good', but he summarises the overall impact as 'ecomessianism' (p173; and see also Sachs and Shiva in the same volume).

As I have demonstrated in chapter 4, the use in development discourse of gender relations is ubiquitous, and it is a concept which, as one of its effects, widens and deepens the remit of development and aid workers. It is, in one way or another, referred to by nearly all of my interviewees as being a critical consideration in their work. For some, such as Joanne, it is a concept which is taken more seriously by the workers than by their organisations: 'I personally don't feel very happy about the strategic plan ... where gender is not a specific area of work because I don't really see how gender is going to be a focus'. In contrast, another interviewee commented that having to explain her project to the funding organisation in terms of its implications for gender was a case of having to use 'the jargon'. And, whilst supporting an increased emphasis on gender in general, a third worker commented that 'local [i.e. Nicaraguan] NGOs in particular have become very good at designing their programmes so that they have a gender component so that they are more likely to get international funding'.

As we have seen, gender is frequently the justification for work which is intra-personal in its focus, and which attempts to change the way individuals feel or function, either by improving self-esteem or by, for example, focusing on male identity – 'what it means to be a man in Nicaragua, what are the forces that make you into a man in Nicaragua – the family, religion and social aspects'. Thus the development worker re-establishes the legitimisation to explore any aspect of Nicaraguan life which she/he has defined relevant and appropriate.

The importance of gender is also reflected in much of the official literature of the development agencies. Oxfam has set up a Gender and Development Unit (GADU), to stimulate and advise on a more gender-sensitive approach within the organisation, and many Oxfam offices around the world have had workshops on gender issues. During the time I was in Nicaragua, the Oxfam representative flew to Brazil to attend a three-day gender workshop which was being attended by all of the Oxfam personnel in the Caribbean and Latin America. In discussing Oxfam's setting up of women's networks which hope to link women 'South-North and South-South' Julia Mosse cites the overall goal as 'a united women's movement in the last', which carries within it 'the potential for social change and transformation'. Possible differences in power relations within that movement, though, are explicitly disavowed, and Mosse quotes Carrel Carbajal, from a 'Third World' organisation, who maintains that 'Black and white distinctions between the First and Third World are neither useful nor accurate any more' (Mosse, 1993, p206). We have explored in the previous chapters in more detail the process whereby trying to establish links along one axis, in this instance, gender, seems to entail the erasing of power differentials along other axes, in this case 'Black and white'– and to perpetuate the idea of gender as a separate power issue.

The following represents the viewpoint of the World Bank:

> The effort to reduce gender inequality (has) moved from the national to the international stage and reached out to women the world over. That

... is transforming nearly *every facet* of contemporary life for women – and for men and children as well ... Illiteracy amongst women is declining, fertility rates are falling, and women are entering the labor force in ever-rising numbers (World Bank, 1995).

Though the ostensible interest is with gender equality, I would argue that the priorities of the World Bank are here encapsulated in the expressed goal of encouraging increasing numbers of 'Third World' women into the labour force, though probable levels of remuneration, and the impact of poverty-income levels remain unmentioned. Fertility rates are linked with population growth which, in turn, is linked to sustainable development, thus re-implicating the South in being the root cause of the problem. Again, 'every facet' of the lives of people in the South is open to interpretation, intervention and, according to the World Bank, transformation.

5.4 CONCLUDING COMMENTS

To summarise – what are the connections between the overarching discourses of development – progress and modernisation – and the role of whiteness, and how might they be contributing to unequal global power relations? There are demonstrable connections between Western discourses and practices, from the time of the European encounter with the indigenous peoples of the Americas, through the critical period of colonialism and imperialism to present day discourses of development and modernisation, including globalisation. The links are expressed through a consistent emphasis on the supposed superiority of the way of life, in all aspects, of the more powerful regions of the world; there are discernible patterns throughout the period, with the allocation of superiority and inferiority on the basis of the attainment of Western-defined stages of progress and modernisation. Clearly this does not translate simply or absolutely into a black/white binary, but such a broad division is very apparent both in the bigger picture and in detailed analysis of development texts, as I have illustrated through the interview material. This is also an aspect which has been relatively ignored.

Rahnema describes the connection between colonialism and development as follows: 'The former subjugates through a traditional master-slave relationship, where the otherness of each is maintained. By contrast, development aims at colonising from within. It acts as the "intimate enemy" setting out to change every vernacular person into an economic agent ...' (Rahnema, 1997, p119). Thus it could seem as if 'Third World' development is the ultimate assimilationist approach, with the goal of transposing Western economic models and values as completely as possible. I argue, though, that the process of racialisation ensures that assimilation can never be complete for, simultaneously, the dynamic of rejection is also at work, often expressed through essential-ist characterisations of what are perceived to be peculiarly 'Nicaraguan' (or any other 'Third World' country) ways, and therefore never likely to be good enough.

The constant repetition of the superior/inferior binary is buttressed by the pervasive usage of essentialist stereotyping, which I discussed in chapter 4. In a unchanging circularity, the use of such 'pathological stereotyping' (Gilman, 1985) of 'Third World' peoples becomes an important enabler in allowing the more powerful party to continually establish reasons for discourses of superiority and subsequent 'devel-opment' interventions. As we have seen, such stereotypes are often expressed in relation to possession of a particular nationality, but there can be no innate quality of Nicaraguan-ness which could define the essential nature of an NGO or a person or anything else. And it is not hard to find similar comments in relation to 'Third World' countries in general – it is a constant in everyday conversation as well as in media representations of the 'Third World'. The essential 'nature' of the Nicaraguan (as with the African, etc) is always utilised to demonstrate who is superior to whom.

Of course 'First World' organisations too are subject to criticism for being too bureaucratic, corrupt, inefficient; but the significant differ-ence is that in the case of the 'First World' the criticism is specifically located rather than put down to the very fact of being, for example, British (the phrase 'look at any British NGO' does not, I think have the same kind of meaning and would imply a definite and particular issue rooted in a specific geographical location). Bhabha summarises the connections between stereotyping, discrimination and colonial discourse as follows:

> An important feature of colonial discourse is its dependence on the concept of 'fixity' in the ideological construction of otherness. Fixity, as the sign of cultural/historical/racial difference in the discourse of colo-nialism, is a paradoxical mode of representation; it connotes rigidity and an unchanging order as well as disorder, degeneracy and daemonic repe-tition. Likewise the stereotype, which is its major discursive strategy, is a form of knowledge and identification that vacillates between what is 'always in place', already known, and something that must be anxiously repeated ... As if the essential duplicity of the Asiatic or the bestial sexual licence of the African that needs no proof, can never really, in discourse, be proved (Bhabha, 1994, p66).

Thus there are certain attributes in the portrayal of 'Nicaraguan NGOs' that have to remain fixed in place – in order to possess an essence – but the link also has to be made with disorder and inferiority and, as I have illustrated, such stereotypes are constantly repeated in an attempt to eliminate any doubts as to their reality. The 'race' element is not explicit, but emerges through resonances with stereotypes frequent in the colonial era, which were in those times more openly attributed to 'racial' inferiority. The power of the coloniser over the colonised has not disappeared; rather, it has dispensed with imperial borders and, in this supposed post-colonial moment, 'has criss-crossed the globe' (Hall, 1996, p76).

NOTE:
1. For an overview see Kay 1989; Munck 1985.

6

CORNERSTONES OF
DEVELOPMENT PRACTICE:
EXPERTS AND PROJECTS

The purpose of this chapter is to apply the arguments set out through-out this book to those absolute essential components of development practice – the project and the expert.

Firstly, I explore the responses of the interviewees to perceptions of their role as 'Western expert'. I describe their views about this, offering an analysis of those practices which might be argued to constitute a definition of 'expert'. I have then chosen to explore the role of knowl-edge in more detail, and the ways in which this relates to defining who is in a position to be allocated the role of expert, whether they welcome the role or not. I then, through the evidence offered by the intervie-wees, analyse some aspects of the project mechanism: firstly, the decision-making process with regard to the setting up of development projects; secondly, planning processes; and lastly, issues raised by the practices of documenting and recording.

The racialisation of the process of defining expertness and who has it goes back at least to colonial times (see Memmi above), at which stage the justification was already propounded that colonisation promoted progress and welfare and, furthermore, that the European countries had a duty to help 'savage' nations become civilised. However, the role of the expert as a distinct, identifiable carrier of development discourse does not emerge until later. Some writers (e.g. Escobar, 1995a and Sachs, 1992) date the emergence of development experts from a speech made by President Truman on 20 January 1949 when he announced that:

> More than half the people of the world are living in conditions approaching misery. Their food is inadequate, they are victims of disease. Their economic life is primitive and stagnant. Their poverty is

a handicap and a threat both to them and to more prosperous areas. For the first time in history, humanity possesses the knowledge and the skill to relieve the suffering of these people ... I believe that we should make available to peace-loving peoples the benefits of our store of technical knowledge in order to help them realise their aspirations for a better life ... What we envisage is a program of development based on the concepts of democratic fair dealing ... Greater production is the key to prosperity and peace. And the key to greater production is a wider and more vigorous application of modern scientific and technical knowledge (quoted in Escobar, 1995a, p3).

Escobar argues that this speech reflects many of the Western assumptions in relation to development, and closer analysis of this speech identifies a number of themes which will re-emerge in the analysis of my interviews, carried out more than fifty years later. Who, for example, does Truman actually mean by 'humanity'? He identifies those who possess knowledge and skills. His use of the word 'we' is highly inclusive and correspondingly exclusive – he includes the white, Western, developed world and excludes the largely black, not materially wealthy, Southern world, referring clearly to 'these people' or 'them', who are very definitely 'not us'. Furthermore, the source of the problem of poverty is defined as entirely distinct and separate from whence will appear its solutions. The expressed intention in this speech is, as Escobar points out, highly ambitious. Truman is arguing for an assimilationist approach, 'replicating the world over the features that characterised the "advanced" societies of the time – high levels of industrialisation, and urbanisation, technicalisation of agriculture, rapid growth of material production and living standards, and the widespread adoption of modern education and cultural values' (Escobar, 1995a, p4).

This is no simple, straightforward agenda; it calls for a multitude of committed people who, either in an employed or a voluntary capacity, could transmit these features from one half of the world to the other. They were needed to move from the 'advanced' world into those societies defined as in need of their assistance and expertise. In some cases, the movement is not one of bodies from North to South, in that 'local' people themselves become development experts – but only after they have received (usually) Western schooling or higher education and Western training on a development or Third World Studies course. The organisations set up to work in this field vary from the global regulatory agencies such as the World Bank to a vast panoply of NGOs. Michael Watts argues (1995, p55) that:

development experts inhabit these institutional environments as cosmopolitan intellectuals, members of a new tribe. They are the scribes

who oversee the production and reproduction of knowledge and practices which purport to measure well-being and poverty, national growth
and standards of living, who negotiate the re-entry of national economies
into the world market through the science of adjustment, who attempt to
'mobilise' and 'animate' peasants in the name of basic needs.

Clearly, few people would willingly put their hands up and plead guilty
to such a massive indictment. Not surprisingly, many of those who
work for NGOs, and particularly the more politically aware, would
want to deny that they are a part of Truman's army or its successors.
Certainly, the development world is far from homogenous and, for
example, there has been much criticism of the World Bank by organisations such as Christian Aid and Oxfam in the UK; there seems to
exist some awareness that being an expert – and specifically a white,
advantaged expert travelling from the North to the South – is no longer
unquestionably a good thing. Certainly, my interviewees wanted to
distance themselves as much as possible from the whole concept; but I
will argue that their/our position is nonetheless implicated.

Much of the literature produced by the organisations themselves
stresses their identification with such notions as the 'grassroots', participation or working in partnership in an attempt to deny, or at least
mitigate the 'expert' position. For example, the World Bank marked its
increasing drives to work more closely with NGOs, which it considered closer to the grassroots, by producing, in March 1995, a book
entitled *Working with NGOs: A Practical Guide to Operational
Collaboration between the World Bank and Non-governmental
Organisations*. This was followed up, in 1996, with the publication *The
World Bank's Partnership with Non-government Organisations*, which
sets out, in the introduction, reasons for increasing such partnership
with NGOs: 'The World Bank recognises the important role that
NGOs, both local and international, play in meeting the challenges of
development. NGOs and community based organisations (CBOs)
often have the closest contact with the poor, are best able to help them
directly, and are well suited to helping them identify their most press-
ing concerns and needs'.

Broadly speaking then, within the 'development hierarchy', it
becomes clear that each level of organisation is making greater attempts
to consult with, to offer participation to, to work in partnership with,
that level below it which is (by their own definition) that much closer
to the poor. In itself, this is unlikely to effect real change, and some
organisations have taken additional steps to try and reduce the power
differentials implicit in the person of the expert. For example, all
CIIR's core workers in Nicaragua are now Nicaraguans and this results
from deliberate policy change. The British workers in Nicaragua have
the title *co-operante*, implying co-operation or skill sharing rather than

imposition. This structure is deliberately designed to move away from the development expert model. There is an apparent desire to demonstrate a closeness with the poor, or the grassroots, and a corresponding disavowal of the expert role. Jan was probably the bluntest of the interviewees on this question. She described how, in her work with a girls' group, she sets up training for the other workers but does not do the training herself: 'I don't want to be the trainer – that's just what I'm trying to avoid. I don't want to be seen as the expert *chela*'. With hindsight, I would stress the significance of the phrase 'to be seen as'. Similarly, in relation to a five-week course on formulating project proposals which she had just attended, Jan pointed out that she attended with her Nicaraguan counterpart, 'so she has the same expertise as me'. So, following the course, the Nicaraguan project co-ordinators will do the work of preparing the project proposals: 'they will do it live, so to speak, but with me around'.

One way of distancing ourselves from being an expert is to level the charge at others whilst dismissing its appropriateness to oneself (as happened in relation to acknowledging power relations of whiteness). Peter does this very effectively: 'It's a mistake', he says, 'to come in as a technician and expert', and he offers the cautionary tale of the North Americans (quoted above in Chapter 1) who enter the situation 'with their First World views' as self proclaimed experts, thus allowing Peter to distance himself from both the objectionable North Americans and the taint of expertness.

In her interview, Meg is very explicit in her desire not 'to be seen as God' (a choice of words with strong resonance with the history of imperialism), and she describes how, in schools where she works, she likes 'more horizontal' relationships with the other teachers. She tells me that the teachers with whom she works are always 'thrilled that they're being trained by other teachers; they are intimidated by NGOs but they accept me as I always say I'm a teacher. I don't say I'm a *metodolgia* or any of the other words'. '*Metodolgia*' is a Nicaraguan Spanish word used for someone in the role of educator – usually with quite a specialist service, and with distinct 'expert' undertones. Later in the interview, she is very critical of the 'whole idea of skills training' and, in spite of its being an attempt by NGOs to get away from the white, Western expert model, Meg links it quite bluntly with racism. It is worth quoting her here:

> People don't recognise it, skills sharing, as racism – but that's what it is. Okay, there are ninety-nine things you could say about the way Nicaraguans administer projects … 'I could achieve twice as much as this lot …', quite a normal reaction, but in another way it's racist because the only logic you're looking at is your own logic … it's to do with thinking your own way of doing things is better, which comes

from imperialism. The whole idea of skills training fosters that, because we've come out to teach these incompetent natives how to do things right. The whole idea is based on racism really.

Interestingly, the person for whom the word 'expert' was not anathema was a Nicaraguan (referred to by Joanne). She describes him as a *metodolgia* who feels frustrated, as 'they hired me as I'm an expert and have experience – and they don't want to know'. Thus are the overall power patterns maintained.

I will argue below that the denial of expertness has a great deal more to do with the ways in which those of us from the West wish to be perceived, than with the reality of what is actually practised. A more detailed examination of the role of knowledge, particularly 'expert' knowledge, will indicate the continued effectiveness of the white, Western expert in practice.

6.1 ROLE OF KNOWLEDGE

The role of knowledge in development has several crucial elements. First there are the 'facts' and opinions, collected by workers and travellers about the 'Third World' and then used to create or reinforce 'First World' images and views about the 'Third World'. This 'knowledge' is, as we have seen, often utilised to underpin the white racism expressed within Western countries towards their black citizens. Secondly there is knowledge which is formulated in Western institutions, and subsequently transferred to the 'Third World'. There is also the knowledge which is extracted from the South – for example, knowledge about plants of medicinal value – and then exploited in the West (such exploitation forms an important part of overall North/South relations but it is not my direct interest here). 'Development', says Escobar (1995a, p213), 'can best be described as an apparatus that links forms of knowledge about the Third World with the deployment of forms of power and intervention, resulting in the mapping and production of Third World societies ... individuals, governments and communities are seen as "underdeveloped" and treated as such'.

Thus – following on from Truman's speech – the social, economic and cultural life of those countries designated as Third World became subject to intense scrutiny and research which, when taken back to universities or organisations based in the First World, led to the formulation and reformulation of definitions of underdevelopment and its solutions. There is also the more informal knowledge, collected by travellers and development workers, which then feeds back into the dominant myths held in the First World. The ubiquitous stories of Latino machismo, for example, are reflected back to NGO workers in the materials handed out to them by their organisations, thus keeping the circle closed. For example, the Overseas Service Bureau (the Australian equivalent of VSO) offers some advice for dealing with what it calls 'a machista country': 'If you are a female, you are likely to be whistled at or called out to while walking along the streets and even told that you look fat (a compliment, so for those of us who come from a society that values being thin, don't despair)'.

The other application of knowledge by development workers is the offering or giving of it to those deemed to be lacking and in need of it. The decision to impart this knowledge is rarely made by the potential recipient. Development workers, as I have demonstrated, are highly knowledgeable about a wide range of subjects, varying from computer technology to human relations work. The introduction of Western technologies has been described by Otto Ullrich (1992, p284) as a major factor in ensuring the continuance of 'friendly imperialism', one which constitutes an insidious invasion, insidious because the decision-making is rarely in 'local' hands and can frequently be seen to have entirely unhelpful results. For example, the project Joanne described to me aimed to computerise the 14 departmental offices and the national office of the Nicaraguan Community Movement. She bought the equipment, set it up, delivered basic computer training and then withdrew. She told me some three years later that the aims of the project had not been fulfilled, largely because when the computers broke down there was no way of getting them repaired. Maria is also involved in establishing more technologically advanced methods of working; she tells me her organisation was recently donated a computer which no-one can use: 'it's like those donations of medicine that are already out of date – donating a computer that's all configured wrong'. So it was a part of her job to get someone in to mend it and then: 'me learning what it can do, so I can teach the team how to use it'. So, even in a situation where no-one has current expertise, the assumption is that the first to obtain it will be the person with the pre-given (though denied) and accepted expert role. This must be reinforced with the ease with which Maria then moves into the teaching role.

It is not difficult for people from the 'First World' to obtain teaching work in the 'Third World'. Increasing numbers of British school leavers do just that as part of their gap year, with little or no experience and, in many cases, without the rudiments of the host language. It is, however, a very fraught activity for those who do not wish to be seen as the expert. I asked one worker, an English teacher in a secondary school, whether she also taught primary children. She replied that they now have an hour a week: 'that's to do with me opening my big mouth and saying "Oh, it would be wonderful if primary school children could learn English" – and it was time-tabled on for the next week'. The instant impact approach! Also striking is the assumption of the unquestioned benefit children would obtain from learning English –

though it has been clear from the arrival of Colon that the dominant Western language would be imposed, whatever the means.

Both Bob and Peter discussed their own roles and knowledge bases in relation to human relations work. Part of Bob's job is to 'organise the team who work directly with the teenagers – one step back from the team – and see what their needs are for training. I look at the structures of the organisation'. These apparently simple statements actually reflect a massive body of Western-based knowledge around organisational theory, group dynamics, needs assessment, etc. Jack uses a number of verbs to describe his work around the gender workshops. He is, with his team, responsible for setting them up, for facilitating, analysing, synthesising and evaluating – these are all words which suggest quite complex, cerebral activities. At a certain stage of the workshop, the workers contribute knowledge directly to the participants: 'and we say, and this is what gender theory says about the construction of male identity – so they (i.e. the participants) can actually feel it in their own words – we complement it with a bit of jargon. To illustrate it's a more general issue'. This is, I think, a good summary of the role of development knowledge. 'First World' personnel organise an input, be it a computerised network or a human relations workshop, for or with their 'Third World' recipients, and it is then almost invariably the role of the Westerner to feed in whatever theoretical input is considered necessary. This includes gender theory, which will, almost without exception, have been formulated in the West.

An assumption of superior knowledge is, then, far-reaching in development discourses; it impacts upon every aspect of development practice and is integral to the formation and maintenance of power relations. It can only travel in one direction, from the white West to the black South, and, thus it both constitutes a part of white racism operating on a global basis, and is itself constituted by global racism.

6.2 WHO SETS UP THE PROJECTS?

There is undoubtedly a real problem for the aid agencies in choosing within their recipient countries those with whom they should work and assist financially. Current jargon stresses the organisational principles of working in partnership, and consultative dialogue – it is argued that such decisions should generally be a two-way process; in the words of one representative, 'we respond to requests from them'. How projects actually get set up is, however, indicated through some of the other discussions which I had with a number of aid workers. One such discussion proceeded as follows:

> *Me* How do the projects actually get set up, I mean how do you decide what to do, because there must be huge numbers of things you could put resources and support into?

Carrie Well, since I've been working in Nepal until this year we haven't started any new projects. So it's lost in the sands of time how we, why we, ended up dealing with a particular place. Often, it's a contact that we have, somebody will go to a new country and they'll make contacts and one thing will lead to another. Or somebody, somebody connected with the organisation, will go to a country and say 'well, where's the most, let's look at the most deprived province or department, and the one that still has the working capital'; and that's where we end up working.

This view was supported by the narrative offered by Mary, a worker based in Nicaragua, working for the same organisation. The way she came to work for this organisation was 'because I knew someone that knew the doctor that wrote up the project'. The doctor, who was white and British, and who originated this project, had visited this area of Nicaragua with his partner, a woman, 'and they went and talked to different people who were working or living there and in the surrounding countryside. And then set up, well, wrote a proposal for the project that we more or less eventually set up'.

When Mary arrived she did not immediately start work on the project, rather spending time talking to people: 'some of it's about how you find out what maybe is the feeling in a place, or what the needs are, what people felt their needs are and there is a lot ... About giving people time and letting them be able to feel they can talk to you, stuff like that.' This approach then would seemingly accord with the principles of needs-led, people-first partnership, although perhaps there is an intimation of who really makes the decisions with the phrase 'letting them be able' – the active subject is here clearly identified. Even more fundamentally, the basic decisions about the nature of the project were not up for debate; the essential criteria had been established long before Mary's arrival. The very fact that the subject was a Western professional, in this case a doctor, would be what actually defined the substance of the project, and this definition then proceeds virtually unquestioned. Mary continues:

We had meetings in the communities ... and, mostly, we worked *in partnership* with the women's organisation. We also worked with anyone that we could get, like the health workers who were run by Catholic nuns and in one place our main contact turned out to be the Mayor of the town. So those people that were within the community would call a meeting. We would talk at the meeting about what we – asking them what they wanted – but, basically, in a way, *all we were going to offer was a health project*. If they had said 'we are perfectly happy with our health' presumably we'd have had to go somewhere else. They weren't, anyway.

The official version of working in partnership, within the space of one paragraph, has come to mean 'all we were going to offer was a health project' (see also Noxolo, 1999).

The role of voluntary work does not differ greatly from the examples offered above. Michael, a student spending a year in Nicaragua, wanted to find 'something to do in the mornings': 'I did entertain myself for a while but then I heard about the job through a friend of mine, a Frenchman who was living with me at the time'. The Nicaraguan organisation which he joined works with street children in Managua and has an unusual way of recruiting volunteers:

> It relies on word of mouth and there's one place, a hostel called El Sol, which a lot of people stay in, and Oliver, the Belgian man (now working on the project) lived there for a while, so he put his feelers out there and collected people from there. Sometimes, there's quite a lot of volunteers, up to four or five, and then they get split.

The who-knows-whom can get highly complex, as when he was explaining the setting up of a street theatre project in which he was hoping to take part:

> Rick knew Susan from school, they went to drama college together and so Susan invited him to Nicaragua a while ago and he saw what Susan was doing and met Oliver and Oliver said 'you know, when are you going to come back and do that theatre project?' And so he said, 'oh yea, no problem', but it took him two or three years to get going. He set up his own little charity to raise the money for it in Belgium.

The purpose here, as throughout the book, is not to pass judgement on the benefits of the individual project (which, in this case, involved a number of street children travelling around Nicaragua with the theatre group, putting on plays and other street based entertainment), but to highlight that at no point is any kind of consultation or Nicaraguan participation indicated. The question must also be put – no matter how beneficial the actual experience of street theatre for the children at the time – about what happens afterwards. Following a period of intensive but time-limited input, there would be no volunteers around to see how the children reacted to the end of the project, the demise of which might make more sense to the organisers than to the participants. This, I would suggest, is a frequent issue with the space-bounded, time-limited approach inherent in the nature of the project approach so beloved of current day developers.

I have already described my own experience of obtaining voluntary work in Nicaragua more than a decade ago, which was very similar in its inception (see Introduction). The same avenues are still available to me, in spite of a, hopefully, increased level of awareness. I recorded in my diary on 26/4/98:

> I was talking to Claire (a Peruvian friend who has lived in Nicaragua for over ten years) about my social work career in England and that recently I have been involved in various aspects of social work education. She is aware that I would like to return to Nicaragua to live some day – at least for a while – and suggested that I could put together a proposal for a project in social work education, take it to the UCA (University of Central America) and they would be delighted to take me on. 'You could take over where Linda left off' (Linda has now returned to Australia). 'Funding wouldn't be a problem; just go to Z (one of the biggest British organisations operating in Nicaragua).'

Again, the privileges implied here are extensive in relation to my choices, my desires being fulfilled, and my needs being met, and are embedded in and reproduced by the constant recurrence in the interviews of the importance of 'personal contacts'. This essential core would hardly be altered in any meaningful way by undertaking consultation meetings with the possible 'beneficiaries' of my intervention. I am not arguing that all aid relationships are necessarily as narcissistic and self-serving as this, but it is clearly 'our own physical and psychic equilibrium' (Herreros, 1996) which dominates, and certainly it is a feature which must be taken account in any discussion pertaining to rights or partnership.

To make a direct connection between the way projects are set up and the power and privilege of whiteness, I will quote further from my diary: on the 20 April, 1997 I wrote:

> Yesterday was Sunday. I went to El Ranchon – a post-Sandinista leisure development, with 3 swimming pools of different sizes, swings, live music, food – in short, all one could ask for a day's entertainment. I had invited several of my friends from Andreas Castro (a barrio in Managua) and Zelda and I were the only chelas there. At some point in the afternoon, I was approached by a light skinned guy, well dressed, strong smell of after-shave and a soft, squishy handshake – did I know anything about disabled children? He explained that he has a 15 year old daughter with severe learning disabilities living in Miami with his estranged wife. He wants her to come and live in Managua, but cannot find a school for her. Did I know of any? No. Then would I care to set one up 'for we must do something for these children'. I gulped for air – was this serious, something about him suggested it was; 'don't worry about the money, I have an NGO and I can raise funds in Italy, Switzerland, wherever necessary'. 'How did you know about me?', I finally got round to asking him. 'I just saw you here, playing with your

daughter and wondered if you were working with disabled children here'. Me – 'No, I live in England, I'm only here for 2 weeks more'. Miami Man – 'Why don't you come and live here and run a school?' There is no question it was the colour of my skin which marked me out for such an offer.

The chele's choice – whether or not to pursue this opening. And whatever I think of him and however I describe the event to my friends (with not a little embellishment of his gold jewellery and his two rather scary looking 'henchmen', expanding into Mafia connections, etc), I was flattered and somewhat tempted. It is hard to turn an offer down, even when you know it only comes your way because of your privileged position.

The official language may be of systems, planning and rationality or even of partnership, but the practice, certainly at the stage of initiating projects, is dominated by personal contacts and the ideas and desires of visiting white, Western professionals. Thus the expressed goals of the NGOs are rarely met, but the underlying impetus to maintain existing global power relations is sustained, with the British organisations and workers making the major decisions at every level, thus confirming the superiority of the West. My personal experience links this directly with the privilege of whiteness. I also reveal, in the above diary extract, how I have unwittingly contributed to the essentialist stereotypes of Nicaraguan and 'Third World' people, in this case by not sticking to the facts, as I observed them, but choosing to embroider the situation in such a way as to feed into predominant Western images of 'Third World' masculinity.

6.3 THE IMPORTANCE OF PLANNING

The concept of planning is central to the notion that, through the systematic application of certain techniques and procedures, the 'Third World' will, at some point, catch up and begin to partake of Western progress and development. The role occupied by planning and its associated procedures have been critiqued by Escobar (1992, p132).

> Perhaps no other concept has been so insidious, no other idea gone so unchallenged. This blind acceptance of planning is all the more striking given the pervasive effects it has had historically, not only in the Third World, but also in the West, where it has been linked to fundamental processes of domination and social control. For planning has been inextricably linked to the rise of Western modernity since the end of the 18th century. The planning conceptions and routines introduced in the Third World during the post-World War II period are the result of accumulated scholarly, economic and political action; they are not neutral frameworks through which 'reality' innocently shows itself. Thus they bear the marks of the history and culture that produced them. When

deployed in the Third World, planning not only carried with it this historical baggage, but also contributed greatly to the production of the socio-economic and cultural configuration that we describe today as underdevelopment.

There is frequently an assumption or an explicit statement that what has 'gone wrong' with many 'Third World' countries is that their planning procedures have not been good enough, and that if only planning could be increased in quantity, speed and efficiency, then all would be well. As I indicated earlier in this chapter, there is, simultaneously with the pressure for greater commitment to the processes of planning, a realisation that, in order for any project to be effectively carried through into implementation stages, the involvement of 'local' people in planning procedures is crucial. There is an avoidance of criticism of the actual concept of planning, but an apparent attempt to reform and render it more responsive to the needs of its recipient communities. To this end, many current-day development workers and agencies would ague that they have moved away from top-down approaches to planning. As the earlier quotes from the World Bank indicate, there now appears to be a degree of satisfaction that things are being done differently, in a more grassroots, close-to-the-people sort of way. 'Western rationality', says Escobar at the conclusion of his chapter, 'has to open up to the plurality of forms of knowledge and conceptions to change that exist in the world' (p143); and many would argue that they are engaged in a process of attempting to do precisely that.

Most of the workers and agencies are keen to demonstrate an awareness of the importance of involving their Nicaraguan partner organisations or co-workers in the setting up or planning of a project. However, a look at the everyday narratives suggests some of the limitations on such involvement. Maggie, for example, would like more involvement from her Nicaraguan counterpart and says that the main factors preventing this are lack of time and that 'the school has not thought deeply enough about this – how do teachers and volunteers fit together?' She goes on to state that a further difficulty preventing her working jointly on the curriculum with her counterpart is that 'he has only just started learning English'. Thus in order to contribute his Nicaraguan viewpoint to the planning process, he first has to Westernise himself still further. It is a somewhat contradictory way of trying to get closer to the grassroots. Maggie was also learning Spanish, but nonetheless pinpointed his lack of English rather than her own lack of Spanish as the difficulty blocking closer co-operation.

Joanne also tells a story which illustrates the limits on participation in planning and how these limits are set by those in the situation who are the most powerful and therefore seen as most expert. She tells how a women's conference came about within the Nicaraguan Community

Movement for the first time. The push for that, she is clear, 'came from the grassroots upwards'. When the conference was first suggested, the national leadership of the NCM wanted the departmental co-ordinators to be present, but of the 14 co-ordinators only two were, at the time, women. This idea, explained Joanne, 'was anathema to the Project Co-ordinator – who was a volunteer'; she argued that it was not acceptable. I asked her what were the views of the 'grassroots women' on this but, in Joanne's words, 'the issue never got to them. It was fought out at national level and it was the volunteer, who's a woman, who said – no, no this is not acceptable'. The situation becomes even more complex: I had, until this point in the story, seen the national leadership as exclusively male but, in fact,

> In the national leadership, there are three people – two of whom (the Vice Co-ordinator and Treasurer) are women – the National Co-ordinator is a man. In the meeting discussing the Women's Conference, the idea that the departmental co-ordinators should attend was put forward by the two women on the leadership – I don't know if that was tactics on their part, if it had been suggested by the National Co-ordinator and they fell into line or if they really felt it was a good idea – who knows?

It would seem no-one took the step of asking the two women in the national leadership what their views were. Whatever the justification for this, it is evident that the involvement of the 'grassroots' in this particular piece of planning was negligible, and the views of the women in the national leadership were not only disagreed with but potentially disbelieved, certainly by Joanne and possibly by the volunteer. Disbelieved, but not, apparently, openly challenged so that at least a more genuine mutual sharing of views could be achieved. It is hard to imagine a more undermining approach to participatory planning processes, and I would argue that this could only take place in a situation where the rhetoric of the inferiority of (Nicaraguan) women is actually reinforced by the practice of Western development. I would argue that this is deeply influenced by a determining factor: the racialisation of discourses of inferiority and superiority.

6.4 SYSTEMS, DOCUMENTATION AND INFORMATION

It is very striking how high a proportion of the time and energy of NGOs is spent on setting up or running systems for dealing with information – its collection, storage, retrieval, recording. The emphasis would seem to be moving away from doing work directly with people and into the organising of information about them. It is possible that this links with the aid worker's fundamental role in modelling, or at least reflecting, Western styles of living to those who need some prompting to catch up and integrate themselves more fully as consumers of information and technology; this is part of the assimilationist approach to the 'Third World'. The desire for ever more complex forms of information and technologies would seem to be an end in itself, and something of a Western fetish, and it certainly links with the increasing managerialism evident in the West. Britain, notably under the Blair government, has become obsessed with the need to relate actions to targets, standards, monitoring; all of which require ever more detailed documentation.

Because of its degree of importance, I will explore in more detail the advancement of information technology in Nicaraguan society. In recent years there have been a number of aid projects whose remit is to computerise what remains of Nicaraguan public services. The Health Centres, for example, were computerised by a British aid agency in order to provide up-to-date information on the numerous, and very different, health units, e.g. children's centres and rehydration units. Some two years after the aid agency work was completed, it was clear that there was not the infrastructure available to use these computers for their original purpose. A number of them had ceased to function altogether. Some of the problems must surely have been apparent before the project began, but I would suggest that the Western appetite for technology obliterates everything in its path. A very basic question, clearly not always asked, must be where computers can be repaired and whether replacement parts (as well as discs, printer cartridges etc) are locally available.

Bob has had involvement in introducing computers into his organisation and he is also tackling other information systems. He says:

> Like any organisation, it's grown organically to a big organisation, but the structures haven't been put in place, so chaos reigns after a while because there's no filing system. It is there, but it's not imposed enough, so that people really understand – so that's where I'm at, at the moment – redesigning the case files for the teenagers, making them easier to use, printing them out in a format which is easier to read and means they (the team) can do effective interviews without having to invent questions themselves. I'm standardising the information for questions.

For Peter, the information aspects of his work are really important and he enjoys them; the workers tape everything which is said in the (two-day) workshop and he says:

> I like doing the reports from the tapes and the men allow us to tape everything – it takes ten to twelve hours to transcribe. It is interesting hearing it again. Then I put it all together in thematic reports. Reports are primarily for people in the workshop, but they're also published as materials on a theme, which can be used by other organisations –

they're anonymous, though there are quotes and the men don't mind having their photos in.

At first sight, such activities seem relatively harmless, though one could perhaps question the degree of priority apparently afforded them. They are also, though, examples of what an expert does, and activities around information can be powerful tools in establishing who is fundamentally in charge. The organisation of information is no more a neutral activity than its production (see knowledge section). For example, organising transcribed information into themes involves the perceptions and judgements of the writer, which will be imbued with his/her cultural baggage and history.

Escobar comments that development is a top-down, ethnocentric and technocratic approach, which treats people and cultures as abstract concepts, statistical figures to be moved up and down in the charts of 'progress'. Given how dependent development workers and agencies are on their documentary systems, it is important that there is an awareness of how they contribute to an extension of those practices through which power is actually exercised. Once knowledge has been documented it becomes the property of the organisations rather than of the locally active people who originally produced it. So, as Peter illustrates, what happened between a group of men then becomes an objectified analysis, presented, not by the individuals involved, but by the organisation – and this happens in spite of his efforts to ensure the reports are primarily for the interests of the men themselves.

6.5 CONCLUDING COMMENTS

As I said in the Introduction, projects and experts never happen the other way round. Nicaraguans (or other 'Third World' peoples) are never invited to a Western country to set up and run a project, importing their own experts and expertise. Projects and experts, apparently neutral working tools of development, are not, as I have demonstrated, immune from the issues of power which pervade development discourses generally. The particular contribution of whiteness is decisive in the sense that the whiter the person, the less to prove there is in relation to expertness or even competency.

It is not, then, simply a question of who possesses greater specialist knowledge and understanding of development, but of who has the self-allocated right and the capacity to move into another's space, make decisions and begin organising projects across the whole range of human activity. It is, as I have demonstrated, more a question of the possession and practice of superior power, often directly connected to the threat or use of force, or the promise of wealth and money, but always underwritten with the mark or badge of superiority – whiteness.

7

A CASE STUDY – HURRICANE MITCH AND POSOLTEGA

This chapter presents a case study to further illustrate some of the issues I have explored throughout the book. The focus is on a part of Nicaragua where I had first-hand experience of the devastation wreaked by Hurricane Mitch, and of the subsequent arrival of development and aid agencies whose remit was to try and repair some of the damage – both physical and psychological – particularly that resulting from the mudslide. I would argue that this kind of scenario is not restricted to Nicaragua, nor indeed to Central America, but is replicated across the 'Third World'.

On 30 October 1998, Hurricane Mitch smashed into Nicaragua and neighbouring countries, causing what some have referred to as the worst natural disaster of the twentieth century. Days of torrential rain and winds of up to two hundred miles per hour laid waste to huge areas of the country. Many thousands of people died, whilst houses, crops, livestock, roads and bridges were simply swept away. Certainly, one way of portraying the catastrophe was as a purely natural event, of which it was the latest in a long catalogue (the earthquake of 1972, for example, almost totally destroyed the capital city, Managua); and this was how it was portrayed in Britain in the immediate aftermath. In the first days following its impact, the British press as well as the Minister for International Aid, Clare Short, spoke insistently of a purely natural, meteorological disaster. A week later this had shifted somewhat, with Radio 4's Sunday lunchtime news (*World This Weekend*, 8.11.98) declaring that the disaster was largely man-made. There was a passing reference to global warming and then the allocation of blame began, with the real villains of the piece being interviewed in person: in Choluteca, Honduras, where the river burst its banks so forcefully as to leave behind a virtually lunar landscape, washing away twelve entire neighbourhoods, a couple of local farmers were interviewed, who admitted that they were guilty of cutting down trees for firewood and thus exposing the soil to the ravages of the most serious storms the region has experienced in over two hundred years. Their basic human needs were re-interpreted as human greed and incompetence; 'sometimes we only have ourselves to blame for our problems', one of them is conveniently quoted as saying.

What this approach does is place the blame solely on the victim, airbrushing out of sight the culpability of much larger players who are not likely to present themselves in person to be interviewed, who probably indeed have rarely set foot in either Honduras or Nicaragua. There is a long history of multinational involvement in Central America, and the vast majority of these companies operate with very little concern either for the well-being of their local employees or for the impact their activities have on the surrounding environment. Their concern is to provide their mostly Western customers with the cheapest possible goods, whilst maintaining the highest possible quality, and their products include timber, bananas, coffee and minerals. All of which have their own story of environmental degradation to tell, each unique in some ways, and yet taken in combination they add up to the human toll being reported daily on TV screens and in our newspapers.

This type of degradation actually started with the Conquest by the Spaniards, who undertook large scale de-forestation across El Salvador and Honduras to plant what was, in 1783, the number one export, indigo. The heritage of bald hills is still visible to today's traveller. Later came coffee, which led to further destruction of the region's forests, especially in this case in the volcanic uplands; it also led to the expulsion of many rural people from their lands. It is estimated that all of El Salvador's forests will disappear in the next eight years, and all of the water-bearing surfaces not destroyed by Mitch will be eroded by 2020 (see ENCA, 2000).

Travelling through Honduras in 1997 by bus and coach, it was impossible not to be struck by the sight of one completely de-nuded mountain after another flashing by. The sides of almost every peak have been completely laid bare, it is a grey landscape with a remaining tree or two standing isolated on the skyline. Pour into this scenario two feet of water in the space of six hours and the result will be one hell of a mudslide. Certainly the land-hungry squatters and *campesinos* are responsible to a degree, but there are other developments which go unreported. In the early 1990s, the Honduran government, under pressure from international organisations to meet its international debt repayments, did a deal with a Chicago-based paper manufacturer, the Stone Container Corporation, to exploit for forty years the unique tropical pine forests to be found in eastern Honduras and Nicaragua. This proposal was ultimately defeated due to the pressure of conservationist groups, but only to be replaced by US mining companies searching for gold in the hillsides.

Not only does the lust for precious metals destroy forests and water supplies, particularly in the exploratory stages, but the method for extracting the gold from ore involves digging cavernous open pits where cyanide solution, used to treat the rocks, is stored. One such mine, La Mina Limon, owned by Canadian mining company Triton, is located in the area of Nicaragua close to where the volcano Casita erupted destroying a number of communities. The cyanide lake is now vulnerable to flooding, with incalculable effects on the entire region.

The region around the Rio Coco, which forms the border between Nicaragua and Honduras, was also badly hit by Hurricane Mitch – a week after the impact some three thousand people were still cut off from all contact with the outside world, and a joint British and Nicaraguan army rescue operation was set up. The rescue operation was well-covered in the press, but hardly mentioned was the fact that the forest in this area had been recently exploited by a Korean company, initially called SOLCASA. The Nicaraguan government had revoked its licence after intense local and international opposition. The company responded by re-starting operations under a different name, PRADA, and with a Nicaraguan businessman fronting it. It is common practice for the current government of Nicaragua, which, it must be remembered, is under massive pressure to pay back foreign loans, to grant concessions for the logging of its few remaining stands of rainforest to foreign companies who can afford to exploit them.

Even a commodity as apparently benign as a banana exacts a price on its host country. The profits made by the huge US plantation owners – Chiquita, Dole and United Fruit – are extracted from Central America and taken to the US; workers are paid minimal amounts and, indeed, following the devastation of Hurricane Mitch many were immediately sacked. These companies regularly use highly hazardous chemicals with aerial spraying, and some of the substances used, such as paraquat, can have fatal results. Soil and water become poisoned, with the effects spreading over even larger areas by flood waters. Even something as small as the blue plastic bags which cover the ripening bananas in order to produce the required colour and shape are potentially dangerous. Not properly disposed of, they collect just under the surface of the earth, thus making it harder for flood water to be absorbed. In addition, the companies' habit of diverting natural water courses for the purpose of irrigation increases the likelihood of flooding, as was the case with the floods in Costa Rica in 1996.

Many Hondurans and Nicaraguans see the hurricane as of religious, end-of millennium significance, a view encouraged by the proliferation of evangelical churches in the region. Like so much else, this development is inter-connected with ever increasing poverty, which is itself linked to the levels of foreign debt, the structural adjustment programmes and the activities of the largely Western-based multinational companies. They pay poverty level wages, oppose the formation of trades unions, and are not averse to removing people, particularly indigenous peoples, from lands they want to exploit; and as well as all this they reduce the capability of the land itself to absorb the impact of disasters. Far from being solely the responsibility of the *campesinos*, we in the West should look to our own greed for consumables as well as our contribution to global warming.

7.1 POSOLTEGA

This section is based on diary entries and an article written after a visit to Nicaragua in 1999.

I wanted to go to Posoltega. I was in Nicaragua for a five-week stay over Christmas 1999 to visit old friends and see how things were working out, plus I was keen to spend the millennium in a place where complete absence of the Dome would be assured. Posoltega is a small community in north western Nicaragua, which became one of those 'events' which catapult an otherwise small and insignificant 'Third World' country into the headlines of the British press when, on 30 October 1998, a vast mudslide, one of the deadly consequences of Hurricane Mitch, devastated the region. People had precisely seven seconds from the moment they heard the first deadly rumble foretelling that the volcano was about to blow to the moment the mudflow hit them. Seven seconds in which to try and save themselves and their children.

Like many others in Britain who know Nicaragua personally and have contacts there, I felt deeply affected, and became almost obsessed with the updates on the rising figures of the dead and dispossessed, and pictures of destruction, which, for a while, were broadcast on a daily basis and transmitted via e-mail. I became quite frantic for a day or two, concerned for the fate of friends and acquaintances, and rushed about doing my bit to raise as much awareness and cash as possible.

Having seen the graphic photographs of the impact of the mudslide devouring everything in its path, I wanted to see how the aid agencies had responded and how effectively they were repairing the damage. That, at least, was the conscious motive for my journey to Posoltega.

So I wanted to go and I wanted to interview people affected by the hurricane. I was lucky inasmuch as an old friend from Britain was working for a British NGO and was actually living in Posoltega. I persuaded her to introduce me to people whom she thought would have something interesting to say. The first person she took me to visit was Petronella.

Petronella has been interviewed several times before and, because of this my friend was a little reluctant to 'use her like that again'. I like to think retelling her story to me was helpful to her. I also prefer to repress the memory that returns to me now as I write that I terminated the interview in something of a hurry as a taxi was waiting to return me to town. She won't read this or, unless I make a special effort, see the numerous photographs I took of her and her adopted son. I shall tell her story in the hope that it validates in some way my exploitation of her experiences and feelings.

Her father, husband and three daughters were swept away during the mudslide in Posoltega. For several days she did not know their fate, searching for them, hoping against hope that they would turn up alive somewhere. A neighbour told her that bodies were being held in a convent, and that three of them fitted the description of her children. She travelled there, but was not allowed in to see if her daughters were among the dead.

Petronella now takes care of two children who were orphaned during the hurricane. They live in the tents of Santa Maria, where three hundred and fifty families are still awaiting the first sign of a new house. Many people are in black plastic tents – in the heat of the day it is like entering an oven. No school has been built – but Petronella, together with some of the other parents, does her best to teach the children on a voluntary basis.

As well as teaching, Petronella also does heavy manual work clearing the land for eighty hours a month. This is in exchange for her family's basic rations – eight pounds of beans, maize and four litres of oil per month. They used to get rice as well, she is not sure why that stopped. She earns no money and therefore cannot buy soap or clothes or vegetables, and is dependent on handouts for such 'extras'. This is the 'Work for Basic Necessities Scheme' which provides the only source of employment for most of the dispossessed families.

Over sixty non-governmental organisations (both Nicaraguan and international) have been involved in the region since October 1998. Nonetheless, there is no free or regularly available healthcare. Petronella showed me an injury to Daniel's head (her nine year old adopted son), sustained when he crashed into a tree as he was swept away by the force of the mudslide. She does not have the hundred cordobas (about eight pounds) to pay for the X ray which her doctor considers essential.

Whilst I was in Santa Maria, word went round that a doctor from one of the NGOs was visiting. He would be there for the afternoon and would see fifty people on a first-come, first-served basis. No-one knew where he had come from or whether he would be back. Petronella thought if she hurried she might be lucky and get her injured foot seen. I do not know whether she was successful.

One thousand four hundred families were made homeless by the mudslide. Sixteen months later two hundred and twenty five have been re-housed. Another one hundred and twenty houses were started in January 2000. One aid worker told me that, as time goes on, it gets harder for the NGOs to decide who are the 'real survivors' of the hurricane and therefore 'deserving' of rehousing, and who are the 'hangers on' who only want a new house because of the standard reasons of poverty.

The hurricane hit an area of Nicaragua already ecologically and economically very fragile. Until the 1980s the agricultural basis of the region was cotton, but it was completely devastated by the slump in world prices, leaving behind a legacy of soil so full of pesticides that nothing else could be planted. The local industry of embroidered cotton shirts was, in the process, also destroyed. Many people, whether directly affected by the hurricane or not, are experiencing life way below the poverty line. The NGOs assess some as more deserving than others.

Raul Martinez is the Director of the Health Centre in Posoltega. In the first days after the hurricane no help arrived from either the Nicaraguan government or the NGOs. He, together with some local volunteers and students from the nearby town of Leon, went from house to house giving everyone they could find a bottle of chlorine and advice on how to avoid cholera and leptospirosis. That was how an epidemic was avoided. And this was in the context of disease generally being on the increase in Nicaragua (for example, in 1999 there were six thousand more cases of malaria than in 1998).

At the same time, this thirty-two-year-old, with the assistance of the local Chief of Police, had the responsibility of supervising the burning of over two thousand human bodies, as well as disposing of innumerable decomposing cattle, horses, pigs, chickens. Even now, when they get together socially, their main topic of conversation is the pain and anguish of this task. It took two months to complete.

One eighth of Posoltega's population was killed.

After a few days, the NGOs began to arrive. Of the sixty operating in the area, twenty of them were concerned with health. Some of them informed Raul of their presence and their plans. Others did not. Some of them attended meetings designed to co-ordinate objectives and resources. Others did not. One or two asked Raul what help he needed to carry out his job more effectively in the circumstances, but most didn't. He showed me the cupboard where the out-of-date (some by years) drugs donated by the First World are stored. He remembers a Minister from England visiting in a helicopter and flying over the town. The helicopter did not land. In Santa Maria he says there are so many organisations that he has no idea who is who and who is doing what.

The different organisations are most visible in the small town centre of Posoltega, where the aid workers sport distinctive NGO logos on the sides of their four-wheel drive vehicles and T-shirts. One aid worker commented to me that the giving of presents to children at Christmas seemed to owe most to good photo opportunities.

Having lunch in Alejandra's eating place in Posoltega, I notice that, as well as cooking and serving food, she is handing out bars of medicated soap to the customers. Nobody requests it and it is received without comment. Alejandra tells me it's a donation which just arrived, she does not know where from. She doesn't quite know what she is supposed to do with it, so gives it to whoever happens to be passing through. There may well be trouble later when the soap is all gone, but word has got round and people turn up looking for their free gift. I hear other stories of donations just arriving out of nowhere and people fighting over plastic chairs, sewing machines, cooking pots and other necessities. Raul comments that the increasing culture of dependency on aid is undermining the local community

The last words should go to Petronella and Raul. Petronella smiles as she says she is hopeful that the government and some of the NGOs are co-operating more now and that perhaps the year 2000 will see them work together sufficiently to start building a proper school for the community of Santa Maria. Raul's hope for the new Millennium is that the outsiders who arrive, well meaning and well resourced, will 'ask us rather than tell us what we need'. I say my farewells, moved by their stories and above all so impressed by the continual optimism that things can and will improve in their lives and those of their neighbours.

I revisited Posoltega in August 2002. Petronella feels she has benefited enormously from a small-scale aid project which gave her the resources to start up a successful chicken farm, producing eggs for sale. She is also proud of her house and is currently constructing an additional room at the back.

I asked her why half the houses in the newly built village were boarded up, though, giving the place a somewhat 'ghost-town' feel. 'There is no work here', she says, 'and not everyone can run a chicken project – otherwise there would be too many eggs'. She says this with a smile but her final comment is sad: 'most of the people who have gone are illegal immigrants in Costa Rica. It's the only way they can get work'.

8

'THIRD WORLD' RACISM AND DEVELOPMENT – IS THERE AN ALTERNATIVE?

As we have seen, a number of writers are deeply critical of development discourse and practice, some to the extent that the 'cure might worsen the ill' (Rist, 1997, p1); Esteva (1992, p6) maintains that in saying 'development' most people are saying the opposite of what they want to convey. Is it possible to conceive of an alternative model/s of development and, in particular, a non-racialised version?

It is fair to say that 'Third World' development is not quite what it seems, nor what it says it is. In spite of the rhetoric exhorting increased grassroots participation and the 'People First' approach, it is clear that any important decisions are invariably taken by white, Western-based workers and agencies. This parallels the argument put forward by Slater (1994, p116) that the West, in general, has not shown a great deal of interest in listening to views from the 'Third World'. He says: 'That the non-West Other has contributed, is contributing and will in the future contribute to the global growth of analytical knowledge and reflection is an idea that often seems beyond the Occidental imagination'.

It is not just about listening more carefully, however, and although improved communication and genuinely mutual dialogue could help redress the power imbalances somewhat, I would argue that relationships which are essentially unequal and racialised pervade too many aspects of life and have penetrated too deep into the psyche, to be resolvable through dialogue alone. All of the examples quoted in this book are taken from individuals or particular agency documents and, though they do not represent a large statistical sample, they are illustrative of widespread attitudes and practices. Furthermore, I have demonstrated the existence of a regular pattern of dominance in the context which surrounds discourses and practices of 'Third World' development and aid. This has been the case wherever I have looked, and, as I have demonstrated, this pattern is apparent from academic to popular writings, from committed workers to volunteers, from media commentary to my own diary jottings, from discourses about globalisation to tourism. Development and aid does not operate in a hermetically sealed vacuum protected from the influence of other aspects of North/South geopolitical relations. Development and aid workers and agencies are not the only ones to embody the superior position occupied by the West; but their role is a pivotal one in maintaining the fiction that the objective of the West is merely to assist with the progress of the undeveloped countries of the South. Our outward marker of whiteness rapidly signifies a massive weight of imperially and geopolitically based white power.

It is also extremely doubtful whether development and aid achieves its stated goals in the material sphere, in terms of individual projects, or experts actually succeeding in lifting (a significant word, again! Who lifts whom?) significant numbers of 'Third World' peoples out of poverty. There is constant dislocation between aims and outcomes, but this rarely results in any examination of the fundamental tenets of development – rather the recommendations for improvement are always along the lines of more of the same. There is frequently a subtext which blames the recipients of development for its non-efficacy, and this feeds, in turn, into discourses of how black and 'Third World' peoples are inevitably inferior to their white, Western would-be rescuers: they do not really understand or appreciate what is being done to help them and therefore cannot respond in the correct way to attempts to help them.

When I first visited Nicaragua, I was struck by the pervasiveness of the debates around the dynamic of the gender power relationship amongst my co-visitors. As I have frequently pointed out during the course of this book, there is a contrasting silence surrounding racialised relationships (both at individual and at global level), particularly regarding the critical role performed by the symbolic value of whiteness. I would suggest that the gender relationship is more straightforward for white, Western women (particularly, though not exclusively) to address, as it allows for instant expressions of solidarity, based on an (otherwise discredited) sense of global unity amongst women. It also allows for, in this case, Nicaraguan men to be identified and challenged as the oppressors. Whilst having some basis in reality, it is nonetheless significant that in this analysis other power factors must be disavowed, particularly whiteness. Any resonances with the historical power relations of colonialism and imperialism, or current day power configurations of geopolitics, are thus effectively denied. It is imperative to bring all the power struggles together, and this means acknowledging and working with those wherein we occupy the role of oppressor. To quote Nora Astega again:

In Nicaragua we cannot conduct a struggle of a Western feminist kind. This is alien to our reality. It doesn't make sense to separate the women's struggle from that of overcoming poverty, exploitation and reaction. We want to promote women's interests within the context of the wider struggle.

To view power relations as crucially interwoven also means, in this context, undertaking a fundamental rethink of the basic concepts of development. Development as discourse has to be understood as totally and perhaps irrevocably saturated with the most potent attributes of Western power, particularly the values of global capitalism. Certainly development and aid can be shown to play a part in the spread of consumer capitalism, from the unrecognised but potentially significant impact of development workers (plus friends and family) in demonstrating a generally materially more affluent way of life (from flying in and out, to consumption and therefore importation, of non locally available goods) to their explicit attempts to transpose Western values (via the construction of discourses extolling the virtues of superior means of transport, information technology as well as explicit attempts to communicate the self-defined values of Western civilisation). There are a number of processes by which workers and agencies also unwittingly support the increasing effects of the homogenising effects of Western culture – from acting as a role model to a quite explicit insistence that progress can only be made once everyone understands and speaks English. Thus ways of thinking and languages become uniform, as well as ways of valuing. To recall the extract at the beginning of Chapter 3: Nicaraguan people, women, rural people, disabled people were all in one sweeping remark found lacking in something (not specified); so much so that some form of advancement is required (again unspecified but preferably quick). The people thus defined then come increasingly to judge themselves by the benchmarks of the more powerful, and so can come to believe in their own inferiority, which can lead to consequent abjection and eventual dependence on whatever forms of Western intervention are on offer, in the hope (if not the expectation) that the ever-present promise of progress will be realised. As I remarked earlier in relation to sex and money, broken promises seems to be a feature of the West's relationship with the South – perhaps there is a similar thread through the development edifice.

I would argue that concepts such as progress and modernisation demand a classification of less/more in order to underwrite discourses and practices effective in development work, and this leads imperceptibly into imputations of worse/better and inferior/superior. Echoing the racialised stratification of imperial times, the current global power balance can be maintained and strengthened whilst the apparent relationship is one of helping and improvement. The racialised discourse of global power relations, of which development and aid are one component, allows for the exploitation of those so deemed inferior, and in some respects encourages it, by offering a subliminal justification and mitigation of consequences.

The crucial role of whiteness in this is to act as an instantly visible, indelible marker which serves both to emphasise the effects of superiority (associated with and inscribed with greater wealth, better education, more 'modern' forms of transport and communication, etc) and to re-locate the origins of superiority in non-explicit but nonetheless present racialised discourses. The development worker unintentionally reinforces this with the inevitable assumption and self allocation of the expert role – for why would s/he be here in the first place if not to offer something which is unavailable locally and which therefore must be brought in from afar? And with all that effort involved, the something brought in from afar must be very special indeed. However, familiarity with the processes and outcomes of development might lead to a certain level of disillusionment in some quarters, and contribute to a narrowing of interest, until it focuses solely on what is on offer in terms of 'money bags'. Though at first sight antithetical to the aims of development (which has a far wider remit than material life alone), actually I would suggest that such encouragement to increasingly think 'money bags' – i.e. consumerism – is fundamental to the constant push and expansion of corporate Western material goals.

The acknowledgement of our role as embodying Western-ness is often a painful one and demands recognition of history – something which is always contestable but nonetheless has observably patterned outcomes – and current day geopolitics. To take a position which allocates the role of baddy within Central America entirely to the US is, I would argue, somewhat disingenuous; and it is very important to try and unpack how the actions and discourses of Western individuals can feed into and fortify the global constructions of power. For example, at the very least we in the West need to be aware of the irony of trying to impose a western-defined value system which exhorts poor Nicaraguans not to throw rubbish away when, globally speaking, as individuals, as communities and as a nation, they are probably among the least culpable (the poor buy less and recycle more); furthermore, they are geopolitically part of that section of the world which is deemed fit to act as a dumping ground for accelerating amounts of toxic and hazardous waste transported from the 'developed' countries. This kind of doublethink, which is common in development discourse, shows the need for a re-thinking of how – and why – the split between the Western 'inside' and the othered 'outside' is constructed (Slater, 1998).

Whiteness as an emblematic sign assures the conferring, sustenance and general acceptance of a whole range of privileges; and these do not disappear – rather in some ways they become accentuated – when the white person chooses to live and work in a country where his/her levels of remuneration (though they may be low-ish in the country of origin), and habitual travel by plane and the ubiquitous four-wheel drive really stand out against the general poverty; such benefits serve to underline the high self regard of the Westerner, especially when coupled with a resolute belief in one's own essential rightness (both as an individual and as an inhabitant of the West), and the unquestionable importance of one's work. The possession and routine deployment of such attributes is absolutely not considered worthy of note when it is done by whites, even if they have elected to be present in the tenth poorest country of the world. When imitated, however, by the (in this case) Nicaraguan middle or upper classes, the professional set, then that causes considerable discomfort and attempts at distancing on the part of the whites.

Whiteness has a further advantage as a symbol of power and authority – it cannot be disposed of in any way. One cannot lend it for a while to a close Nicaraguan friend in order to assist with their visa to visit England. One cannot choose to leave it at home for the day in order to taste a different 'racial' experience. In spite of the increasing understanding that separate 'races' as such do not have a biological nor a genetic reality, the marker of skin colour still retains enormous impact on people's lives – materially, culturally and emotionally. And the marker of superiority, whiteness, is ultimately unattainable for those who are deemed lacking or differently marked. What's more, the huge effort some non-whites put into 'acting white' is also unacceptable, as some of my interviewees made clear. And yet the whole purpose of development work is to encourage less developed countries to become as much like the West as possible. This sets up a highly contradictory no-win atmosphere. The possible psychological impact of such persistent double messages (both on giver and receiver) cannot be explored here, but I would suggest that it is a significant aspect of the processes of development work and its consequences.

The power of whiteness is not obvious to whites – it rather emerges through a number of referent themes which inter-link in a mutually supportive fashion, and whose lineage can be re-traced to discourses dominant in an era more comfortable with the overt and obvious expressions of racialised thought. The motifs associated in the colonial and imperial epoch with all-round inferiority are still very much present in development discourse today. The open ascription of such characteristics as belonging to an othered 'race' is certainly less present in current day development discourses, and they may indeed be conspicuously disavowed, but I would argue that it is to the endurance of these themes that we should look for continued indications that relationships between the West and the Rest are much as they always have been. These themes are of fundamental importance in the West's perception of itself, and in the ways it translates itself to other parts of the globe. They reflect and re-create the essential touchstones of the white, Western way of life and way of thinking and, crucially, the Western self-belief in our own immutable superiority.

Some of the themes to be found in the material quoted in this book resonate with the time/progress dynamic. For example, there are a number of references to countries such as Nicaragua being 'backwards', or 'at the back of beyond'. These are relative terms, but the complementary 'forwards' or 'at the front of ...' cannot be specified for fear of illuminating the latent discrepancies. It is so much easier to talk about what 'not advancing quickly' might indicate than to look too closely at where advancing quickly might be leading! Meshed in with these temporal references are spatial metaphors, also employed to create an ethos of otherness – which is invariably at a great distance from where it is apparently preferable to be. Nicaraguans 'live on the edge', and their voices are sought 'from the other side'. The word 'local' is also frequently used to mean Nicaraguan, with its undercurrents of less cosmopolitanism and less sophistication. Comparisons between less developed transport and (tele)communication systems and those in the West trace temporal and spatial figurations of the superiority/inferiority polarity. Information technology and its accoutrements also seem to have become a major component of development practice, even in situations where there is clearly not the available infra-structure to support functioning computers, fax machines, etc. This is in some ways perhaps the most potent symbol of the power of the West, and I have suggested that their aggressive introduction into countries such as Nicaragua has more to do with the marketing strategies of vast and wealthy Northern corporations than with people-centred development.

On the whole, overt references to motifs with transparent connections to evolutionary raciology are avoided in development discourse. There are, however, significant mentions of the idea of a ladder, with associated images of who is at the top and who at the bottom – and who would be helping whom to take the next step upwards (spatial referents again). This also incorporates the idea of whiteness as light – climbing further up the ladder signals getting closer to the light, to purity, to God. The theme of Nicaraguans and other 'Third World' peoples as less than pure is also picked up by those interviewees who attribute an unhealthy inclination for the 'money bags' aspect of development. The further allusion to 'bees around the honey pot' uses a simile from the insect world, which though perhaps not deliberately unflattering in itself does link into the pervasive animalisation of 'inferior races' from earlier, less squeamish times. As does the image of Nicaraguans as children (though this was intentionally renounced by the interviewee quoted, it was nonetheless established as an integral part of our conversation and thus the image becomes a valid one), with all that that implies in terms of who it is that takes on the parenting role of nurturing, and, of course, meting out necessary discipline. Here, the very use of the concept of development becomes highly significant, for it is used extensively within Britain and other 'developed' nations in relation to children (though not in relation to children of the 'less-developed world'). This strengthens the self image of certain nations as protectors and providers in relation to others; and as undertaking the same role in relation to the 'smaller' nations of the world as parents do with their children. The discourse of dependency contributes further to this. Thus each of these referents, whilst not necessarily in themselves of huge significance, feed into and off each other, and this allows for a semi-explicit but we-all-know-what-is-meant tapestry to be woven. And when viewed at a distance each stitch contributes to the overall meaning understood by both speaker and listener. The use of essentialisms to refer to Nicaraguans would not in itself imply allusions based on racist categories, but they perform a crucial role in upholding the deepening division of the world into lesser beings (inevitably the poorer and black part of the world) and those of supposedly greater worth.

I now turn to the question which I anticipate from readers: what do I think can be done to change the situation? I will try to offer a few tentative suggestions here. This is not primarily a problem for the development and aid world, though a place to start might involve a redefinition of development and aid. If the West is serious about helping the South then why not consider paying back some of our own debts to Africa, Asia and Latin America? And if that is too much to swallow, then at least we could redefine discourses of development to respond to requests for help rather than continuing with the imposition of Western notions of what help is needed and how it should be administered.

Of course, development workers could play a critical part in such changes but, given that power inequalities are a global feature of overall North/South relations, it is clearly the responsibility of all of us who inhabit the North to work for change. To complicate this somewhat, I would also argue that the more we (as individuals, as members of organisations including nations) benefit from or have benefited from the racialised exploitation of the 'Third World', the greater is our corresponding responsibility. This responsibility must be exercised in two main ways. Firstly, the current balance of power must be challenged at all levels, and discrepancies between statements of official policy and outcomes must be continually registered, both in the development world and elsewhere. Secondly, the benefits of the unequal relationship must be fundamentally readjusted. The division of the globe into a

South which serves as supplier of cheap goods, a dumping ground for unwanted rubbish and an exotic holiday location, and a West with ever increasing consumption and therefore demands, is fundamentally unjust. One of the major discrepancies, which I have discussed in some detail, is the constant portrayal of the South as dependent on the West (and the corresponding view that aid is a favour), which totally obscures the extent to which the West is dependent on the South, both in material ways and in defining its own identity as everything the South is deemed not to be. Paradoxically, challenging the overall racialisation and inequality of global power relations would reinforce an insistence on particularity of place as a way of countering the 'standardised solutions' of Western development (Escobar & Harcourt, 1998, p3).

The cost for the West, and those of us who identify as Westerners, of not challenging the current situation is the destructiveness of living with such deep and pervasive discordances. The deeper they become, the more essential for maintaining the status quo will become processes of stereotyping, victim-blaming and anxious repetition of superiority. Denial, projection and narcissism are known to be deeply destructive psychic processes within the individual, and it is possible that, acted out on the global stage between camps of nations, they could be even more so. Apparent enough in the discourses of development, such tendencies are likely to be even more strongly present in relations between governments, or in the public justifications of transnational companies. Given the unfashionableness of advocating world revolution, though emphasising the importance of a 'wider struggle' as defined by Nora Astega, I would like to end on a note of encouraging all individuals to consider their own role in the processes of accumulation. Perhaps we could begin to concentrate on the possibility that I/we consume enough or too much, instead of following the temptation to invariably consider that consuming more and bigger equates with progress, and advancing towards the dawn of enlightenment. Perhaps the responsibility of the West lies more in examining and challenging ourselves than in deciding what is best for 'others'.

Appendix

VERSIONS OF HISTORY

A potted – and inevitably selective – history of Nicaragua

Thanks to Hazel Plunkett (1999)

2000 BC – Earliest known civilisation, thought to be connected to the Aztecs and the Maya.

16th century – Spanish colonial empire expanded into Nicaragua. Disappointed by the relative lack of gold and silver, the Spanish instead exported slave labour to the mines of Panama and Peru. In 40 years, the indigenous population had fallen from 1 million to 30,000.

1838 – Independence

1856 – A North American, William Walker, declared himself ruler of Nicaragua and reintroduced slavery.

1909 & 1912 – US marines invaded Nicaragua to protect US commercial concerns in coffee, bananas, gold, timber production.

1916 – US granted the right to select Nicaragua's presidential candidates.

1920s – Nationalist opposition to US marines built up, led by Augusto Sandino. US used planes to bomb the northern town of Ocotal where Sandino's forces were based.

1932 – North Americans left Nicaragua. Anastasio Somoza, with the backing of the US, began his rise to power.

1937 – Somoza became Nicaragua's leader. He ruled with extreme violence, using torture and murder to deal with opposition. He owned most of the country's gold and silver mines, sawmills, factories, cattle ranches and cotton estates.

1956 – Somoza assassinated by a poet. His sons took over the reins of power. If anything, they ruled even more viciously than their father.

1961 – National Sandinista Liberation Front (the FLSN) formed in Honduras. During the 1960s the number of recruits rose steadily and by the 1970s, successful military operations were being mounted against Somoza's hated National Guard.

1972 – Earthquake destroyed the capital city, Managua. Much of the destruction is still visible today. 30,000 killed. The Somoza boys pocketed the emergency aid money. This had the effect of alienating some of Nicaragua's small but influential middle class and crucial media figures.

1979 – Sandinista troops march into Managua and Daniel Ortega became President.

1980 – National Literacy Crusade launched.

1983 – World Health Organisation declared that Nicaragua's emphasis on health prevention and education should be a model for developing countries.

1980 – Ronald Reagan elected President of the US. Between 1981-1986, $100 million were officially transferred to the Contra forces opposing the Sandinistas. The war lasted over nine years. There were at least 60,000 casualties. One third of the casualties were civilian doctors, teachers and farmers living in the war zone.

1985 – The US instituted a trade embargo on Nicaragua.

1986 – The Iran-Contra scandal broke.

1990 – The Sandinistas lost the election, though they held onto 40 per cent of the vote. UNO, a coalition of opposition parties, won.

1990s – FSLN beset with internal divisions and accusations of corruption.

1996 – FSLN again lost an election. Daniel Ortega was also facing accusations of sexual abuse by his step-daughter. This time Arnoldo Aleman took power. He is a ferocious 'moderniser', who sets about privatising every Nicaraguan institution and introducing charges for health, education etc. The market economy takes hold and gang-based crime, prostitution and drugs start to become major problems.

Nov 2002 – Election time again. When it looked as though the FSLN might just win this time, George Bush (post September 11) declared Ortega a 'terrorist', and the US Ambassador to Nicaragua stated publicly that the US marines were ready to intervene. The FSLN narrowly lost.

SOME MORE HISTORICAL PERSPECTIVES

The following extracts from the more recent history are intended to convey a number of messages. Firstly, I hope to assist any reader new to Nicaragua to become more familiar than I was at the beginning of my journey. I also hope to indicate how the positioning of Nicaragua in its geopolitical context manifests significant continuities from previous eras into recent decades. The decisions and actions of Northern aid agencies are often represented in the Northern media as being greatly affected by local (i.e. 'over there') events, especially wars and disasters, but as if divorced from global (or Western) forces and pressures. This section cannot address the impact of accumulated historical processes in great detail, but rather offers a few 'fragments of the ... mosaic' (Galeano, 1987, p xv) in order to demonstrate that the processes of development and aid do not exist in a vacuum but have to be located in their context, both spatially and temporally. In presenting a selection of more recent history from a range of texts, I hope to illustrate how different standpoints can impact upon the readers' understanding of history. The majority of Western writers are not explicit about their standpoint, which must therefore be inferred.

Cristina Rodriguez – A Nicaraguan Story

In 1962 the struggle to regain the indigenous land began in Subtiava. The land of the Indigenous Community of Subtiava ... over the years the governments had been encroaching on these lands until by the 1960s all the area had been fenced in and the indigenous people could not enter onto the land even to gather a little low grade firewood ... In 1960 there was a battle over the land and the Sanchez family called in the National Guard, led by Silvio Arguello Cardenal, who was also Somoza's vice-president, so that we could not take back our lands.

One time in 1962 Sanchez had the Guard posted along the fence to stop us. We decided to hold a march. We made a huge banner saying 'Indigenous Community of Subtiava' and we women carried it. The guards thought it was just a procession of women, but what they did not know was that behind us, hidden by the banner, were the men. By the time they realised what was happening they were surrounded by all the Indians. The Indians took all their rifles and gave each one a pair of wire-cutters and that night it was the Guards who cut the wire at rifle-point. They kept them cutting until the whole fence was down. Early in the morning the Indians delivered the Guards back to the barracks with their rifles tied up in bundles like firewood. Imagine the surprise of the Major when he saw that instead of the Guards having the Indians prisoner, the Indians had captured the Guards and made them the laughing stock of the people.

The Revolution happened because the National Guard had come to be hated among the people, not only in the city but in the countryside as well. Somoza sent the National Guard out like a fury against the people of Nicaragua with orders to murder local people.

In 1978 my daughter, Isabel, was killed by the National Guard, murdered when she was pregnant. She may have been in a few demonstrations and things, but she was a pregnant woman ready for the midwife and the National Guard did not respect even that and killed her. They attacked the defenceless. To my mind that is what the people revolted against; all the poverty, the ignominy and the ignorance there was in Nicaragua.

Rodriguez, 1997, p53.

Clearly the Rodriguez account is highly personalised and I would not wish to elevate the 'truth' of her version above others nor to romanticise it as the authentic 'native' voice; however such a perspective is increasingly promoted within a feminist and solidarity approach, certainly in Britain.

John Pilger – Distant Voices

In 1979, it was because President Carter was preoccupied with the American hostages in Iran that Nicaragua was spared the usual intervention when its people rose up against the tyrant Somoza, of whom Richard Nixon had said; 'Now that's the kind of anti-communist we like to see down there.'

Exploiting their luck, the Nicaraguans went on, precariously, to lay the foundations of a decent society unheard of in most of the countries of the region. Indeed, they smashed the stereotype; no more did they work on 'Somoza's farm'; no longer were they victims, accepting passively their predicament.

Many in the West may have forgotten, if they ever knew, the political subtlety of the Nicaraguan revolution. In the early days there were Stalinists, Maoists liberals and even conservatives among the Sandinistas, but the dominant strain were genuinely non-aligned radicals and visionaries, who were probably closer to Mexico than Havana, and to 'liberation theology' than Marx.

They offered to their neighbours, all of them suffering under murderous Washington-sponsored tyrannies, a clear demonstration of regional nationalism ... consequently, they represented a threat. During the second half of the 1980s, they were attacked by the United States, using a Contra army funded, equipped and trained by the CIA, often secretly and illegally, whose speciality was the terrorising and murder of civilians. Today, only the United States stands condemned by the World Court for the 'unlawful use of force' against another, sovereign state – Nicaragua.

Pilger, 1992, p317

John Pilger's interpretation is presented as very sympathetic to those opposed to the rule of Somoza, but I would argue that his stance is nonetheless somewhat patronising, inasmuch as he refers to 'luck' and 'victims accepting passively their predicament', thus failing to acknowledge the rebellion and resistance evident in the testimony from Rodriguez.

Eduardo Galeano – 1984; Esteli – Believing

They preside over childbirth. Giving life and light is their profession. With practised hands they straighten the child if it's coming out wrong, and communicate strength and peace to the mother.

Today, the midwives of the Esteli villages and mountains close to
Nicaragua's border are having a party to celebrate something that truly
deserves joy; for a year now not one new baby in this region has died of
tetanus. The midwives no longer cut umbilical cords with a machete, or
burn them with tallow, or tie them off without disinfectant; and pregnant
women get vaccines that protect the child living inside.

This region, this war zone, suffers continual harassment by the invaders.
'Here we are in the alligator's mouth'
Many mothers go off to fight. The ones who stay share their breasts.

Galeano, 1990, p275

Significantly, in terms of global power relations, the accounts written
from northern perspectives rarely make their connections to the
prevailing configurations of power explicit (including the more sympathetic approach of Pilger), whereas Galeano is transparent about his
motivation:

I did not want to write an objective work – neither wanted to nor could.
There is nothing neutral about this historical narration. Unable to
distance myself, I take sides; I confess it and am not sorry. However,
each fragment of this huge mosaic is based on a solid documentary
foundation. (Galeano, 1987, p xv).

Contrast this clarity about the role of objectivity with the majority of
Western based commentators, where its existence is usually just
assumed.

Paul Johnson – The History of the American People

Under Reagan, National Security Council officials Admiral John
Poindexter and Colonel Oliver North had been accused of conducting
secret arms sales (via Israel) to Iran, hoping for goodwill to free US
hostages ... and in order to use profits from the $48 million sales to
finance democratic Contra rebels seeking to undermine the Communist
regime in Nicaragua. This was said to be in violation of the Boland
Amendments, passed by Congress on December 21, 1982 ... In 1989
both Poindexter and North were found guilty of misleading Congress,
but an appeals court overturned both convictions and other charges
against them were dropped.

The witchhunt served only to reveal a waning popular backing for
proceedings against officials who had merely acted in what they thought
American interests, even if they had technically broken the law ... The
continual fear of prosecution engendered what has been called a 'culture
of mistrust' in American government and led to an unwillingness of

public-spirited citizens to run for high office or to accept presidential invitations to serve. One critic of the intermittent witch hunting of the executive by Congress noted that 'a self-enforcing scandal machine' had come into existence.

Johnson, 1997, p781

Johnson, who would aspire to a greater degree of objectivity than would perhaps be reasonable to expect of North (see below), still remains mired in a totally North Ameri-centric view of the war, dismissing its illegality as a trivial issue, and showing considerably more concern for the impact on the quality of America's public servants than he reveals for the recipients of the US policy.

Oliver North – Under Fire

On November 25, 1986, at five minutes past noon, President Ronald Reagan and Attorney General Edwin Meese marched into the crowded White House briefing room to face the press and the TV cameras. As I watched from my office in the Old Executive Office Building, the President explained that he hadn't been told the whole story of our secret arms sales to Iran, and that he had asked the Attorney General to look into the matter. He then announced that Admiral John Poindexter, his national security adviser, had resigned, and that Lieutenant Colonel Oliver North had been 'relieved of his duties' on the National Security Council staff.

What?

Before I could catch my breath, the President turned over the microphones to Attorney General Meese and left the room.

Then Ed Meese dropped the bomb: 'In the course of the arms transfer, which involved the United States providing arms to Israel and Israel, in turn, transferring the arms – in effect, selling the arms – to representatives of Iran, certain monies which were received in the transaction between representatives of Israel and representatives of Iran were taken and made available to the forces in Central America who are opposing the Sandinista government there.'

North, 1991, p5

North says volumes more than he may have intended in this brief quotation. He is writing an autobiography, and this certainly encourages introspection and a focus on the self interest of the author, but this does not render North immune from criticism, especially as he is of the opinion that the rest of the US population should share his sense of priorities. The lack of reference to Nicaragua in a book of almost 450 pages is striking. There are seven references to the Sandinistas, who constitute precisely the threat which placed America 'Under Fire' (the title of the book). He offers no commentary on the impact of his actions on the lives of Nicaraguan people and I find his use of the word 'bomb' in this context particularly ironic. O'Tuathail and Dalby add a further interesting dimension by questioning the impact of gender issues, suggesting that for North 'masculine subjectivity is an insecure and ultra-patriotic warrior masculinity' (1998, p6).

BIBLIOGRAPHY AND FURTHER READING

Alexander, Titus, *Unravelling Global Apartheid*, Polity Press, Cambridge 1996.

Anthias, Floya, and Yuval-Davis, Nira, *Racialized Boundaries – race, nation, gender, colour and class and the anti-racist struggle*, Routledge, London 1993.

Anzaldua, Gloria, *Borderlands / La Frontera –The New Mestiza*, Aunt Lute Book Company, San Francisco 1987.

Barnes, D., *Disabling Imagery and the Media*, The British Council of Organisations of Disabled People 1992.

Barnes, T. & Gregory, D. (eds.), *Reading Human Geography – The Poetics and Politics of Inquiry*, Arnold, London 1997.

Barrios de Chungara Domitila with Viezzer Moema, translated by Ortiz Victoria, *Let Me Speak! Testimony of Domitila, a Woman of the Bolivian Mines*, Monthly Review Press, New York 1978.

Bauman, Zygmunt, *Postmodernity and its Discontents*, Polity Press, Cambridge 1997.

bell hooks, *Talking Back*, Sheba Feminist Publishers, London 1989.

bell hooks, *Aint I a Woman?*, Pluto Press, London 1990a.

bell hooks, *Yearning*, South End Press, Boston 1990b.

bell hooks, *Killing Rage–Ending Racism*, Penguin, London 1996.

Bendana Alejandro, 'The Politics of Hurricane Mitch in Nicaragua', personal e-mail communication 1999.

Benko, Georges, and Stohmayer, Ulf, *Space and Social Theory; Interpreting Modernity and Postmodernity*, Blackwell Publishers, Oxford 1997.

Berkeley Students, *Central America on the Loose*, Fodor's Travel Publications, New York 1993.

Bernal, Martin, *Black Athena; The Afroasiatic Roots of Classical Civilization, Vol 1; The Fabrication of Ancient Greece 1785 – 1985*, Free Association Books, London 1991.

Bhabha, Homi, *The Location of Culture*, Routledge, London 1994.

Beverley, John, Oviedo, Jose and Aronna, Michael (eds), *The Postmodern Debate in Latin America*, Duke University Press, London 1995.

Bond, George C., and Gilliam, Angela (eds), *Social Construction of the Past – Representation as Power*, Routledge, London and New York 1994.

Bonnett, Alistair, *Radicalism, Anti-Racism and Representation*, Routledge, London 1993.

Bonnett, Alistair, *White Identities: Historical and International Perspectives*, Prentice Hall, Harlow 2000.

Boyce Davies, Carole, Black Women, *Writing and Identity – Migrations of the subject*, Routledge, London and New York 1994.

Bradshaw, York W., and Wallace, Michael, *Global Inequalities*, Pine Forge Press, California 1996.

Brah, Avtah, *Cartographies of Diaspora*, Routledge, London 1996.

Briggs, Ann, 'Special Needs – Bullying, Racism, The Last Taboo?' *Soundings* 14, 63-73, 2000.

Bunting, Madeleine, 'Stop. I Want to Get Off', *Guardian*, 29.11.99.

Burman, Erica, *Deconstructing Developmental Psychology*, Routledge, London 1996.

Butler, Judith, and Scott, Joan (eds), *Feminists Theorize the Political*, Routledge, London 1992.

Cardoso, Fernando Henrique, and Faletto, Enzo, *Dependency and Development in Latin America*, Urquidi, M. M (transl.), University of California Press 1979.

Carmen Raff, *Autonomous Development – Humanizing the Landscape – An Excursion into Radical Thinking and Practice*, Zed Books, London 1996.

Chambers, Iain, 'Signs of silence, lines of listening', in Chambers, Iain, and Curti, Lidia, *The Post-Colonial Question; Common Skies, Divided Horizons*, Routledge, London 1996.

Chambers, Iain, and Curti, Lidia, *The Post-Colonial Question; Common Skies, Divided Horizons*, Routledge, London 1996.

Chaudhuri, N. and Strobel, M., *Western Women and Imperialism; Complicity and Resistance*, Indiana University Press, Bloomington 1992.

Chomsky, Noam, *The Chomsky Reader*, Peck, James (ed), Serpents Tail, London 1988.

Chomsky, Noam, *Deterring Democracy*, Vintage, London 1992a.

Chomsky, Noam, *Chronicles of Dissent*, AK Press, Stirling 1992b.

Chomsky, Noam, *Powers and Prospects – Reflections on Human Nature and the Social Order*, Pluto Press, London 1996.

Chomsky, Noam, 'Power in the Global Arena', in *New Left Review*, No 230 July/August 1998.

Collins, Patricia Hill, *Black Feminist Thought – Knowledge, Consciousness and the Politics of Empowerment*, Unwin Hyman, London 1990.

Corbridge, Stuart, 'Post-Marxism and Post-Colonialism: the needs and rights of distant strangers', in D. Booth (ed), *Rethinking Social Development – Theory, Research and Practice*, Longman, London 1994.

Corragio, Jose Luis, and Carmen, Diana Deere (eds), *La Transicion Dificil – La Autodeterminacion de los Pequenos Paises Perifericos*, Editorial Vanguardia, Managua, 1987.

Cowen, M. P. and Shenton, R. W., *Doctrines of Development*, Routledge, London 1996.

Crosby, C., 'Dealing with Differences', in J. Butler & J. Scott (eds), *Feminists Theorize the Political*, Routledge, London 1992.

Crush, Jonathan (ed), *Power of Development*, Routledge, London 1995.

Curtis, Mark, *The Ambiguities of Power – British Foreign Policy since 1945*, Zed Books, London 1995.

Curtis, Mark, *The Great Deception – Anglo-American Power and World Order*, Pluto Press, London 1998.

De Landa, Friar Diego, W. Gates (Trans), *Yucatan – Before and After the Conquest*, Ediciones Alducin, Merida Mexico undated.

De Leon, Arnoldo, 'Initial Contacts; Niggers, Redskins, and Greasers', in Delgado, Richard, and Stefanic, Jean (eds), *The Latino/a Condition – A Critical Reader*, New York University Press, New York 1998.

Delgado, Richard, and Stefanic, Jean (eds), *The Latino/a Condition – A Critical Reader*, New York University Press, New York 1998.

Department for International Development, *Eliminating World Poverty*, The Stationery Office, London 1997.

Donald, James, and Rattansi, Ali (eds), *'Race', Culture and Difference*, Sage Publications, London 1992.

Duncan, Kate, and Karidis, Electra, *Beyond Solitude – Dialogues between Europe and Latin America*, University of Birmingham, Birmingham 1995.

Dyer, Richard, *White*, Routledge, London 1997.

The Economist, *The World in 2002*, London 2001.

Ellwood, W., *The No-Nonsense Guide to Globalization*, New Internationalist Publications, Oxford 2001.

Escobar, Arturo, 'Planning', in W. Sachs (ed), *The Development Dictionary – A Guide to Knowledge as Power*, Zed Books, London 1992.

Escobar, Arturo, *Encountering Development – The Making and Unmaking of the Third World*, Princeton University Press, Princeton New Jersey 1995a.

Escobar, Arturo, 'Imagining a Post-Development Era', in J. Crush (ed) *Power of Development*, Routledge, London 1995b.

Escobar, Arturo, and Harcourt, Wendy, 'Creating "Glocality"', *Development*, 42, 2 June 1998 pp3-5.

Esteva, Gustavo, 'Development', in W. Sachs (ed), *The Development Dictionary – A Guide to Knowledge as Power*, Zed Books, London 1992.

Fanon, Frantz, *The Wretched of the Earth*, Penguin Books, Harmondsworth, Middlesex 1985.

Fanon, Frantz, *Black Skin, White Masks*, Pluto Press, London 1991.

Ferguson, Margaret, and Wicke, Jennifer (eds), *Feminism and Postmodernism*, Duke University Press, Durham, North Carolina 1994.

Foucault, Michel, *The Archaeology of Knowledge*, A. M. Sheridan Smith (transl), Tavistock Publications, London 1972.

Foucault, Michel, *Power/ Knowledge*, Harvester, Brighton 1980.

Foucault, Michel, *The History of Sexuality Vol. 1*, Penguin, London 1990.

Frank, Andre Gunder, *Critique and Anti-Critique – Essays on Dependence and Reformism*, Macmillan Press, London 1984.

Frank, Andre Gunder, and Gills, Barry K., *The World System – Five Hundred Years or Five Thousand?*, Routledge, London 1996.

Fryer, Peter, *Staying Power – The History of Black People in Britain*, Pluto Press, London 1991.

Fuss, Diana, *Essentially Speaking – Feminism, Nature and Difference*, Routledge, London 1989.

Galeano, Eduardo, *Open Veins of Latin America–Five Centuries of the Pillage of a Continent*, Monthly Review Press, New-York 1973.

Galeano, Eduardo, 'To Be Like Them', in M. Rahmena and V. Bawtree (eds), *The Post-Development Reader*, Zed Books, London 1997.

Galeano, Eduardo, *Genesis*, Methuen, London 1987.

Galeano, Eduardo, *Century of the Wind*, Minerva, London 1990.

Gates, Henry Louis (ed), *'Race', Writing and Difference*, University of Chicago Press, Chicago 1985.

George, Susan, *How the Other Half Dies – The Real Reasons for World Hunger*, Penguin, London 1986.

Giddens, Anthony, *The Third Way*, Polity Press, Cambridge 1998.

Gilman, Sander L., *Difference and Pathology; Stereotypes of Sexuality, Race and Madness*, Cornell University Press, New York 1985.

Gilman, Sander L., 'Black bodies; white bodies; towards an iconography of female sexuality in late nineteenth century art, medicine and literature', in Donald, J. and Rattansi, A. (eds) *'Race', Culture and Difference*, Sage, London 1992.

Gilroy, Paul, *Between Camps – Race, Identity and Nationalism at the End of the Colour Line*, Penguin, London 2000.

Glaister, D., 'Travails with my Camera', *Guardian* 8.10.96, p2.

Green, Duncan, *Silent Revolution – The Rise of Market Economics in Latin America*, Cassell, in association with the Latin American Bureau, 1995.

Grillo, R. D. and Stirrat, R. L. (eds), *Discourses of Development; Anthropological Perspectives*, Berg, Oxford 1997.

Gronemeyer, Marianne, 'Helping' in W. Sachs (ed), *The Development Dictionary – A Guide to Knowledge as Power*, Zed Books, London 1992.

Guardian, 'A "Tasteful" Way to Keep the Mexicans Out', *Guardian*, 10.12.97, p16.

Gudynas, E., 'The Fallacy of Ecomessianism; Observations from Latin America', in Sachs, W. (ed) *Global Ecology; A New Arena of Political Conflict*, Zed Books, London 1993.

Hadgipateras, Angela, *Women's Rights in Nicaragua – Aleman's Fundamentalist Agenda*, Central American Report, Winter 1997.

Hall, Catherine; *White, Male and Middle Class – Explorations in Feminism and History*, Polity Press, Cambridge 1992.

Hall, C., 'Histories, Empires and the Post Colonial Moment', in Chambers, Iain, and Curti, Lidia, *The Post-Colonial Question; Common Skies, Divided Horizons*, Routledge, London 1996.

Hall, Stuart, 'The Local and the Global – Globalization and Ethnicity', in King, A. (ed), *Culture, Globalization and the World System*, Macmillan, Basingstoke 1991.

Hall, Stuart (ed), *Representation – Cultural Representations and Signifying Practices*, Sage Publications in association with the Open University, London 1997(a).

Hall, Stuart, 'The Work of Representation', in Hall, Stuart (ed), *Representation – Cultural Representations and Signifying Practices*, Sage Publications in association with the Open University, London, 1997(b).

Hall, Stuart, 'The Spectacle of the "Other"' in Hall, Stuart (ed), *Representation – Cultural Representations and Signifying Practices*, Sage Publications in association with the Open University, London, 1997(c).

Hall, Stuart, and Gieben, B. (eds), *Formations of Modernity*, Polity Press, London 1992.

Haney Lopez, Ian F., 'Chance, Context and Choice in the Social Construction of Race', in Delgado and Stefanic (eds), *The Latino/a Condition – A Critical Reader*, New York University Press, New York 1998.

Harding, Sandra (ed), *Feminism and Methodology –Social Science Issues*,

Indiana University Press, Bloomington and Indianapolis and Open University Press, Milton Keynes 1987.

Hartsock, Nancy, 'Foucault on Power: a theory for women?', in *Feminism/Postmodernism*, L. Nicholson (ed), Routledge, London 1990.

Hayter, Teresa, and Watson, Catherine, *Aid; Rhetoric and Reality*, Pluto Press, London and Sydney 1985.

Herman, Edward, and Chomsky, Noam, *Manufacturing Consent – The Political Economy of the Mass Media*, Vintage, London 1994.

Herreros, J.L. Trechera, 'Narcissism: The Epidemic of our Time', in *Envio*, September 1996, pp30-38.

Hirshman, M., 'Women and Development – A Critique', in Marchand, M. & Parpart, J. (eds), *Feminism/Postmodernism/Development*, Routledge, London 1995.

Hoogvelt, Ankie M.M., *The Third World in Global Development*, Macmillan, Basingstoke 1987.

Hooker, Ray, 'Problems of the Atlantic Coast', in Marcus, B. (ed), *Nicaragua – The Sandinista People's Revolution – Speeches by Sandinista Leaders*, Pathfinder Press, New York 1985.

Hooks, Margaret, *Guatemalan Women Speak*, Catholic Institute for International Relations, London 1991.

Jackson, Peter, *Maps of Meaning; An Introduction to Cultural Geography*, Routledge, London 1989.

Jackson, Peter, and Penrose, Jan (eds), *Constructions of Race, Place and Nation*, UCL Press, London 1993.

Janovitz, T., 'I Saw People with Adorable Asian Babies, Like Dolls. That's What I Wanted', *Independent on Sunday*, 24.10.99.

Johnson, Hazel, 'Women's Empowerment and Public Action; Experiences from Latin America', in M. Wuyts, M. Mackintosh & T. Hewitt (eds), *Development Policy and Public Action*, Oxford University Press, Oxford 1992.

Johnson, Paul, *The History of the American People*, Weidenfield & Nicolson, London 1997.

Jordan, June, *Moving Towards Home – Political Essays*, Virago, London 1989.

Karidis, E., 'Introduction', in K. Duncan and E. Karidis, *Beyond Solitude – Dialogues between Europe and Latin America*, University of Birmingham, Birmingham 1995.

Kay, Cristobal, *Latin American Theories of Development and Underdevelopment*, Routledge, London and New York 1989.

Keith, M., and Pile, S. (eds), *Place and the Politics of Identity*, Routledge, London 1993.

King, A. (ed), *Culture, Globalization and the World System*, Macmillan, Basingstoke 1991.

Kobayashi, A., and Peake, L., 'Unnatural Discourse: "Race" and Gender in Geography', in T. Barnes and D. Gregory (eds), *Reading Human Geography – The Poetics and Politics of Inquiry*, Arnold, London 1997.

Kothari, R., *Rethinking Development: In Search of Humane Alternatives*, Ajanta, Delhi 1988.

Korten, D., *When Corporations Rule the World*, Kumarian Press, Bloomfield 2001.

Kovel, J., *White Racism; A Psychohistory*, Free Association Books, London 1988a.

Kovel, J., *In Nicaragua*, Free Association Books, London 1988b.

Lagarde, M., *Claves Feministas para el Poderio y la Autonomia de las Mujeres*, Puento de Encuentro, Managua 1998.

Lancaster, Roger, 'Skin Colour, Race and Racism in Nicaragua', in *Ethnology*, 30, 4, pp339-53.

Landa, Friar Diego de, *Yucatan; Before and After the Conquest*, William Gates (transl), Ediciones Alducin, Mexico 1994.

Landry, Donna, and MacLean, Gerald (eds), *The Spivak Reader*, Routledge, London 1996.

Larrain, Jorge, *Ideology and Cultural Identity – Modernity and the Third World Presence*, Polity Press, Cambridge 1994.

Larsen, Neil, 'Postmodernism and Imperialism; Theory and Politics in Latin America', in Beverley et al (eds), *The Postmodernism Debate in Latin America*, Duke University Press, London 1995.

Latouche, S., R. Morris (transl), *The Westernization of the World; The Significance, Scope and Limits of the Drive Towards Global Uniformity*, Polity Press, Cambridge 1996.

Leys, C., *The Rise and Fall of Development Theory*, James Currey, London 1996.

Linear, Marcus, *Zapping the Third World: The Disaster of Development Aid*, Pluto Press, London and Sydney 1985.

Lorde, Audre, *The Audre Lorde Compendium – The Cancer Journals, Sister Outsider and A Burst of Light*, Pandora, London 1996.

Lutz, Helma, Phoenix, Ann, Yuval-Davis, Nira, *Crossfires; Nationalism, Racism and Gender in Europe*, Pluto Press, London 1995.

Marchand, M. and Parpart, J., *Feminism/Postmodernism/Development*, Routledge, London 1995.

Marchand, M., 'Latin American Women Speak on Development – Are We Listening Yet?', in Marchand, M. and Parpart, J., *Feminism/Postmodernism/ Development*, Routledge, London 1995.

Marcos, subcommandante, J. de Leon (ed), *Our Word is Our Weapon – Selected Writings*, Seven Stories Press, London 2001.

Marcus, Bruce (ed), *Nicaragua – The Sandinista People's Revolution – Speeches by Sandinista Leaders*, Pathfinder Press, New York 1985.

Marnham, P., *So Far From God – A Journey to Central America*, Penguin Books, London 1985.

Mason, Mike, *Development and Disorder – A History of the Third World since 1945*, University Press of New England, Hanover 1997.

Massey, D., 'A Global Sense of Place', *Marxism Today*, June 1991, pp24-29.

Massey, D., 'Politics and Space/Time', in Keith, M., and Pile, S. (eds), *Place and the Politics of Identity*, Routledge, London 1993.

Massey, D., 'Entanglements of Power: Reflections', in Sharp et al (eds), *Entanglements of Power: Geographies of Dominance/Resistance*, Routledge, London 2000.

McClintock, A., *Imperial Leather: Race, Gender and Sexuality in the Colonial Conquest*, Routledge, London 1995.

McGee, T. G., 'Eurocentrism and Geography – Reflections on Asian

Urbanization', in Crush, Jonathan (ed), *Power of Development*, Routledge, London 1995.

Memmi, A., *The Colonizer and the Colonized*, Earthscan Publications, London 1990.

Menchu, Rigoberta, *I, Rigoberta Menchu – An Indian Woman in Guatemala*, Ann Wright (transl), Verso, London 1983.

Miles, R., *Racism and Migrant Labour*, Routledge, London 1982.

Mohanty, Chandra Talpade, 'Feminist Encounters: Locating the Politics of Experience', in Barrett and Phillips (eds), *Destabilizing Theory*, Polity Press 1992.

Momsen, J., *Women and Development in the Third World*, 1991.

Momsen, J., and Townsend, J., *Geography of Gender in the Third World*, University of New York Press, London 1987.

Monbiot, G., 'Both Saviour and Victim', *Guardian*, 29.1.02, p15.

Morley, David, and Chen, Kuan-Hsing, *Stuart Hall – Critical Dialogues in Cultural Studies*, Routledge, London 1996.

Morrison, T., *Playing in the Dark – Whiteness and the Literary Imagination*, Picador, London 1992.

Mosse, J., *Half the World, Half a Chance; An Introduction to Gender and Development*, Oxfam, Oxford 1993.

Munck, R., *Politics and Dependency in the Third World – The Case of Latin America*, Zed Books, London 1985.

Nederveen Pieterse, Jan, *White on Black; Images of Africa and Blacks in Western Popular Culture*, Yale University Press, New Haven and London 1992.

Nicholson, Linda, J. (ed) *Feminism / Postmodernism*, Routledge, London, 1990 – photos.

Noble, John, et al, *Mexico–a Lonely Planet travel survival kit*, Lonely Planet Publications, London 1995.

North, Oliver, *Under Fire–An American Story*, Harper Collins, New York 1991.

Noxolo, P., 'Dancing a Yard, Dancing Abrard: Race, Space and Time in British Development Discourses', Unpublished Thesis.

O'Connell, H., *Dedicated Lives; Women Organising for a Fairer World*, Oxfam, Oxford 1993.

Ohri, A., *The World in Our Neighbourhood – Black and Ethnic Minority Communities and Development Education*, Development Education Association, London 1997.

Oquendo, Angel R., 'Re-imagining the Latino/a Race', in Delgado and Stefanic (eds), *The Latino/a Condition – A Critical Reader*, New York University Press, New York 1998.

O'Shaughnessy, Hugh, *Latin Americans*, BBC Books, London 1988.

O'Tuathail, G., and Dalby, S. (eds), *Rethinking Geopolitics*, Routledge, London 1998.

Pajaczkowska, C., and Young, L., 'Racism, Representation, Psychoanalysis', in Donald. and Rattansi (eds), *'Race', Culture and Difference*, Sage Publications, London 1992.

Parpart, Jane L., 'Post-modernism, Gender and Development', in Crush, Jonathan (ed), *Power of Development*, Routledge, London 1995.

Pearce, Jenny, *Under The Eagle – US Intervention in Central America and the Caribbean*, Latin American Bureau, London 1982.

Peet, Richard, 'Social Theory, Postmodernism, and the Critique of Development', in Benko, Georges, and Strohmayer, Ulf (eds), *Space and Social Theory; Interpreting Modernity and Postmodernity*, Blackwell, Oxford 1997.

Perea, Juan F., 'The Black/White Binary Paradigm of Race', in Delgado and Stefanic (eds), *The Latino/a Condition – A Critical Reader*, New York University Press, New York 1998.

Pilger, John, *Distant Voices*, Vintage, London 1992.

Plunkett, H., *Nicaragua – A Guide to the People, Politics and Culture*, Latin American Bureau, London 1999.

Power, Marcus, 'The Dissemination of Development', in *Environment and Planning – Society and Space*, 1998 Vol. 6 No 5, pp577-598.

Quijano, Anibal, 'Modernity, Identity and Utopia in Latin America', in Beverley et al (eds), *The Postmodernism Debate in Latin America*, Duke University Press, London 1995.

Radcliffe, Sarah, and Westwood, Sallie, *Viva – Women and Popular Protest in Latin America*, Routledge, London 1993.

Radcliffe, Sarah, and Westwood, Sallie, *Remaking the Nation – Place, Identity and Politics in Latin America*, Routledge, London 1996.

Rahmena, Majid, with Bawtree, Victoria (eds), *The Post-Development Reader*, Zed Books, London 1997.

Ramirez, W., 'Today We Speak Naturally of Atlantic Coast Autonomy', in Marcus, Bruce (ed), *Nicaragua – The Sandinista People's Revolution – Speeches by Sandinista Leaders*, Pathfinder Press, New York 1985.

Ransom, D., *The No-Nonsense Guide to Fair Trade*, New Internationalist Publications, Oxford 2001.

Rattansi, Ali, 'Changing the Subject? Racism, Culture and Education', in Donald and Rattansi (eds), *'Race', Culture and Difference*, Sage Publications, London 1992.

Rattansi, Ali, and Westwood, Sallie (eds), *Racism, Modernity and Identity on the Western Front*, Polity Press, Cambridge 1994.

Reeves, Frank, *British Racial Discourse – A Study of British Political Discourse about Race and Race-related Matters*, Cambridge University Press, Cambridge 1983.

Richards, G., *Export Processing Zones in Nicaragua*, One World Action, London 1998.

Rist, Gilbert, *The History of Development – from Western Origins to Global Faith*, Zed Books, London 1997.

Robinson, William, and Norsworthy, Kent, *David and Goliath – Washington's War Against Nicaragua*, Zed Books, London 1987.

Rodriguez, Cristina, *A Nicaraguan Story*, The Nicaraguan Return Visit Committee, Dublin 1997.

Rooper, Alison, and Smith, H., 'From Nationalism to Autonomy; The Ethnic Question in the Nicaraguan Revolution', *Race and Class*, 1986 Vol. XXVII No.4.

Rushdie, S., *The Jaguar Smile – A Nicaraguan Journey*, Pan Books, London 1987.

Sachs, Wolfgang (ed), *The Development Dictionary – A Guide to Knowledge as Power*, Zed Books, London and New Jersey 1992.

Sachs, Wolfgang (ed), *Global Ecology; A New Arena of Political Conflict*, Zed Books, London 1993.

Said, Edward, *Orientalism*, Penguin, London 1991.

Said, Edward, *Culture and Imperialism*, Chatto and Windus, London 1993.

Sale, Kirkpatrick, *The Conquest of Paradise – Christopher Columbus and the Columbian Legacy*, Hodder and Stoughton, London 1991.

Schumann, M., *Towards a Global Village; International Community Development Initiatives*, Pluto Press, London 1994.

Shanin, Teodor, 'The Idea of Progress', in Rahnema, Majid, with Bawtree, Victoria (ed), *The Post-Development Reader*, Zed Books, London 1997.

Sharp, J., Routledge, P., Philo, C. and Paddison, R. (eds), *Entanglements of Power: Geographies of Dominance/Resistance*, Routledge, London 2000.

Sheehan, Daniel, and Ortega, Daniel, *Assault on Nicaragua; The Untold Story of the US 'Secret War'*, Walnut Publishing Co., San Francisco 1987.

Shiva, V., 'The Greening of the Global Reach', in Sachs, Wolfgang (ed.), *Global Ecology; A New Arena of Political Conflict*, Zed Books, London 1993.

Shorris, Earl, 'Welcome to the Old World', in Delgado and Stefanic (eds), *The Latino/a Condition – A Critical Reader*, New York Press, New York 1998.

Short, Clare, *The Role and Functions of the Department for International Development*, Department for International Development, London 1997.

Shrestha, Nanda, 'Becoming a Development Category', in Crush Jonathan (ed), *Power of Development*, Routledge, London 1995.

Sibley, D., *Geographies of Exclusion – Society and Difference in the West*, Routledge, London 1997.

Sibley, D., 'The Racialisation of Space in British Cities', *Soundings* 1998, Issue 10, pp119-128.

Silva-Michelina, J. (ed), *Latin America; Peace Democratization & Economic Crisis*, Zed Books, London 1988.

Slater, David, 'Challenging Western Visions of the Global; The Geopolitics of Theory and North-South Relations', in *The European Journal of Development Research*, Vol. 17, No.2, December 1995 pp366-388.

Slater, David, 'Geopolitics and the Postmodern; Issues of Knowledge, Difference and North-South Relations', in Benko, Georges and Strohmayer, Ulf (eds), *Space and Social Theory – Interpreting Modernity and Postmodernity*, Blackwell, Oxford 1997.

Spivak, Gaytari Chakravorty, *The Post-Colonial Critic – Interviews, Strategies, Dialogues*, Harasym, Sarah (ed), Routledge, London 1990.

Spurr, D., *The rhetoric of Empire – Colonial Discourse in Journalism, Travel Writing and Imperial Administration*, Duke University Press, Durham 1994.

Stanley, Liz and Wise, Sue, *Breaking Out Again – Feminist Ontology and Epistemology*, Routledge, London 1993.

Tercier, J. (ed.), *Whiteness*, Lawrence & Wishart, London 2000.

Thrift, N., 'Entanglements of Power: Shadows', in Sharp, J, Routledge, P, Philo, C & Paddison, R. (eds.), *Entanglements of Power: Geographies of Dominance/Resistance*, Routledge, London 2000.

Townsend, Janet Gabriel, *Women's Voices from the Rainforest*, Routledge, London 1995.

VSO, '6 Ways to Change Your Life', in association with *The Guardian*, 2001.

VSO, *Working Overseas with VSO – The Facts*, VSO Publications London, undated.

Wade, Peter, 'Representation and Power: blacks in Colombia', in *Social Construction of the Past – Representation as Power*, edited by Bond, George C., and Gilliam, Angela, Routledge, London and New York 1994.

Wallerstein I. (ed.), *World Inequality – Origins and Perspectives on the World System*, Black Rose Books, Montreal 1975.

Ware, V., *Beyond the Pale; White Women, Racism and History*, Verso, London 1992.

Watts, Michael, 'A New Deal in Emotions – Theory and Practice and the Crisis of Development', in Crush, Jonathan (ed), *Power of Development*, Routledge, London 1995.

Watts, Michael, 'Mapping Meaning, Denoting Difference, Imagining Identity: Dialectical Images and Post-modern Geographies', in Barnes, T. & Gregory, D. (eds.), *Reading Human Geography – The Poetics and Politics of Inquiry*, Arnold, London 1997.

Waugh, D. & Bushell, T., *Key Geography: Interactions*, Stanley Thornes, Gloucester 1993.

Wells, B., 'Editorial', in *Developments*, Issue 3, Department for International Development, London 1998.

Wearne, P., *Return of the Indian; Conquest and Revival in the Americas*, Cassell, London 1996.

Werbner, P. & Modood, T. (eds.), *Debating Cultural Hybridity – Multi-Cultural Identities and the Politics of Anti-Racism*, Zed Books, London 1997.

Williams, Patrick and Chrisman, Laura (eds.), *Colonial Discourse and Post-Colonial Theory*, Harvester Wheatsheaf, Hemel Hempstead, 1993.

Winant, Howard, 'Racial Formation and Hegemony; Global and Local Developments', in Rattansi, Ali and Westwood, Sallie (eds.), *Racism, Modernity and Identity – On the Western Front*, Polity Press, Cambridge 1994.

World Bank, *Working with NGOs: A Practical Guide to Operational Collaboration between the World Bank and Non-Governmental Organisations*, The World Bank, Washington DC, 1996a.

World Bank, *Annual Report*, World Bank, Washington DC, 1996b.

World Commission on Environment and Development, *Our Common Future*, Oxford University Press, Oxford, 1987 (also known as the Bruntland Report).

Worsley, P., *The Third World*, Weidenfield & Nicolson, London 1967.

Yorkshire Post, 'Ten Years that Changed a World', 20 March 1999, p15.

Young, Robert, *White Mythologies–Writing History and the West*, Routledge, London and New York 1992.

Young, Robert, 'Egypt in America; Black Athena, Racism and Colonial Discourse', in Rattansi, Ali and Westwood, Sallie (eds.), *Racism, Modernity and Identity – On the Western Front*, Polity Press, Cambridge 1994.

Young, Robert, *Colonial Desire – Hybridity in Theory, Culture and Race*, Routledge, London and New York 1996.